Roger, Tom, and Joyce have written an important book on a critical management issue. Their blend of research and practical advice makes this an unusually valuable read.

> Pete Smith, President of the Private Sector Council and Former CEO, Watson Wyatt Worldwide

***Impending Crisis** is a valuable Flight Plan to avoid turbulence. Organizations who put their people and their future people needs first will be the big winners in the next expansion cycle. Leadership, people and corporate governance go hand in hand to improve the bottom line. Roger, Tom, and Joyce have nailed the issues and offer us a pathway around the turbulence.*

> Howard Putnam, Speaker, Author and Former CEO, Southwest Airlines

*In **Impending Crisis** Roger Herman, and this time with Tom Olivo and Joyce Gioia, offers another down to earth book that not only explains what is happening in terms of workplace and workforce trends but what to do about them. Take their advice — pay attention—start to plan now or risk losing competitive positioning—or worse yet, fail totally.*

> Michael R. Losey, SPHR, CAE, President & CEO (Retired) Society for Human Resource Management, Executive Consultant

*I really value books like this one that are so inventive and dynamic that you just must stop and immediately tell somebody about some gem trapped within its pages. Not to be taken lightly, **Impending Crisis** is a book essential to the future of your company. I have known Roger Herman for a long time and it is safe to say that he has terrific vision. And because he has been so far in front of the curve with his other books, I'd even say he's a bit the clairvoyant. Now, he and his co-authors warn: "Employers, particularly in the United States, are in serious trouble…and few realize it." Take them seriously and buy this book to learn how to stave off the crisis.*

> Jack Covert, President, 1-800-CEO-READ

This is a substantive work on an alarmingly important area for every business and for all corporate leaders. Read it now to prepare for the future. Share it with your team to plan for a successful approach to build a competitive edge in a demanding environment.

Nido R. Qubein, Chairman, Great Harvest Bread Company and Founder, National Speakers Association Foundation

__Impending Crisis__ is great. Lots of good statistics, made a good case, and really gave senior executives a wake-up call. Showing what the labor shortage is doing to healthcare and then saying "this is will happen to you soon" was a great way to bring the lesson home.

Todd Raphael, On-Line Editor, *Workforce Magazine*

If you had the opportunity for professional business futurists and a professional business measurements expert to sit with you and openly discuss their combined perspectives on a single issue that will affect every aspect of your organization in the very near future, would you create the time to listen??? This is your chance. This book needs to be read and then reread.

Bob Crumley, Senior Vice President/Personnel Services, Boddie-Noell Enterprises, Inc.

Once again Roger Herman and Joyce Gioia have brought their delicious combination of future challenges and pragmatic possibilities to a fresh business equation. Every business and every reader will find that unique combination of challenge and solution which makes every Herman/Gioia book worthwhile. Tom Olivo's contribution takes their work to a new level.

Bob Danzig, Author, Speaker, Teacher and Former CEO, Hearst Newspapers

I enjoyed the book and agree that the shortage of human capital is real and it is off the radar screen for most companies. The authors give a data-backed definition of the issue and sound advice on how to deal with it.

Bob Pierce, Retired CEO, Two National Restaurant Chains

Startling and informative! Now senior executives have no excuses. For some leaders, the coming labor crisis will be career-changing . . . maybe even career-ending. Other executives will be inspired to make some significant changes in how they lead people and their organizations in a whole new environment.

Sandy Vilas, CEO, Coach U

This is an important book. Herman, Olivo, and Gioia offer insights on the future of managing a critical corporate resource—talent.

Richard J. Semenik, Ph.D., Dean, College of Business, Montana State University

*I found this book very easy to read and enjoyable. Perhaps the greatest testament is that I actually looked forward to the next reading session instead of forcing myself to sit down and pick up the book. Obtaining the knowledge from some business books is an exercise in discipline. The knowledge in **Impending Crisis** was the reward in itself. I agree with your message completely. Perhaps now others will better understand why I have been preaching the sermon and taking the actions they seemed reluctant to accept. I will certainly urge our senior managers and HR staff to read the book, discuss, and act.*

Willie Wooldridge, Director of Human Resources, Unifi, Inc.

*Every business in America will face employment challenges during this decade. Reading **Impending Crisis** will help corporate executives prepare with valuable knowledge and advice to weather this storm. This book is consistent with all our research and writings. Heartily recommended.*

Bob Nelson, Ph.D., Author, *1001 Ways to Reward Employees*

*The **Impending Crisis** is wake-up call for corporate executives everywhere. With skill and precision, Herman, Olivo, and Gioia chart the seismic demographic forces that are reshaping the workplace. Smart leaders will heed this book's compelling message—and transform an impending crisis into a bold opportunity to reinvigorate their companies.*

Daniel H. Pink, author, *Free Agent Nation*

Groundbreaking work! Full of powerful act-on-it-now information. The healthcare example effectively brings the future into present focus.

Randall L. Scheel, Director, Association of Professional
  Futurists

Impending Crisis *is a book with a daunting message for business leaders everywhere: get moving, or else! But if you're serious about building your business and sharpening your edge, here you'll find solid advice and tested solutions to some of the scariest scenarios we all face now.*

Nancy K. Austin, Co-Author, *Passion for Excellence*

Impending Crisis *presents convincing evidence that the US is headed for an unprecedented shortage of workers that could lead to the failure of many businesses of all sizes. The good news is that this book also offers solid advice on how to meet the challenge. Executives who want to ensure their companies' future success would be wise to follow this book's advice.*

Tom Lucas, Senior Vice President, Human Resources, Adecco
  Employment Services

(Author's note: Adecco Employment Services is the nation's—and the world's—largest staffing services company.)

Impending Crisis

BOOKS BY THE AUTHORS

By Roger E. Herman

Keeping Good People
The Process of Excelling
Signs of the Times
Turbulence!
Disaster Planning for Local Government (out of print)
Emergency Operations Plan (out of print)

By Roger E. Herman and Joyce L. Gioia

Lean & Meaningful
Workforce Stability
How to Become an Employer of Choice
How to Choose Your Next Employer

Impending Crisis

Roger E. Herman
Thomas G. Olivo
Joyce L. Gioia

Oakhill Press
Winchester, VA

10   9   8   7   6   5   4   3   2

Book design and production by Bookwrights Design
Jacket design by Barbara King
Printed in the United States of America

Library of Congress Cataloging-in-Publication Data
on file with the Publisher

ISBN 1-886939-53-5

Oakhill Press
461 Layside Drive
Winchester, VA 22602
800-32-BOOKS

DEDICATION

Each of us is a teacher. We teach our children, our employees, our clients, and so many others. It is because there are so many wonderful teachers in schools, businesses, and life that our world is blessed with learners who make a difference.

At a higher and more meaningful level are coaches. In our consulting work, we have seen that people who coach others to higher achievement are the real heroes. It's more difficult to coach than to teach—and more rewarding. The focus is on achieving results, more than just imparting information.

Tom dedicates his work on this book to his most significant coach, his father. Thomas J. Olivo invested his life in the public schools teaching, but was a particularly effective coach in mathematics, music, and tennis. He remains a highly valued coach in life as it could—and should—be led. His inspiration continues.

Coaching is vital to organizational success. So is professionalism—knowing what to do, how to do it, and doing it well. Committed professionals make a profound difference in their performance and the inspiration they share—often unintentionally—with others who watch them work.

Roger dedicates his work on this book to Keith M. Clance, M.D., Jake Hochrein, M.D., Jay Kaplan, M.D., and Jeff Todd, M.D., the doctors who have kept him alive and relatively healthy. And a special thanks to the cardiology unit at Moses Cone Hospital in Greensboro, North Carolina. It is because of them that Roger is able to continue his education and coaching of corporate leaders.

Joyce dedicates her work to her high-achieving daughters, Belinda and Melissa Fuchs and Samantha Gioia with her gratitude for the numerous opportunities they give her to practice her leadership skills.

TABLE OF CONTENTS

LIST OF FIGURES

Chapter 5

Chapter 6

Chapter 7

Chapter 9

Appendix B

ACKNOWLEDGMENTS

One of the toughest challenges for authors is to remember all the people who should be thanked for their help in putting a book together. This concern is even deeper when a book, backed by research, seeks to break new ground in a controversial arena. So, if we have missed anyone, we humbly apologize.

Here are the folks we remember with sincere appreciation for their contribution to the thought process and the data that has brought this work to fruition: Steve Ahnen, Senior Vice President, American Hospital Association; Ned Albee, Senior Vice President, Human Resources, Lancaster General Hospital; Karen Berman, Business Literacy Institute; William Bliss, Bliss and Associates, Inc.; Chuck Bohlen, Director, Performance Consulting, VHA, Inc.; Carol D'Amico, Assistant Secretary of Education for Vocational and Adult Education; Scott Degraffenreid, Behavioral Statistician; Robert Gately, President, Gately Consulting; Lillee Gelinas, R.N., M.S.N., Vice President and Chief Nursing Officer, Clinical Affairs, Voluntary Hospital Association; Greg Hessel, Heidrick & Struggles; Jay Kaplan, M.D., Vice President for Emergency Services, Arizona Region, Banner Health System, and Medical Director, Studer Group; Joanne Kassebaum, Director of Marketing, Adecco; Keith Kosel, Ph.D., Director of Outcomes Management, Clinical Advantage, VHA, Inc.; David Lloyd, Vice President, Operations, The ViaLink Company; Garry Mathiason, Senior Partner, Littler Mendelson, L.L.P.; Don Reynolds, Senior

Vice President, Salomon Smith Barney; Phil Rones, Assistant Commissioner, Bureau of Labor Statistics; Richard Scaldini, President, Hiram College; Ernie Shippey, Senior Consultant, VHA, Inc. Consulting Services; and Sandy Vilas, President, Coach University. Thanks to Don Mitchell and Carol Coles, authors of *The Ultimate Competitive Advantage* (Berrett-Koehler, 2003) for their contribution to Chapter 8.

Special thanks also go to Philana Burton, Carol McKinney, and Yolonda Tayo with The Herman Group. Roger and Joyce thank Trudy Arnold, Bill Brooks, Traci Capraro, Nido Qubein, Terry van der Werff, and our professional colleagues on The Herman Group Consulting Team. Tom thanks Bob Bennett, Karen Berman, Bill Brown, Diane Camet, Rick Culley, Thom Handley, Ron Malone, Justin Martin, Annah Moore, William Olivieri, Steve Pringle, Mike Reilly, Darcee Richmond, Kelly Tilleman, and Ken Thuerbach, who have generously contributed to Success Profiles, Inc., over the years. And a salute, of course, to our editor, "JK" Fuchs, and Ed Helvey and Marty James from Oakhill Press.

Our families deserve our appreciation as well. Research, writing, editing, and other tasks are time-consuming and eat into family time. Thanks for your love, patience, and indulgence. Here are your names in print! Samantha, Jennifer, Scott and Renee, Belinda, and Melissa in North Carolina, Ohio, New York, and Massachusetts. Katie, Christine, and Sarah in Montana.

INTRODUCTION

Many authors describe the writing of a book as a labor of love. For us, this book is part of a mission. In our consulting, forecasting, and measuring for our corporate clients, we discovered a major crisis situation just around the corner. In fact, some organizations were already experiencing the crisis, most notably in healthcare.

As we were doing some more research, digging into this situation, we were engaged by VHA, Inc. to help with their attack on the problem. Roger became the National Chairman for the Tomorrow's Workforce Collaborative and Tom joined the team to help guide the measurement aspect of the project and to serve as the national spokesman for the business case. This opportunity enriched and sharpened our awareness of the workforce shortage. As we learned more, working with these dedicated healthcare professionals, our passion intensified. We knew we had to produce this book—and as quickly as possible.

Employers, particularly in the United States, are in serious trouble . . . and few realize it.

A dangerous worker shortage, more severe than most people expect, is compounded by deep systems problems in the way companies operate today. Senior corporate executives, often including owners, perhaps unwittingly, are aiding and abetting corporate homicide by continuing to aggressively support systems and philosophies that inhibit the stability, the success, and the future of their organizations.

Our reward system for senior executives—the leaders who guide the future of the organization—is counterproductive to long-term achievement. In so many cases, Wall Street rewards the opposite behavior to what is really needed. The market has historically rewarded companies executing large-scale layoffs with temporary short-term stock price boosts—and, not so coincidentally, also rewarding the executive option holders. Chief executive officers win points (and huge bonuses) for cutting costs, directing employee layoffs, and concentrating on the short-term gains that make the numbers look good for the market.

What they do not realize—or choose to ignore—is that in the long run the most profitable companies are those that take care of their people. In fact, some investment analysts look carefully at employee turnover before recommending a particular stock. They know that without good, qualified people who are happy and productive, the company's long-term prospects are mediocre at best. The needed strategic shift to an appreciation of the importance of human capital is coming, but it will be damagingly slow for most companies. The chickens have come home to roost; no longer can executives put off these problems "for the next guy to worry about."

There is an old story about dropping a frog in a pot of boiling water. The frog will come leaping out of the pot—doesn't like that environment at all! But, if you put the frog in a pot of room-temperature water and gradually turn up the heat, you can boil the frog alive. It's become very comfortable in the overheated environment. (Don't try this at home.)

The moral of the story is that if conditions around us change *gradually*, we don't realize quite what's happening to us—and we could be in a pretty precarious situation. We suggest that this evolution is precisely what has happened to corporate executives—and boards of directors—over the years. The Enron Revelation and other corporate, uh, discomforts have raised the awareness. How many executives and boards will have the courage to be the pioneers and early adapters in new ways of strategic leadership?

The climate for business is changing. Merely paying attention to the day's weather obscures the view of the climate. Leaders need to move to a higher level of perception.

Will your company's leadership "get" that a stable, productive workforce can be your secret weapon? Or perhaps a not-so-secret weapon? Are you attracting and holding top talent? Savvy investors, like Warren Buffett, evaluate investment opportunities by studying how management takes care of people. They routinely avoid investing in companies that do not devote enough attention to human resources. They watch for *compassionate* layoffs, emphasis on retention of high-level talent with knowledge of the business, and open and deliberate development of the human resources that drive organizational success to incredibly high levels. They concentrate on the human resources as being the competitive edge.

> A major systemic change in leadership thinking—and performance—is imperative. CYA must shift to CYF. "Cover Your Anatomy" must shift to "Create Your Future." And the key is people.

The interviews we have conducted in our research for this book have been stimulating, educational, rewarding, and unsettling. We've encountered thought leaders who are at least as fervent as we are, and every one of them is worried that employers won't get the message in time. Unfortunately, a number of companies are racing headlong towards extinction.

We can't save the world, but hopefully we can help you save your organization. We have built this book with an aggressive enthusiasm that has fueled some strong writing . . . and speaking. A special thanks to the audiences that have heard us speak as we have put this book together; your energized feedback has been meaningful and inspiring.

Some Caveats

Your coauthors come to you with some background and biases that will be helpful to understand.

Roger is founder and chief executive officer of The Herman Group, consulting futurists concentrating on workforce and workplace trends. A great deal of Roger's work has been to help corporate executives understand—and reduce—the negative impacts of uncontrolled employee turnover. In working with a wide range of clients, he has seen firsthand the damage that can be done . . . and how the damage can be repaired.

In his work, Roger has seen companies crippled and hindered by the inability to serve customers, benefit from their own research and development, bring products to market, and maintain their leadership role in the marketplace—all unnecessarily. He has wrestled intellectually with executives who cannot see the wisdom in a relatively small investment to build workforce stability in order to gain a huge multifold increase in net return on investment. He has seen companies fail because they were penny-wise and pound-foolish.

Because of what he has seen, and what he discovered in his trends research (you'll read some of his critical findings in this book), Roger is dedicated to helping employers avoid the dangers that unquestionably lay ahead. Undaunted by the knowledge that some people reading this book will leap into denial, Roger is sounding the Paul Revere–like wake-up call in hopes that astute leaders will get the message and take action.

During the 1990s, the second decade of his consulting career, Roger focused on helping employers do the things that would make them more attractive to the kinds of employees they wanted to hire—and keep. He has been ahead of the curve from the time he wrote the first edition of *Keeping Good People* in 1990. Employers thought he was an off-center alarmist when he warned of unprecedented employee turnover while people were lined up at the unemployment office. They soon discovered he was right and his book on retention became—and still is—a best-selling business book. Demand for his consulting and speaking services rose.

Joyce is president of The Herman Group. She brings to the book her perspectives developed over decades of experience as a publishing and marketing executive, having spent the last ten years working with Roger in the realm of "internal marketing." Joyce coined this term to describe her application of external marketing techniques *within* the organization to attract, optimize, and hold the best employees. For some years now, marketing professionals have been focused on internal marketing communications to reinforce the bonds the organization enjoys with its *internal* customers.

A key component of Joyce's philosophy is the concept of "adding value." Employers that want to be successful in winning the talent wars will add more value than the competition. Enlightened organizations recognize that in order to continue to become more profitable, they must keep finding new ways to add value for *all* the stakeholders.

To strengthen their messages and provide more tools to employers, Roger and Joyce wrote several more books: *Lean & Meaningful*, *Workforce Stability*, and *How to Become an Employer of Choice*. They became sought-after speakers, often cited in the news media.

Tom describes himself first as a coach. He is justifiably proud of his accomplishments as a coach in the sports world and the business world. In his coaching work (he was NCAA Coach of the Year in 1985), Tom has learned to emphasize that measurement is the key to success. It is impossible to make improvements unless you know where you are, where you've been, and where you want to go. It's all measurement—know the numbers.

Measurement, however, has limited value, unless you put the knowledge to work. Once you have the knowledge from the measurement and the evaluation of what it means, it is essential to take action. In his consulting career, Tom has been amazed and saddened by executives who measure, absorb, and withdraw. They don't share the information with others and don't lead the campaign to make changes that are obviously needed. These senior corporate executives—some company owners—act like managers instead of leaders. They direct instead of coach, ignoring the fact that it's *coaching* their people want and need, not managing.

> **"You can't make major business decisions with minor information."**

Tom asserts that those executives must comprehend human capital requirements, just as they understand their operational and financial performance factors. They can no longer be afraid to act, hiding behind some corporate policy or external environment excuse. Referring to the expression, "You can't make major business decisions with minor information," Tom urges corporate executives to carefully evaluate relevant data to fully understand their circumstances, relative to the facts presented in this book. Now is a time for action, and those organizational leaders who do not act decisively on the information in front of them will be in serious trouble.

As president of Success Profiles, Tom has participated in measurement of factors that influence business success in hundreds of organizations in the United States and other countries. His company's measurement practices, described later in this book, have produced a wealth of data that will be helpful for our readers. Tom observes that leading an organization does not have to be difficult, if you measure, coach, and maintain good life-work balance. He discovered a long time ago that fly-fishing in Bozeman, Montana, can be done in the middle of a workday without limiting success.

A futurist is sometimes suspected of being somewhat disconnected from reality. Yes, out-of-the-box thinking is a requirement for effective future-thinking. A good base of research combined with the depth of specialization brings that futurist's perspective to a higher level. People focused entirely on measurement might be suspected of just looking at the numbers without understanding—or caring about—what they mean. But a specialist in how those numbers influence success operates at a higher level. Put the powers together and you get the team that has prepared this book, this tool, for you.

Learn, grow, *act.*

FAMILIAR ROLES, NEW MEANINGS

Each member of the executive leadership team has a role to play in the normal operation of the business. In the face of the Impending Crisis, senior executives will have additional roles to play in building the organization's human resource strength. As you read about your particular role, in the big picture, you'll note a particular perspective from which to read this book.

Here are some important reminders and thought-provoking alerts for your consideration. As you discuss these issues with your colleagues around the "strategic table," these insights may stimulate a greater awareness for things that must be done. Think of them as spotlights, highlighting opportunities.

The Chief Executive Officer's Role

Most CEOs recognize that the people issue is critical to their success. Many, however, are not fully aware of the current convergence of trends—the storm clouds on the horizon. In times past, you might have delegated people issues to the folks in Personnel, now Human Resources. While they have a vital role to play, our rapidly changing environment calls for significantly stronger leadership from the most senior executives.

You know it is up to you to provide a strong sense of direction. You simply cannot abdicate the leadership role that will determine the future of your organization. Sure, it will be tempting to off-load this "soft" stuff to your chief human resource

9

officer, but as you'll see in this book, managing the impending crisis in the workforce is a critical bottom-line issue. HR isn't so soft anymore; there are hard numbers to contend with. Frankly, the survival of your company is at stake. You don't want to delegate that exposure to *anyone*, regardless of your level of trust.

Watch your numbers. While you are closely monitoring financial, operational, and market-price metrics, carefully watch your human-capital metrics. As we move through the decade, your greatest vulnerability will likely be the strength and volatility of your *human* resources. You cannot afford to ignore or delegate this risk—there are too many potential impacts that could affect every aspect of your organization. Set the example by staying on top of this issue and insist on regular reports from all members of your senior team. Do not let your senior executives push the issue to Human Resources without continuing to be highly involved—personally.

To maximize your effectiveness, encourage every member of your leadership team to read *Impending Crisis*. Emphasize the critical nature of this problem and demand solid plans of action. Beware of elaborate plans that never get implemented. We've all seen too much of that lack of follow-through. Not this time: the risk is too great. Insist on results.

The Chief Operating Officer's Role

Your CEO is faced with a challenge. Reading this book, he/she will become acutely aware that the organization is facing a crisis. Your company is not alone. This crisis will confront every employer—in the United States and overseas. As you might imagine, your boss will probably be a bit shaken up by the realization of the facts. We're not soft-pedaling your situation. This is serious business.

We recommend you plan to spend some extra time with your senior leader discussing this situation. You'll have an opportu-

nity to serve as a strong, solid sounding board. Be sure to think—
and act—"out of the box." Meeting this evolving challenge leaves
no room to anchor yourself to tradition. "We've always done it
this way" won't work anymore.

You will probably play a strong role in implementation of
your organization's plans to deal with this looming crisis. Don't
let up. The natural temptation will be to atrophy, to return to
customary work patterns, to become complacent about the urgency of the shortage of capable workers. Every organization
already has a tremendous current workload competing for attention with future-thinking.

Your organization will need to change many aspects of the
way it does business. It's time to reduce your dependence on
human resources, to reduce your exposure to the volatility of
unexpected and uncontrolled employee turnover. Are your other
types of resources being used to the best advantage? Look carefully at cost-benefit.

Examine *all* of your processes. Do they still make sense, or
should they be modified or even eliminated? You may have to
drive the examination in your organization. Expect some turf
wars. Consider yourself the designated referee. Establish clear
criteria. Measure. Move into new ways of doing things to better
achieve your objectives.

Pay special attention to silos. If your organization is like most
others, you have formal and informal silos all over the place.
They confound operational efficiency and effectiveness, driving
costs much higher than they need to be. As chief operating officer, you have the positioning to bring various factions of the
company together, to build cohesiveness, communication, consistency, and collaboration.

Expect resistance. While many people sense that economic
and workforce issues may be a problem, few understand the far-
reaching implications we'll discuss in this book.

The Chief Financial Officer's Role

In these pages, we will link a number of measurements together to present new perspectives. Even though we're talking about people and some soft issues, your company's exposure will come in hard dollars—and a lot faster than most people think. In your position, you have a unique vantage point for spotting the numbers, the values of any picture presented to you and the company. As you know, employee turnover and profitability are inversely proportional. Your input can help other senior executives comprehend the need for taking fast, positive action. You will see many numbers here from a variety of sources, all presented to validate the very real predicament facing most employers today.

Many executives are not aware of the full impact of turnover on the bottom line. Many of *your* organization's leaders may benefit from your assistance to understand—and accept—the numbers that are presented in these pages . . . and to see how they relate to your organization. Help them "get" the full impact of the graphs and charts that illustrate this book. As your co-leaders design a whole new strategy for your organization, measurement will be essential.

With your help, human resource metrics will rise to a new level of importance and value. Alone, the numbers are interesting. Connected to your company's financial metrics, they tell a powerful story. You and your financial management team must not only link those numbers, but assure that every leader in the company—regardless of discipline—understands the deeper meanings and far-reaching implications of the measurements and the trends. This level of detail will require a competency in activity-based-cost (ABC) accounting.

In most organizations, personnel costs are the highest expense category. In most situations, it's simply imperative that we have live people out there doing the work; machines and automation simply can't do it all. Undoubtedly, you are highly sensitive to the people costs—wages and salaries, benefits, incentives, perquisites, training, and all the rest of the categories. However, are you attuned to the costs of uncontrolled employee turnover?

In this book, we'll present some compelling evidence about the real costs of losing people and replacing them. The numbers are astonishingly higher than most people, even astute chief financial officers, are aware. We'll tell you about a tool to measure the direct and indirect costs to an amazing level of depth and accuracy, and we'll *show* you abbreviated case studies to present the numbers. When you see what we've presented, you will better understand why we're happy that *you're* reading *Impending Crisis*. There's a job to be done, and you're a vital player.

The Chief Human Resource Officer's Role

The Impending Crisis is clearly a people issue. This book is filled with people issues put to numbers music. You'll revel as you flip through the pages. Someone is finally singing your song. You've argued that the human resource is the most vital resource for the organization. Now, more than ever before in history, your senior leaders *must* focus on the human resource, in the short-term future *and* in the long-term picture. Your colleagues may come to you for help and advice.

Fight the temptation to express some snide comments like "Where have you been?" or "It's about time you saw the light." Instead, answer questions, teach your colleagues about your profession, and help others design and implement the new strategies that must become a part of what your organization does. Don't assume that everyone will rush to you to worship at the new altar of Human Resources. It doesn't work that way. While there will be heightened awareness of the people side of the business, there will also be considerable attention given to how people and the bottom line connect. It is imperative that you participate *actively* at the strategic table, which means you must learn how to business-speak.

If you are not already very familiar with human resource metrics, it's time to invest in some in-depth education. As we continually assess the return on investment in this vital asset, measurement will be the name of the game in Human Resources. While the soft-skills aspects of HR will remain important, the language of communication with your fellow leaders will be hard numbers. Emphasis will be placed on how the people numbers link to the bottom line, with intense interest in building the capacity and stability of the workforce.

For years there has been an acceptance of the "warm body" philosophy of recruiting. This approach will not work anymore. It must stop, and you're the traffic cop. If an applicant is not qualified to do at least the immediate job, let alone probable future tasks, do not permit the person to be hired. You'll just cause yourself a lot of headaches . . . and productivity and turnover numbers that won't sit well with your colleagues. Looking for the "A" players will take more work, a lot more work. But it must be done. A very important part of your job will be to assure that everyone who is hired is top drawer—well-qualified and suited to your organization's culture.

Don't fret about being the lone wolf—executive or department—doing this alone. When done well, recruiting is a company-wide effort. Many managers need you to coach and teach them how to attract the candidates they want and how to invite them to join the organization. It's common knowledge that a company's best recruiters are current employees, but rarely do staffing professionals teach other employees how to do this all-important job. Everyone in the company should be a talent scout. Teach, coach, inspire, and reward your company-wide recruiting team.

Retention is a major issue for professionals in Human Resources. But, again, retention is not solely your job. Here again, your roles are teacher, coach, cheerleader, and resource provider. Every manager and executive in your organization should be trained and supported to retain his or her good employees. Yes, "good" employees. If you have people on your payroll who can't do the job, collaborate with their managers to get them up to par or to send them packing.

The Chief Marketing Officer's Role

A significant part of your responsibility is the image and reputation of your organization. This impending crisis may threaten your brand and position in the marketplace, which will, of course, influence your sales and profits. Where's the problem? Employers will have to change the way they do business, including perhaps what markets they are in. You may be called upon to evaluate scenarios to help determine potential new directions for the organization.

Our experience suggests that you should begin now to identify new markets for your company. Analyze sales and determine which markets or products may be wrong for your organization. Prepare to reposition your company in its current marketplace, and/or in marketplaces that are not even on today's radar screen. Think further into the future.

While searching for new customers, you will also be hunting for new employees. Not your job? Well, not directly. However, each company reaches into several markets. Since the critical problem is an unprecedented labor shortage, you may need to reposition your business in the *employment* marketplace. Your organization will be competing for top talent, going head-to-head against a lot of other employers who also want those rare, top-talent resources. Your human resource professionals need your expertise to compete more effectively in the employment market. This shift into some new arenas will be stimulating and challenging, calling into play practically everything you have ever learned in your chosen profession.

In the years ahead, workers will *choose* where they will be employed. They will have plenty of choices, with lots of temptations. Recruiters will be aggressive—to attract not only your company's best candidates, but also your best employees. Everything you do in marketing will take on new meaning as you concentrate on sending overt and subliminal messages to prospective and current employees.

Recognize the importance of having congruent brands for your external and internal marketing efforts. This alignment will be especially critical in the years to come, as workers will evaluate your company based on your brand. If there is a dissonance between the internal and the external, they may judge your corporate culture to be fake—one in which people do not walk their talk.

Without the right employees, your organization will not be able to serve its customers, clients, patients, constituents, or donors—the folks who provide the funds to support your operation. In the future, you may be called upon more and more to provide *internal* marketing assistance. Get ready.

Conclusion

The traditional roles played by senior executives will undoubtedly become more intense in the years ahead. This decade will be the most exciting and challenging in history for corporate leaders. As predictable trends and wild cards converge to create new opportunities at hyperspeed, everything we ever learned will be called into play. Collaboration will reach new levels, as experienced professionals bond together to fight the common enemy of an unprecedented labor shortage.

PART 1

Problems

CHAPTER ONE

Impending Crisis in the Workforce

Employers are not prepared for the impending labor crisis, a dangerously growing shortage of workers that is coming soon. This shortage will be felt most acutely in skilled positions, however all employment will be affected. Without a decisive change in the mindset of corporate executives and boards of directors, employers are seriously vulnerable. The crisis is not limited to the private sector; not-for-profit organizations, government agencies, the armed forces, trade and professional associations, and educational institutions— public and private—have the same exposure. Understanding and moving through the four stages of awareness and understanding is imperative. An important distinction between climate and weather can be applied to human capital. Climatic changes in the work environment could cause some employers to become extinct if they do not respond to subtle changes. Executives who prepare for this Impending Crisis will lead their organizations to a bright future; those who ignore the threat risk dangerous vulnerability. This preparation won't be easy.

Employers lulled into complacency by the demands of economic, stock market, and competitive issues will soon face a crisis for which most are unprepared. The impact could be devastating, causing employers to suffer greatly and, perhaps, even be forced out of business. Frankly, the very survival of employer organizations (perhaps yours) is at risk. We know this sounds melodramatic, but we'll explain.

Many corporate leaders are not even aware that a potential catastrophe looms just around the corner. They have not evaluated their vulnerability or made viable plans to manage the impact on their organizations. They are not aware because executive focus in too many companies is relatively short-term. Not enough corporate leaders are looking at the long-term picture, let alone preparing for future conditions. An amazing number of leaders don't have a clue about the workforce shortage just over the horizon. Do you?

> **Relative to projected levels of employment, the Impending Crisis is a dangerously growing shortage of workers.**

By 2010 we will face a labor shortage of 10,033,000 people.

This figure, from the projections of the Bureau of Labor Statistics of the U.S. Department of Labor, is an attention-grabber. But the problem goes deeper than just an insufficient number of people in the workforce. A number of other factors will cause serious difficulties for employers, making this decade's human resources the most valuable—and the most volatile—in history. The implications demand attention—and action—by every senior executive of every employment organization.

Trends and conditions, which we will detail in this chapter, are exacerbated by the unfortunate fact that too many executives, managers, and supervisors are not currently capable of rising to the challenge. They are simply not prepared for the trouble that we *know* awaits them. In fairness, they have no experience dealing with this kind of predicament. No executive leading an organization today has ever had to confront the employment conditions that will characterize this decade.

What are the emerging conditions? A major shift has occurred in the employment market. Until the mid-1990s, there were always more people than jobs. Finding someone with a specific talent might have been difficult, but there was still an abundance of people in the workforce. The labor shortage of late 1990s gave corporate leaders a taste of what is coming in this decade; many were overwhelmed by even those circumstances. The current decade will be even more challenging.

Without a decisive change in the mindset of corporate executives and boards of directors, a serious vulnerability will threaten employers. This critical shift must occur in the cultural employment environment that is typically reluctant—if not resistant—to change. To overcome this resistance, we need strong, enlightened leadership . . . at a time when we have a dearth of heroic leaders in the world of business. As we experience a dangerous lack of confidence in the ethics, capability, and motivation of those charged with guiding organizations through the turbulent present into an even more daunting future, this dilemma is taking shape.

The problem is serious—of crisis proportions—involving more than just finding enough people to fill our jobs. There is a dollars-and-cents issue. Most executives sense that employee turnover is expensive, but few comprehend the risk to their bottom line. Complicating the corporate predicament, especially for publicly traded companies, is the emerging inclination by financial analysts to pay more attention to workforce capability and stability. Uncomfortably high employee turnover can cause bond ratings to drop and stock prices to tumble, threatening capitalization. The shifting relationship between workforce and finance issues, something most corporate executives have not watched carefully enough, could drive seemingly stable companies out of business.

Lest this discussion miss a point, we must emphasize that the crisis is not limited to the private sector. Not-for-profit organizations, government agencies, trade and professional associations, and educational institutions—public and private—have the same exposure to this workforce virus. The same kinds of vulnerabilities are prevalent in practically every employer organization.

Can this problem be overcome? Yes, but. The "but" depends on the capacity and commitment of organizational leadership, the speed with which leadership moves itself—and others, and how quickly they get started. In this highly charged competitive environment, he—or she—who hesitates is lost.

As we prepared to write this book, by interviewing corporate executives around the country, we were struck by the ignorance—the lack of knowledge—regarding the Impending Crisis. How well do you and your colleagues at your organization understand human capital, the risks that we face today, and tomorrow, and what you can do about it?

You may be stuck in the realm of *unconscious incompetence*, where you don't know what you don't know. Ignorance is bliss. Or, you may have gathered information and experience that gives you a greater understanding, but you're still not sure what to do. Or you may enjoy a competitive advantage, because you see, you understand, and you are ready. Consider these stages and take a guess where your organization might be today.

The Four Stages of Awareness and Understanding

Stage 1: "No Clue." We estimate that about 25 percent of employers fit into this category. Their leaders have been so focused on their company's work that they haven't poked their heads up to see what's going on in the world of employment. Some of our readers may argue that this figure is high. Anyone who reads a newspaper or a magazine, listens to the radio, or watches television must know there's a labor crisis. The question is how many are really paying attention, or does that fact simply blend in with the rest of the news—with the sense of futility that we can't do anything about it anyway.

In this group, we're including those folks who are in denial. There is a surprisingly large group of corporate leaders who believe that the labor shortage is over forever, because they haven't had a problem hiring the people they needed lately. Many of these ostrich-types don't believe the economy will get much better. Life, as it is at this moment in their lives, is just about what life will be for years to come. Or they assume that automation will solve all the problems, and we won't really face a shortage.

Stage 1: "No Clue"

- Human Capital (People) are treated as a liability rather than an asset
- HR mostly administers policies, benefits and problems
- Demonstrate the attitude that "We can always find people to fill the positions and it doesn't cost anything to replace them"
- Site migration to another (cheaper) location is considered strategic thinking and savvy leadership
- No real performance measurement or management competency   (more focused on day to day tactical operations)
- A "business owner" versus a CEO mindset (usually observed in smaller companies)

In cooperation with Scott Degraffenreid

Figure 1: Stage 1: "No Clue"

Stage 2: "Awareness." About 50 percent of our corporate leaders are aware that there may be some sort of a labor shortage. They may not see many indications of the potential problem, but would agree that it's sometimes difficult to find just the right person to fill a particular job. If you asked them about human resource issues, they'd say, "Yes, you're right. Somebody ought to be doing something—but that somebody isn't me."

A number of organizations that fall into this category offer a wide range of benefits, decent pay, and safe working conditions. Their leaders go to seminars and talk about the importance of employee retention, but their efforts are not particularly effective. They don't measure employee opinion, turnover, productivity, or the costs involved. Interestingly, the people who work for the managers and executives of such organizations are much more aware—and sensitive—than their bosses. It's frustrating for them, but the bosses just don't seem to care.

Stage 2: "Awareness"

- It's an HR issue and a *recruiting* problem (beat up on HR)
- May have a director or VP (title) of HR, but the position is not equal to the other senior executives
- Weak measurement processes
- Corrective actions that include: class and compensation studies, exit interviews, increased training for managers and supervisors, lots of meetings, employee referral bonuses, high participation in job fairs
- Performance measurement competency: no employee profiling and weak performance management (reviews)

In cooperation with Scott Degraffenreid

Figure 2: Stage 2: "Awareness"

Thought leaders at the "awareness" stage treat employee turn-over like back pain. Just take some pills and the pain will go away. During economic downturns, these are the people who poke fun at those more concerned, pointing out that the problem took care of itself in the past and will again.

Stage 3: "Appreciation, Preliminary Understanding." Leaders in this category, about 20 percent of the total, are highly concerned about the labor shortage. They feel the angst and are moved to do something about it. These leaders are involved, listening to their people. They're designing strategies for workforce stability and taking proactive steps to position themselves strategically in the employment marketplace. They're looking for the "A" players, understanding the value of having top talent on their team.

These leaders have a significant advantage over their competitors. They are focused on building a workforce that will enable them to compete very effectively—for people, for other resources, for customers, and for profit.

Companies in this category are pretty good places to work. People care about each other and are treated fairly. There's a sense of mission and values, and at least a vague sense among employees of what the company vision is. Exit interviews are conducted, as are focus groups, generating reports to help management keep in touch with how people feel, where the problems are, and perhaps how vulnerable they are.

Stage 3: "Appreciation and Preliminary Understanding"

- Recognize the importance of Human Capital: "It's not just headcount but experience/talent that matter" (match people skills to job requirements)
- Director or VP of HR receives a lot more recognition than in Stage 2, but not on par with other senior executives yet
- Beginning to measure costs of turnover, quality levels, and potential impact on service/satisfaction with customers
- Experiment in initiatives and begin to spend $$$ (convinced that money is the solution and that you can pay people more to solve the problem); "Front end handcuffs" provide temporary relief
- Have initiatives that include: Benchmarking, employee surveying, increased training, competency mapping, and data mining
- Performance measurement competency: Use employee profiling as a basic "litmus test" for employment and have an improved performance management process

In cooperation with Scott Degraffenreid

Figure 3: Stage 3: "Appreciation and Preliminary Understanding"

Stage 4: "Comprehensive Understanding, Internalization." These leaders get it! About five percent of the total, they know that their human resources are clearly their most valuable resource. "A" and "B" players and some "C" players are all diligently working to improve their skills and performance These companies could qualify to become recognized as Employers of Choice^{SM}, because they have addressed the comprehensive range of issues described in *How to Become an Employer of Choice*. This book describes how people use defined criteria to choose their employers. See chapter 10.

Stage 4: "Comprehensive Understanding and Internalization"

- Quantified their Human Capital requirements/metrics and recognize talent (creating job requirements to align with the talent they find)
- Chief HR Officer is on par with other senior executives and HR is often measured as a "profit center" versus an "expense"
- Have comprehensive, integrated measurements for all key performance areas (business practices, business processes, people measures, customer measures, and financial measures)
- Predictive modeling at a valid and reliable statistical level
- Invest money for the long term to attract the best and brightest talent
- Business practices demonstrate highest level of quality and discipline that form the habits and foundation of success (Employer of Choice[SM] positioning as a *brand image necessity,* as opposed to an initiative or program)
- Performance measurement competency: Use employee profiling to select the "right people" for the "right position;" treat values as important as experience and talent; performance management process aligned and integrated with selection and development

In cooperation with Scott Degraffenreid

Figure 4: Stage 4: "Comprehensive Understanding"

Their customers, suppliers, investors, employees, and employee families know that this organization is an outstanding place to work. Employees are so enamored with the place that they don't *ever* want to leave. In fact, some of them work such long hours that they are chastised by their superiors who are concerned about their life-work balance. Enthusiasm runs high because everyone subscribes to the mission, adheres to the values, and supports the vision that will carry the organization toward even greater success in the future.

Organizations move through the stages. It's a process. At the lower stages, you can't leapfrog because you'll leave too many people behind. Gradually you get better and better through continual effort that is clearly focused on improvement. Some organizations can move through the stages rather quickly; others take a lot longer.

The only way to leapfrog aspects of any of the stages is with exceptional leadership. Leadership appears to be the tipping point for any major improvement initiative. Skipping a stage of development is difficult (similar to a baby trying to go from the crawling stage to the running stage—it has no understanding and skill in the area of balance).

One of the factors influencing speed through the stages is the size of the organization. Smaller organizations, where senior leaders are closer to their people on the ground, are able to move through the process faster. The larger the organization, the longer it takes to go through cultural transformation. Regardless of how dynamic the leaders may be, it just takes longer.

To illustrate our point, a speedboat can make a turn pretty quickly. An aircraft carrier making the same change in direction will need a lot more space and time, no matter how well-loved the captain may be. Turns must be made. But today, danger lurks ahead, like the icebergs waiting for the *Titanic*.

This book is your wake-up call.

Our message is a warning, an alert, for leaders in every industry in the United States and every other economically developed country in the world. This disaster-about-to-happen will be obvious to those who pay attention to the signals. Senior executives who ignore this advisory may place their organizations in serious jeopardy and could be subject to a highly uncomfortable career change if no action is taken.

We cannot be any more direct, except perhaps to warn that every executive who reads these words has been served notice. Disregard this heads-up and you place yourself and your organization at peril.

As part of this warning, we stress a sense of urgency. If you delay assessment, planning, and action, you may be at a disadvantage on many fronts. As you understand what employers will face, you will better appreciate why we assert that you cannot wait to get started. If you are not in substantially better shape by 2005, your vulnerability will be corporately life-threatening.

Climate versus Weather

Scott DeGraffenreid, a nationally known social network analyst with an extensive background in the business environment, shared a fascinating concept with us. We'd like to share it with you. It's a way of thinking that relates change and its impact to climate and weather. Consider how these perspectives affect your thinking and behavior as an organization.

Climate is relatively predictable over the long term and changes very little over the short term. Climatic events move too slowly for people to perceive them as a real threat, though climate has produced more extinctions than any other natural event. Contrast the Ice Age and asteroids. The workforce supply over generations is a climatic process; we don't feel the immediate impacts every day. The change takes place over a long period of time.

Organisms that succeed over the long term are those that adapt earliest to climatic changes. They sense the changes coming, similar to the way senior leaders function, strategically watching long-term trends. You, as a senior leader, are responsible for guiding your organization through climatic change, staying ahead of the change to take advantage of trends and not be victimized by them. And if you fail to adjust to climatic shifts, you may eventually become extinct.

> **You can be very successful at reacting to the weather and still become extinct.**

Weather represents fluctuations that occur on a random and frequent basis. While weather is relatively easy to predict in the short term, weather forecasting over the long term is unreliable. Weather changes quickly—interest rates, process changes, day-to-day problems, new product releases, and quarterly financial reports. Managers respond to weather's short-term changes. Weather can make you uncomfortable, but it rarely kills you. However, you can be very successful at reacting to the weather and still become extinct. For example, heavy emphasis on short-term results for stock markets may help you look good in the short term, but you may still become extinct because of insufficient strategic planning and workforce stability.

Unfortunately, companies are motivated by pain or dysfunction to address these problems. As long as they are trapped in the "weather" versus the "climate" paradigm, they are doomed to delay the change initiatives.

The Impending Crisis that is the subject of this book is a climatic change. Corporate organisms must adapt or risk extinction. The choice is yours. Ride the cresting waves on your surfboard, or move to higher ground as the tsunami approaches. Enough of the literary drama. Let us explain what's happening.

The Impending Crisis

> The Impending Crisis is a dangerously critical shortage of qualified people to perform the work of employer organizations. What we will experience in 2003–2010 will make the workforce crisis of the late 1990s seem like a practice session.

A number of trends have converged to create an untenable predicament for employers. These conditions are unprecedented in history and will trigger workforce and workplace turbulence of a magnitude that will be difficult for even the best-prepared employers to navigate. Emerging challenges call for new strategies, new thinking, and substantial shifts in the way most companies do business. We will be drawn rapidly into a much different operational design that will shake traditional management and corporate structure to their very foundations.

We have designed this book for corporate executives: In these pages, we will explain each of the trends, examining both causes and implications. We will present our case with clear evidence and offer guidance to help you steer through the storm. While we are not able to forecast all the eventualities that will flow from the convergence of the trends, we'll shine the spotlight of clarity on as many as we can to smooth your journey.

The first part of the book will explain explicitly what is happening and what will happen during the balance of this decade. The second part of the book is filled with advice about what employers must do to counteract the impact of this Impending Crisis. Then we'll give you more information and insight to digest, as you consider an industry case study and some unknowns that may alter this forecast.

In the well-worn paths of corporate strategic thinking and planning, we have all learned about SWOT analysis: Strengths, Weaknesses, Opportunities, and Threats. The subject of this book is most definitely a threat to your business. Learn about it. Question it. Explore how it might affect your organization, your processes, your success, and your survival. Then, armed with the knowledge you've gained, attack *your* particular situation and do what must be done. *Planning will not be enough. Action is essential.*

"Leaders either *see the light or feel the heat.*"

Please accept our apologies if this prose sounds sensational, but we've chosen these words carefully to get your attention. This is serious. We know it. We've seen it. We want you to see it, then act on it for the good of your company . . . and your own sanity.

Rick Butts, a speaker on change, uses a phrase that aptly describes what stimulates real change: "Leaders either *see the light or feel the heat.*" Regardless of your motivation, it's time for some serious thinking and substantial change.

—————————— Words of Wisdom ——————————

Unless you are consciously and deliberately on the leading edge, you may not know that your competitors have eaten your lunch until it is far too late.

The unprecedented labor dilemma is more complicated because so few corporate leaders are fully aware of their predicament and the implications of this trend convergence. The unfortunate result is that a crisis looms before us: a concurrent shortage of labor and a dearth of experienced leadership. Executives who prepare for these critical circumstances will lead their organizations to a bright future; those who ignore the threat risk dangerous vulnerability and perhaps corporate extinction.

Obstacles to Successful Transformation

The most troublesome obstacle will be the employers them-selves. In spite of enlightened leadership, those organizations will get in their own way of progress. Many companies are deeply rooted in tradition . . . and bureaucracy. Turf wars, silo protec-tion, and not-invented-here attitudes will doom companies that are not vigorously shaken from the top.

Senior leaders will have to drive radical change in structure, social hierarchy, and protocols to save their companies from ex-tinction. Some of these leaders will do a beautiful job, generat-ing the kind of experiences and results that become graduate-school case studies. Others will fail miserably because of their inability to overcome resistance in their ranks.

Aggressive leaders will have to really work hard to convince people to change to a new way of doing business. Some will give copies of this book to every key person in the organization, us-ing this volume as a stimulator to open discussion and change thinking. Others will bring in outside experts and consultants. Still other leaders will be out with their people every day, per-suading and encouraging. And some will bring in motivational speakers and retired sports stars with bright, shiny messages de-void of the content people will need to change the way they do business. It's like detailing a used car that doesn't run very well.

Now is the time to assess your obstacles and your chances of success. Design your strategy, then as quickly as you can, get moving on implementation. There is no time to waste.

We'll show you what's happening, why, and what you can—*must*—do about it. Given the urgency, let's begin by looking at the vital factors influencing our predicament.

Closing Questions

1. What stage of awareness would characterize your organization today?
2. What is the role of HR at your present stage?
3. How well do you measure your Human Capital?
4. Does your leadership consider you to be an Employer of Choice[SM]?

Opportunities for a Competitive Advantage

At what stage of awareness are your major competitors? How long will it take your organization to evolve to Stage 4? And…how much easier would it be for you to recruit and retain talented people if you were formally recognized as an Employer of Choice[SM]?

CHAPTER TWO

Economics and Demographics

Economic and demographic trends converge during this decade. With consumer spending expected to remain strong until at least 2009, companies will enjoy profitable business, but will be challenged to attract and hold the employees they will need. This economic boom will spawn an unprecedented churning in the labor marketplace. Generational drivers will bring together different value sets and attitudes in the workplace. The profile of the American workforce will change as the wave of Boomers ages. The reduced numbers of Generation Xers will again present a serious challenge to organizational executives with stakeholders to serve. Younger folks, looking out for themselves, will move from job to job, seeking training and other opportunities. Job tenure will decrease. Workers will once again find themselves in the driver's seat, in a position to "choose" their employers. As the war for talent heats up, workforce stability will become imperative for profitability and perhaps, survival.

Can an expanding economy be part of the crisis facing business leaders? It can when economic growth places a severe strain on the organization and its [human] resources.

Economic forecasters allege that we are in the midst of a long-term boom. This growth period began in the early 1990s, but wasn't obvious because of a recession and a substantial amount of publicity about how bad things were. So many people were focused on the negative that they didn't realize the recession was over ... until their competitors surged ahead of them.

Looking at the long-term picture, which is what senior corporate executives are supposed to do, most economists see significant growth over the next decade. Sure, there will be some periodic downturns and corrections, but the fundamental strategic picture is that we'll be operating in a boom economy. Though no one can accurately forecast the particular year, presuming that spending patterns maintain. The data and trends point to the boom lasting to 2009 and possibly as long as 2013.

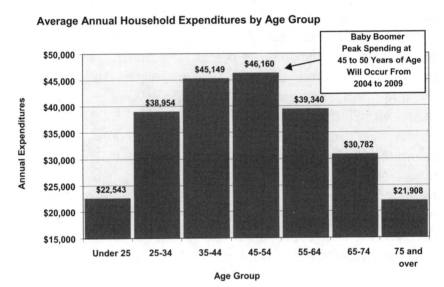

Average Annual Household Expenditures by Age Group

Source: BLS Research 2001

Figure 5: Annual Household Expenditures by Age Group

Statistics show that the peak age of consumption (consumer spending) occurs between ages 45 and 54. If this pattern continues, we should see the peak age of the Baby Boomers reaching this "spending high point" somewhere between 2004 and 2009. Between 2009 and 2013, due to the lower rate of spending of people over the age of 50, the U.S. economy will most likely begin to slow and decrease.

Statistics show that spending on durable goods peaks when people are aged 45–54. Demographically, this trend portends heavy spending 2004–2006, when the largest number of Baby Boomers will be in their mid-forties. Add to the factor of durables purchasing the increased desire for convenience services, and we can anticipate a robust economy. This condition will even be extended, since many Boomers postponed having children and/or married more than once and have second or third families. For these Boomers, the heavier purchasing of durables will be postponed as much as 15 years.

We hearken to forecasters like Harry S. Dent, whose book *The Great Boom Ahead* describes the influence of age waves on economic cycles. Dent asserts that the prosperity in our economy is based on the purchase of durable goods, and that historically consumers in their late 40s and early 50s have purchased more durables than at any other time in their lives. The unprecedented push on the economy is fueled by 76.4 million Baby Boomers in the United States and similar proportions of this age cohort in other countries. The Baby Boom generation began in 1946; add 45 years and, lo and behold, we're at 1991 . . . the start of the economic boom. Dent's theory suggests that we'll see this economic strength continue until the last of the Baby Boomers reaches their mid-fifties. Let's see: the generation ended in 1964. Add 55 years and we're in 2019. Can we sustain this hot economy that long?

There are so many variables that forecasting the economy more than five years out is difficult, at best. Recently we've seen how politics and terrorism can affect the economy—on a short-term basis. Fortunately, employers who have built underlying strength and stability will benefit from their resilience. Should you plan for such a long-running high-energy economy? Our crystal ball (and we use that term only metaphorically) says "yes." Actually, it says, "yes, but."

————————————— Words of Wisdom —————————————

Have contingency plans in place and continually watch the indicators that are important and significant to you. Many factors can influence the economy, sometimes without warning. Be prepared, at least in your thinking, for alternative scenarios.

On a more short-term basis, our consulting economists tell us that gradual growth is anticipated during the first part of the decade. By early mid-decade, most people will have noticed the growth and their thinking will shift more to a healthy economy model. With increased confidence, consumer spending will increase, followed by business-to-business spending.

What will this growth mean to you and your organization? More business. That's the good news. How much can you handle without putting a strain on all your resources? To produce that increased business, you will probably need more people. That's the bad news. The people you will need may not be available, or may not be as available as you would like them to be. Remember, in most situations, you need people who can do the job, not just warm bodies. You need people with skills, education, and credentials.

Broad economic growth, extending across all sectors of the economy, will generate job formation. At first, employers will be back-filling: hiring people to fill the jobs that were vacated during the layoff period of the early part of the decade. This restaffing could happen relatively quickly. Then new jobs will be created. Many organizations will simply swell the ranks of the jobs they have had, continuing to do business in the same way, but on a larger scale. The rise in commerce that will come with this change in perception will cause more companies to increase their hiring, inspiring people to leave jobs and employers they don't like to try the new opportunities.

> We forecast an unprecedented churning in the labor marketplace.

We forecast an unprecedented churning in the labor marketplace, accompanying these shifts. As other trends affect employment decisions, turbulence in the employment market will make the worker movement of the late 1990s seem mild by comparison.

The economy will continue generating jobs for workers at all levels of education and training. However, according to the Bureau of Labor Statistics, growth rates are projected to be faster, on average, for occupations requiring a postsecondary award (a vocational certificate, other certification, or an associates or higher degree) than for occupations requiring less education or training.

Most emerging jobs, however, will arise in occupations that require only work-related training (on-the-job training or work experience in a related occupation), even though these occupations are projected to grow more slowly, on average. This apparent paradox reflects the fact that these occupations accounted for about seven out of 10 jobs in 2000. This picture suggests that there will plenty of jobs for people receiving on-the-job training at the same time that we are encouraging people to upgrade their education and skills.

——————————— Words of Wisdom ———————————

Enlightened employers, sensitive to the need to do things differently, will redesign the way they are structured. They will challenge their processes, their staffing plan, and how people work together to accomplish results. They will keep employees who fit with the new design, and let those who do not move on to other jobs. Then they will carefully recruit just the kind of people they need to operate the company under the modified system. Their studied deliberation will enable them to hire people who will perform better and stay longer.

Generational Drivers

In the 1980s, labor force issues were not the problem that they are today. Shortages were localized or limited to certain specialties. As we moved into the 1990s, the economy was beginning to grow, stimulated by the Baby Boomers' buying power. During the early part of the decade, growth was inhibited by a recession, but the trends were in place. The strong commercial environment created more jobs, many of them at the entry level.

The shift into a boom economy caused unexpected challenges for employers. Several trends converged to change the relationship between employer and employee in ways that no one was prepared for or knew how to manage. The world of employment shifted to a whole new environment.

Customarily young people have filled our entry-level jobs. The generation following the Boomers, The Baby Busters, now known as Generation X, was smaller—about 15 percent smaller. So we had an expanding economy calling for more people to fill jobs, but only 68.5 million people in the entire Generation X population segment to take the positions. Fueled by technological expansion and the dot-com explosion, demand increased at all levels of the employment ladder.

Boomers, who had been fairly stable in their employment relationships, began to change jobs almost as frequently as the twenty-somethings. Across the population, people were changing jobs on an average of every two to four years. Employers who had enjoyed workforce stability throughout their history now found themselves scrambling to hire enough people to get the work done. Competition for competent employees intensified, evidenced by aggressive recruiters going after job candidates like crazed bounty hunters.

Employers were intent on filling those positions on the organizational chart, no matter what. Unfortunately, this thinking was seriously flawed, but employers resisted warnings during the go-go years of the mid-1990s. The problem began in the late 1960s when conservative, cost-minded, productivity-conscious employers were given a wonderful gift: a cornucopia of talent as the Boomers moved into the workforce. There were more people looking for work than jobs for them to fill, so employers had plenty of choices. With all those workers available, and funds available to hire them, many employers expanded their staffing levels. They hired more people, so they could grow their companies. Sadly, the companies did not stop at optimum staffing levels and gradually became bloated. Many employers had more people than they needed; they'd hired workers because people were available, not necessarily because they were needed.

The drop in the birth rate between the Boomers and Generation X created a problem. Employers had become accustomed to having plenty of people to choose from. Now the circumstances were considerably different. There were fewer applicants available, but most companies did not reduce the number of jobs on their organizational charts. Ignoring the statistics and the warning cries, they continued to hire to fill their inflated organizational charts.

The Changing Profile of the American Workforce

Because of a number of factors, the U.S. birth rate changes from year to year and, thus, we have corresponding changes in the number of people of any particular age in each year.

Over the past 25 years Ken Dychtwald, Ph.D., has emerged as the nation's leading visionary on the aging of America. He is a psychologist, gerontologist, and author of nine books, including the bestseller *Age Wave*.

Discussing the Age Wave phenomenon, Dychtwald explains, "We are in the midst of the most extraordinary evolutionary event of all time: the mass aging of our society. Throughout 99 percent of human history, the average life expectancy has been 18 years. In the past, people didn't age; they died.

"During the past century, extraordinary breakthroughs in healthcare have already been eliminating many of the diseases that used to keep us dying young. One hundred years ago, only 3 million Americans were over 65, 4 percent of our population. Today, the over-65 age group numbers more than 33 million, some 13 percent of our population." As people are presented with career and lifestyle choices, the aging of the population holds fascinating, exciting, and challenging implications for employers.

─────────────────── **Words of Wisdom** ───────────────────

The robust economy will provide tremendous opportunities for the older members of our population. Retirement at some predetermined age, a relatively recent phenomenon in our society, will fade in importance and use, as people choose to continue to work. The jobs will be there, income will be available to supplement savings, and people will have the opportunity to remain active, productive members of society. The concept of "retirement" will undergo significant change, challenging employers to build new flexibilities into their relationships with older workers.

Attention to the Age Wave has been focused on the maturation of our largest population cohort, the Baby Boomers. Considerable study has been done of this group over the years—understandably, because a wave of 76.4 million people has a monumental influence on a society. Dychtwald observes, "With the middle-aging of the boomers, we are beginning to feel the impact of the demographic 'age wave,' whose mass and force will ultimately challenge every aspect of our personal, social, financial, and political dynamics."

Well, we take Dychtwald's work another step, into another realm: The Workforce. In our study, we're going beyond the Boomers to look at people older—and younger—than the Boomers. What does the Age Wave of the workforce look like?

The following three figures illustrate the shift in ages in the workforce from 1994 through 2010. Each chart starts on the left side with people born in 1935 and continues to the right side of the graph where we show the proportionate numbers of people born in the 1990s. As you study these charts, watch the change in the aging of the workforce. Note that in the mid-1990s, the largest portion of the workforce was in the late twenties to late thirties. By 2002, that age range shifted to the late thirties to late forties. Look what happens in 2010. If we assume, as we do today, that a great deal of work gets done by people in their mid-thirties, we can see some changes coming.

What implications do these changing demographics have for your organization? As you ponder this question, please bear in mind that, while this is a future-focused book, 2010 is not *that* far away.

The Numbers

As the economy picked up in the mid-1990s, even more jobs were created to respond to the demand from customers—in the business-to-business and business-to-consumer arenas. Few human resource professionals or other executives were paying attention to population numbers and internal metrics at that time. Suddenly, there were not enough people to fill the jobs. In 1994 and 1995, employers began to feel the pinch. Nationally, according to the Bureau of Labor Statistics, we had 134,959,000 jobs to be filled, but only 132,304,000 people to fill them.

Most employers were oblivious to the climatic change that was taking place. They did not respond to the changing demographics with changes in the way they did business. Instead, they showed lots of vacancies on their organization charts and listened to their employees moan about how much work they had to do. They intensified their recruiting and complained about a labor shortage—blaming outside factors, but not exploring the changes taking place within their own organizations.

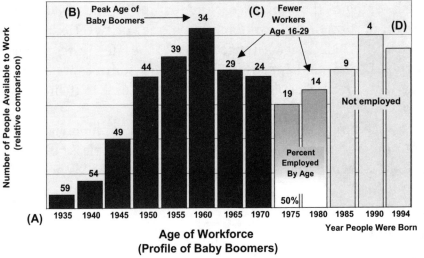

Figure 6: Workforce Age Wave 1994

The employment "age wave" chart illustrates the U.S. population profile of people born between 1935 and 1994 (A). This profile also represents the approximate number of people available for employment by age. Note that in 1994, the peak age of the Baby Boomers that were born in 1960 was approximately 34 years old (B). In 1994, there was approximately the same number of jobs available as there were people in the civilian labor force. There was a relative shortage of workers in the younger ages of 16 to 29 (C) and the next wave of people born between 1985 and 1994 is too young to enter the workforce (D).

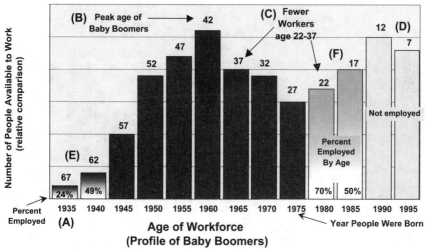

Figure 7: Workforce Age Wave 2002

This "age wave" profile in 2002 illustrates the U.S. population of people born between 1935 and 1995 (A). This profile also represents the approximate number of people available for employment by age. Note that in 2002, the peak age of the Baby Boomers was approximately 42 years (B). There was a relative shortage of workers in the younger ages of 22 to 37 (C); the next wave of people born between 1985 and 1995 was still too young to enter the workforce (D). There was also a shortage of people available to work due to retirement (E): only 49 percent of people aged 60 to 65 were still employed.

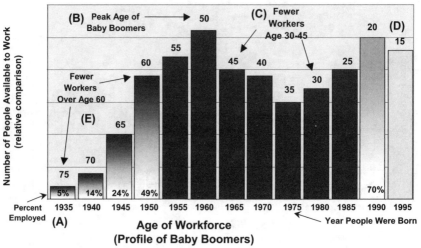

The Workforce Age Wave 2010

Source: BLS Research 2001

Figure 8: Workforce Age Wave 2010

The 2010 "age wave" chart illustrates the U.S. population profile of people born between 1935 and 1995 (A). This profile also represents the approximate number of people available for employment by age. Note that in 2010, the peak age of the Baby Boomers born in 1960 will be approximately 50 years (B). By 2010, there will be approximately 10,033,000 more jobs available than there are people in the civilian labor force. There will be a relative shortage of workers in the younger ages of 30 to 45 (C), and the next wave of people born between 1985 and 1995 is just entering the workforce (D). There is also a shortage of people available to work due to retirement (E) where from age 60 to 75, a significant number of people are no longer employed.

Oh, yes, we went through the reengineering phase. In so many organizations, reengineering was merely a euphemism to describe deep reductions of the workforce. This effort, described by some as "wholesale slaughter," concentrated on reducing headcount and payroll levels, not on changing the work to be done, the way to do it, or the reallocation of resources to address new ways of doing business.

Now, with fewer people in the workforce, employers had to compete in a sellers' labor market to get the people required to get the work done. Throwing money at the problem, like BMW automobiles as sign-on incentives, was classic during this period. This competition for talent pushed up compensation costs, as well as acquisition costs. As employers competed to hold on to their people, uncontrolled employee turnover became a predictably critical issue. Too many employers ignored the human elements, pushing their people even harder to reach productivity numbers and raising pay and perks to almost ridiculous levels.

In the year 2000, the Bureau of Labor Statistics reported a shortage of 4,731,000 people needed to fill the jobs available. Then in 2001, the economy slowed. Layoffs followed downsizings. Plant closings, restructurings, and other strategic corporate moves put hundreds of thousands of people out of work. The newspaper headlines about massive layoffs screened the fact that many of the employers who were pushing people out one door were bringing workers with different qualifications in another door, sometimes in greater numbers than the layoffs! Employers took advantage of the down economy to get rid of workers they didn't want or need.

Even though they weren't filled, the jobs remained. Waiting. Waiting for the economy to pick up again. Waiting to be filled by the same people who left. But those departing employees were looking for greener pastures. Their trust had been violated. Too many employers compromised their fragile relationships with employees when they handled the layoffs and downsizings badly.

—————————————————— Words of Wisdom ——————————————

Animosity continues to run deep. It will be difficult, if not impossible, for many employers to hire back the people they let go. As the economy grows and they need people, those less-than-sensitive employers will be forced to hire strangers, train them, and build a new workforce and a new culture. Consequently, some employers will have an advantage, some a disadvantage.

Let's fast-forward to 2010, a benchmark year for statisticians. Projections from the U.S. Department of Labor's Bureau of Labor Statistics indicate that our economy will support 167,754,000 jobs by the end of the decade. That's great news for prosperity, until you learn that we'll only have 157,721,000 people in the workforce in 2010 to fill those jobs.

167,754,000	openings
-157,721,000	people
10,033,000	shortfall

Today—and tomorrow—we don't have enough people to fill the jobs available in our economy.

Worse, many of the people who are available are not qualified to perform the duties required by those jobs now, let alone what those jobs will become in the future.

Competition will intensify more than ever as employers pursue qualified applicants to join their organizations. Certainly there is a risk of wage inflation, which could drive employers' payroll costs through the roof. This payroll increase is not an absolute; use of nonfinancial incentives may overcome at least part of the need to simply throw money at employees.

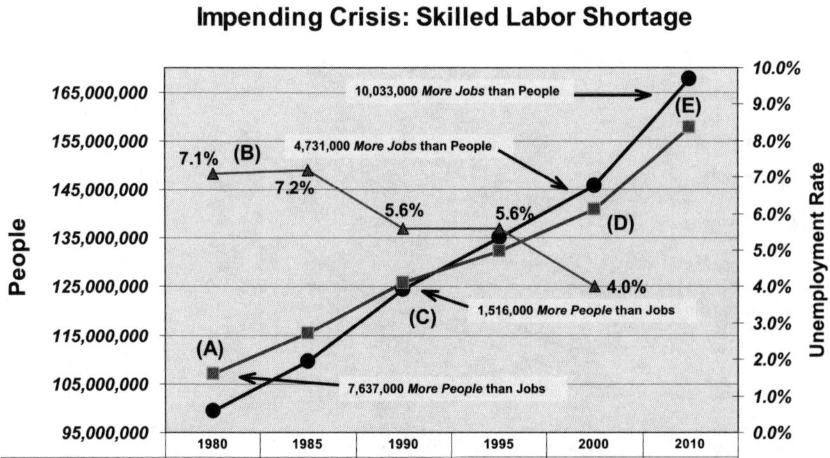

Impending Crisis: Skilled Labor Shortage

	1980	1985	1990	1995	2000	2010
Jobs Available	99,303,000	109,680,000	124,324,000	134,959,000	145,594,000	167,754,000
Civilian Labor Force	106,940,000	115,461,000	125,840,000	132,304,000	140,863,000	157,721,000
Unemployment	7.1%	7.2%	5.6%	5.6%	4.0%	?

Source: BLS Research 2001

Figure 9: Impending Crisis: Skilled Labor Shortage

This chart illustrates three trends in U.S. employment from 1980 to 2010: the civilian labor force, the approximate number of jobs available, and the unemployment rate. The historical and projected employment data is drawn from research by the U.S. Bureau of Labor Statistics. In 1980, the United States had approximately 7,637,000 more people available to work than there were jobs available (A). The unemployment rate in 1980 was 7.1 percent (B). By 1990, the employment condition had changed, but there were still approximately 1,516,000 more people available to work than there were jobs available (C). In 1994, the employment condition reversed itself for the first time in U.S. history where there were now more jobs available than there were people available to work. By 2000, there were 4,731,000 more jobs available than there were people able to work and the unemployment rate nationwide was 4.0 percent (D). The 2010 projection is that the U.S. employment market will have 10,033,000 more jobs available than there will be people to fill them (E).

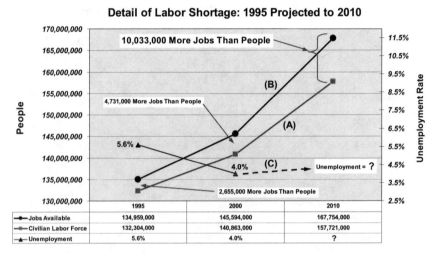

Source: BLS Research 2001

Figure 10: Detail of Labor Shortage from 1995 Projected to 2010

We get up close and personal with this chart as we enlarge the time frame. A closer inspection illustrates the relationships and gaps in three U.S. employment trends from 1995 to 2010: the civilian labor force (A), the estimated number of jobs available (B), and the unemployment rate (C). Although it is impossible to forecast these figures with pinpoint accuracy, most experts agree that the unemployment rate by 2010 will be in the 4 percent range, maybe even lower! An unemployment rate this low, combined with a shortage of younger workers creates an incredibly challenging environment for employers to recruit, hire, and retain skilled workers.

If we are to maintain the levels of productivity that will be required for competitive survival, we must hire competent employees. Productivity rates have accelerated over the years to match—and perhaps exceed—wage rates, demonstrating that we have seen significant improvement. Productivity may be improving at a faster rate than wages, thanks to the application of technology, systems improvement, and other changes in the way we do business.

Organizational charts became heavy with middle managers and other positions that really weren't essential to business operations. The positions were created because there were people available who could be hired to fill the jobs. Some employers engaged in empire building, so they could boast about how many people were employed by the company.

Under these conditions, work that had been done by, say, two people, was now being performed by three. We became accustomed to spreading the workload, then bringing in technology to strengthen productivity even more. Alas, we then had to hire more people to manage the technology. But, at that time, people were available, so it wasn't much of a problem. We had staff hours available for training, so corporate education and development programs flourished. Everything was wonderful until the supply of young workers began to diminish.

———————————— Words of Wisdom ————————————

To overcome the threat of wage inflation, because of a significantly reduced talent pool, we must continue to achieve gains in employee productivity. Therefore, companies must keep the competent people they have and improve their business processes (their efficiency).

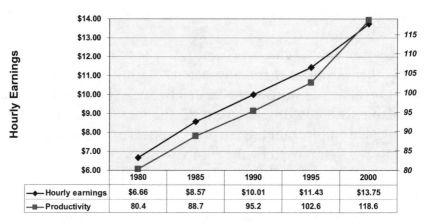

Productivity Compared to Hourly Earnings

	1980	1985	1990	1995	2000
Hourly earnings	$6.66	$8.57	$10.01	$11.43	$13.75
Productivity	80.4	88.7	95.2	102.6	118.6

Source: BLS Research 2001

Figure 11: Productivity Compared to Hourly Earnings

From 1980 to 1995, the two indices of labor productivity and hourly earnings track essentially parallel. In 1995, labor productivity accelerates to grow at a faster rate than the index for hourly earnings. As the economy heated up from 1995 to 2000, these gains in productivity may have contributed significantly to keeping wage inflation in control. There were only two other times in U.S. history that we observed productivity gains of this magnitude (from 1917 to 1927 and from 1948 to 1973).

Worker Movement

So, will people continue to change jobs every two to four years? At least. Workers are no longer loyal to the companies that employ them. They are loyal to their supervisors, coworkers, customers, and the work they are doing. If they are not happy, they leave. This behavior is difficult for management to understand. Many executives were raised in a different era, when people went to work for a particular company and stayed there for a long period of time. Job-hopping was frowned upon and could be a career killer. Work was not supposed to be enjoyable, meaningful, and rewarding. It was just work.

Today the prevailing attitudes and behaviors are considerably different, almost 180 degrees different. People feel that work should be fun, meaningful, and intrinsically rewarding. If someone is not happy in a job or doesn't like a supervisor, it's perfectly all right to just quit. Human resource professionals can tell you all sorts of stories about people walking off jobs and not expecting—or caring about—their final paycheck. People will leave a job on the first day—sometimes after just a few hours, or even not show up for work after having been hired.

To a large extent, society condones this career freedom. People can, do, and will make their own choices about where they work and why they work there. Employers have a responsibility to respond to employee needs and desires, aligning workers' preferences with employer needs.

> Are you that "right employer?" Can you prove that? Then sustain that belief after employment?

In an economy with plenty of jobs, a low unemployment rate, and continual growth, workers understandably feel a high level of confidence about managing their careers. Job change is not a big issue when there are "Help Wanted" signs everywhere you look. Newspaper advertising and on-line job boards make job search easy. There is an abundance of opportunities, practically anywhere in the country. (For more detailed data, see figures 12 and 13 in chapter 3.)

So, with all these choices, why should a worker stay with your company? We'll show you more about employee retention later in the book. For now, recognize that uncontrolled employee turnover is a very serious issue for you . . . perhaps your greatest vulnerability, because people *can* move so easily. They're searching for just the right employer for them. Are you that "right employer"? Can you prove that? Then sustain that belief after employment?

Impact

It's obvious that we have a problem, but looking at these numbers is just scratching the surface. Of course, if we can't get the work done for our customers and clients, we risk losing them to competitors who can meet their needs and expectations in a timely manner. This risk involves serious potential loss, probably permanent, changing the way the business operates . . . if it can even survive.

The solution, it would seem, is to intensify our recruiting campaign . . . to aggressively move to attract and hire the people who can get the jobs done. This approach is fine, in isolation. However, imagine how many other employers will be competing with you to hire the same people. This battle could become very expensive. Competition for scarce resources always is. And paying high prices for scarce resources isn't the answer, particularly when it drives up prices for customers who are already sensitive to being gouged.

The situation becomes complicated, more difficult, and substantially more expensive when those competitors target *your* employees in their recruiting efforts. Employers will be faced with much more than just a recruiting war; as having a stable workforce becomes a strategic advantage in the marketplace, retention will become even more critical. It's a lot cheaper to keep trained, experienced employees than to find replacements and then to invest a considerable amount of time and other resources training and preparing those new hires to do the jobs.

Perhaps an even bigger problem is the potential loss of continuity. Companies with high turnover become inefficient, because critical knowledge and experience has walked out the door. The employees who are targeted by recruiters are the most competent. Consider who will be left to run your business when the competent workers are gone. Scary?

Words of Wisdom

Business owners who see the challenge as insurmountable may attempt to sell their businesses or negotiate some sort of roll-up or industry consolidation. Recognizing that a large proportion of the mergers and acquisitions that have taken place in recent years were done to acquire talented employees, a lack of sufficient staffing may endanger the potential sale of the business.

The workforce dilemma will create a serious vulnerability for employers. Not all industries will be affected the same way at the same time, but all will feel the shortage of qualified workers. Human resources will play an increasingly vital role in maintaining the strength, viability, and profitability of the corporation. Bottom line: A stable, productive workforce will be the competitive advantage. Corporate leaders must recognize this fundamental fact and do everything in their power to attract, optimize, and retain top talent. Workforce stability will be a strategic imperative.

Closing Questions

1. Is your leadership team aware of the coming Impending Crisis in the labor market?
2. Have you analyzed your workforce from an age cohort perspective?
3. Is the average age of your employees increasing or decreasing?
4. Do you have a good understanding of your productivity levels with respect to your present and future human capital needs?

Opportunities for a Competitive Advantage

Would having more mature, experienced employees that were less likely to move to other organizations help you at this time? How much more "market cap" overall value could be added to the total value of your company, if the productivity of your employees increased just 5 percent per year for the next 8 years?

CHAPTER THREE

Influential Trends

When we look at the big picture, a number of significant trends and other factors emerge. Attitudes of workers and managers will shift. In an effort to control their own destinies, workers will move from job to job. As workers evaluate what's really important to them, their values will change, including their placing increasing emphasis on life-work balance. Some employees will choose to telecommute; most will recognize the need to stay marketable. Human resources must be active at the strategic table and forecasting of needed personnel strength through strategic staffing will be vital. Factors like globalization of work, the aging of the workforce, the older workers' choices to keep working, the increasing speed of change, and exponential advancements in technology will all play a part in the workforce/workplace of tomorrow. More women will rise to positions of greater authority, however, this trend will be seriously threatened by the lack of affordable, quality childcare. The Impending Crisis is affected by the inadequacy of workers' education compared with job skill needs. Though immigration will be used to offset some of the shortfall, more highly skilled workers may choose to stay in their home countries. Employer-employee relationships will evolve as will organizational structure. The corporation of the future will be much different that today.

Trends and other factors interact to cause situations that have may not been anticipated by those who will be affected. Without advance warning and understanding of what's happening, people and organizations risk becoming victims of trends rather than beneficiaries.

Forecasting is not an exact science. While based on a wide range of facts, manipulated by mathematical models and other computerized tools for projection and extrapolation, there is a certain degree of intuition that comes into play. Therein lies the risk, because it is not possible to predict with precision what will happen when. However, for most forecasting needs, we can build confidence around approximations based on a collection of assumptions.

We see a convergence of relevant trends that will significantly affect the way employers do business. Can we establish a specific date that all this disruption will happen? Of course not. We do, however, expect that the initial impact will be felt about a third of the way through the 2000–2010 decade, with increasing intensity as time passes.

This convergence is an evolutionary process, with a variety of trends moving together at differing speeds and strengths. Our assumptions are presented below. As you give some thought to what we're observing and sharing with you, you will probably come to similar conclusions.

Job Movement Condoned

While employers don't like it, society has blessed the relatively frequent movement of workers from one job to another. What used to be called "job-hopping" is now accepted behavior. In fact, among many groups of friends or networks of colleagues, if you work "too long" at one job, you may actually get questions from your peers about why you're still there.

This freedom of movement between jobs was not fully possible until the mid-1990s. Prior to that time, there were not enough opportunities for a large proportion of workers to change employment very often at all. As the economy picked up, people saw more "Help Wanted" signs and felt a new sense of mobility in the employment market. Customer demand placed employers in a position of needing more help, stimulating more aggressive recruiting. An unprecedented churning in the labor market began. At its height, this movement saw people changing jobs every two to four years. The average tenure on a job plummeted from 4.6 years in 1990 to 3.5 years in 2000.

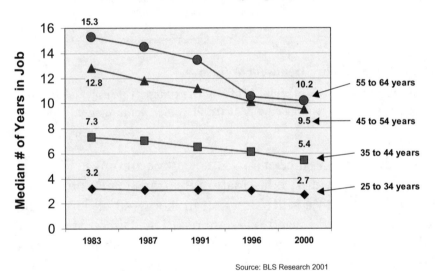

Job Tenure Trends by Age for Men

Source: BLS Research 2001

Figure 12: Job Tenure Trends for Men

From 1983 to 2000, every age group of men exhibited progressively shorter tenures in their jobs. Also, people ages 25 to 44 are now leaving their jobs at the peak of their "tenure equity" and "talent equity," a time when they add significant human capital value. (See chapter 5)

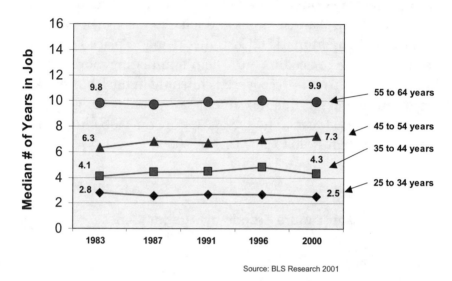

Source: BLS Research 2001

Figure 13: Job Tenure Trends for Women

From 1983 to 2000, most age groups of women exhibited consistent job tenures. Also, note the gap in tenure between men and women in the age groups of 35 to 44 and 45 to 54.

With the abundance of jobs in a healthy economy in the mid-1990s, we watched with fascination the transformation from a buyer's market to a seller's market in labor—at all levels. The leading edge of this trend was centered in the United States, but other developed countries felt the same swing months later. As we moved through the 1990s, the lag time shortened and other economies experienced aspects of the American phenomenon very soon after American employers—and employees—did.

Concurrently, workers became disenchanted with the world of big corporations and felt a desire to have more control over their career destiny. They began to drop out, creating what Daniel Pink describes in his book, *Free Agent Nation*. People were no longer following the established rules, but instead looking toward selling themselves and their services to employers *they* wanted to work with.

In 2001, a survey of 32-year-old workers revealed that their average number of jobs held was 8.6. Corporate loyalty was gone, replaced by a loyalty to oneself, to one's work, to one's customers, and to one's colleagues. The work relationship focused on the bond between the employee and the employee's immediate supervisor. Loyalty became one-on-one, which illuminated serious shortcomings in supervisory training. The professional development of supervisors—at all levels—had fallen far behind the need. A great number of people left jobs because of the way they were treated, or mistreated, by their bosses.

This frequent movement, or at least the open possibility of it, abruptly ceased during the economic downturn of 2001. Though the full effect wasn't seen until later in the year, the reversal was firmly in place by mid-year. As the economy slowed, employers dumped the excess baggage of employees they could no longer afford. They laid off the very people they had competed so aggressively (and expensively) to attract. Unfortunately, with many companies led by relatively unseasoned managers, who had not fully experienced the recession of 1989–1991, the organizations were less than sensitive in the way people were removed from the payroll. Workers who received this ill treatment now became even testier than before and much less likely to feel loyalty or trust toward employers in the future.

> People graduating from college in 2001 are projected to hold an average of 11 jobs in their working lifetimes.

Employer-Employee Relationships

At the height of the seller's market period, there was a major change in the relationship between employees and employers. This relationship shift is an important part of our social fabric yet today, though it is now felt with some degree of animosity.

During the 1970s, the 1980s, and even the early 1990s, workers were "forced" (okay, "motivated") to follow company rules, procedures, and directives. They applied themselves diligently, ever eager for that shining positive performance appraisal that would mean continued employment and, hopefully, a modest increase in compensation. Workers responded obediently to requests from their superiors. The social system was well-ordered and understood by all. Even without the badge of management, older workers commanded respect and honor, especially in the trade occupations with their apprentice-journeyman-craftsman hierarchies.

When workers no longer needed to protect their positions in a company, because there were plenty of alternative employment opportunities available, they no longer had to comply with the establishment's system. Now the worker was king, not the job or the company. If workers were not happy, they left. The time-honored practice of giving two weeks' notice disappeared, as workers jumped to the new job that, of course, needed them right away. Employers now had to deal with new challenges: Critical positions suddenly coming open, not enough people to get the job done, and customers leaving because they could not get their needs met. Workforce stability became a bottom-line issue, though still a great number of employers didn't get it.

The shift to an employee-centered work environment was a totally foreign concept to many supervisors, managers, executives, and company owners. While those who became more aware gave lip service to the new relationship, in most workplaces the acknowledgment was shallow, unproductive, and sometimes even counterproductive. However, in the larger sense, workers now had a taste of something different, something intoxicating: they had value and could actually exert some influence over their careers, their link with their employers, and how they did their work. An emerging sense of worker autonomy became part of the employment environment.

Worker Attitudes

Another factor affecting your predicament is a shift in worker attitudes that we've seen over the past decade or so. These attitudes influence job choice, on-the-job performance, tenure, and relationships within the employment environment. We list worker attitudes as part of the Impending Crisis because of their conflict with management attitudes. Employers must change their relationships with the people who work for them, and that kind of climatic change won't be easy. It must be actively led from the top of the organization, and that fact will often make the change even more problematic.

In years past, workers were accustomed to doing what they were told. The boss was the boss. Orders were given and followed. Management knew what was right and laborers—whether on a production line, in an office, or on the street—were expected to do what they were told. Jobs were not supposed to be enjoyable; work did not have a pleasant connotation. It was something that *had* to be done to earn money to purchase food, clothing, and shelter. As we have stated earlier, it was "just work."

Managers were similar to parents. During this era, children were not permitted to argue with their parents. Respect and obedience were the societal expectation. Teachers and clergy carried the same force of power as parents, so designated by society, and this relationship was even expressed in the form of condoned corporal punishment. Parents were home when children came home from school. Supervision was close at hand.

In the hot economy of the 1970s and 1980s, there were plenty of jobs. Both parents were working as Generation X kids grew up. These children were known as "latchkey kids." They'd come home from school to an empty house, open the door, and get started on fulfilling their responsibilities—chores, homework, and staying out of trouble. These kids learned how to be independent and self-sufficient.

Watching their parents work all the time with insufficient family time, these young people began dreaming of adult lives with more life balance. Work for its own sake, especially all-consuming, was not valued as highly by this younger generation. The older generations seemed to identify themselves by the work they did more than the families they raised.

Then came the recession of the late 1980s and early 1990s. Parents lost their jobs, their income, and their occupational identities. This sudden change in societal status was unexpected. Parents were not prepared, financially or psychologically, to be without work, resources, benefits, or support groups. They felt a sense of betrayal. These workers had trusted their employers to take care of them from cradle to grave, and now they had been thrown out like yesterday's garbage.

The children saw the grieving, the deep emotional reaction that adults exhibited when the rug of life was jerked out from under their feet. They heard the moans of disappointment, of powerlessness. The feelings were similar to those experienced by their ancestors during the Great Depression, but deeper because they were more vulnerable. Their feelings of personal responsibility, self-sufficiency, and fundamental survival were not as strong as they had been for people back in the 1920s. Their children were deeply affected; it influenced the thought patterns and emotions that would stay with them for many years. Those children are today's Generation X workers.

Can you understand why your younger employees have so much trouble trusting employers? Can you appreciate why they are so adamant about managing their own careers? After seeing what happened to their elders, they certainly don't want to put all their eggs in one basket—anyone's basket. They want control over their own lives.

Part of the way to avoid getting too attached—putting too many of those eggs in one basket—is to keep moving. Don't stay too long in any one job. Don't trust supervisors and managers.

And what they tell you to do isn't law. Permissiveness that was learned growing up carries over into the work environment, as does self-sufficiency and personal accountability.

Manager Attitudes

Have your managers been trained in the skills and techniques of working with Generation X workers? A better question: Have your managers been sufficiently trained to supervise others? Have they been trained to lead, and shown the difference between leading and managing? You would be astonished at the deficiencies in management and supervisory training in corporate America—and that includes nonprofits, education, and government organizations.

Too few supervisors ever get the education and training they need to do their jobs well. Let's define the terms, with thanks to Dr. Leonard Nadler, recognized as the "father of the field of human resource development". Education helps learners understand the big picture, the "why" and "what." Training conveys the "how," the skill to do what education says must be done. Most supervisors are in desperate need of both education and training in their roles. We've thrown these ill-prepared bosses into untenable situations and expected them to perform. And we wonder why their people are leaving the company.

Research, conducted by the Corporate Leadership Council in Washington, D.C., underscores the supervisor's role in employee retention. Peter Friere, executive director of the organization's human resource practice, drives home the point when he says that "the relationship between the employee and the employee's immediate supervisor is the single most influential factor in determining how long the employee will stay."

Managers and supervisors—frontline and middle-level—have been trained and reinforced in methods that worked fine a generation ago. These old-style methods don't work as well in today's environment and, at times, are even counterproductive. As we move into the balance of this decade, supervisors using the old approaches will become obsolete and potential liabilities to the organization. Serious retraining is needed, inspired by the company's top leadership, who should also participate—to encourage and to learn themselves.

While you may accuse us of playing with semantics, the big change is that we must now work with fellow employees—at all levels—in a much more collaborative relationship. Your people, your "subordinates," will work *with* you; they will not work *for* you. The days of micromanaging are over once an employee understands the job to be done. Employees are sending a clear message of what they want: "Let's agree on the results, give me the tools I need to get the job done, and get out of my face!" A lot of managers just aren't able to do that. Nor do they know how to intervene when a team member really does need some help.

There is a lot of work to be done to bring managers and supervisors into the new mode of leadership. Many of them are receptive. They sense the changes, the climate shift, but don't know what to do about it. They know they need help and they want it. Other managers will refuse to change, forcing you into making some decisions that may not be too comfortable. They don't know what they don't know. You cannot use yesterday's techniques with tomorrow's challenges and expect to be successful. Period.

An extra heads-up: In some organizations, the changes will not occur because the person or people at the top are still stuck in yesterday. If the senior leaders don't change, they may soon find that all their good people have left. If all your competent employees leave, your workforce will consist entirely of incompetent people. Incompetent employees who cannot serve customers satisfactorily will expose the company to further losses, as unhappy customers take their business elsewhere.

Mercenary Darwinism

We've encountered a number of employers who believe they can solve their job vacancy problems by dangling huge signing bonuses in front of desired candidates. The research we've conducted suggests that this practice does not work, and it's very expensive. Bonuses have become an easy way out for employers who don't have the courage or the leadership to change their business practices. The bonuses also give the illusion that recruiting and retention is getting easier. The problem is that every time an employer "wins" a new recruit, another employer loses.

Looking more closely at the big bonus game, social network analyst Scott Degraffenreid describes what he calls "Mercenary Darwinism." When employers hire people who have demonstrated a tendency to leave for more or quick money, they load their staffs with people whose motives may be questionable . . . and probably out of alignment with the organization's more stable culture. We could call this a "fickle workforce." Their loyalty is to themselves and their investment portfolios.

The plot thickens. Mercenary Darwinism sends strong signals to existing staff that job hopping for bonuses is condoned, even encouraged. Over the years, Scott has observed that signing bonuses have a consistent and extremely deleterious effect on tenure and retention. The practice accelerates both warm- and empty-chair attrition of experienced employees, requiring more hiring of inexperienced "mercenaries." (See chapter 5 for an explanation of warm- and empty-chair attrition.) This recruiting approach is the classic case of a short-term solution generating a much greater long-term problem.

Worker Control Over Their Own Destiny

At the same time, younger workers were exerting more influence over the workplace. Their voices—and their attitudes—

were being heard. When they were just coming into the world of work, these young people, part of Generation X (born 1965–1985), watched their parents get pink slips during the recession of 1989–1991. They felt the anguish as these loyal employees, who expected the company to take care of them from cradle to grave, were suddenly out on the street with no support system and nowhere to go. They were abruptly thrown out of work, losing their all-important occupational identity, with some deep emotional feelings of betrayal. . . and in many cases minimal financial compensation.

These young people learned a vital lesson from their parents' experience: Employers can't be trusted. If you want to succeed in your career, you must manage the process yourself. No longer can you place your career in the hands of an unfeeling, uncaring employer who obviously will not have *your* best interests in mind. The concept of climbing the career ladder in one organization (as in William Whyte's *The Organization Man*) was gone. Evaporated. Now it was (and is) everyone for himself or herself.

To grow and prosper, one must stay alert for new opportunities for growth, challenging assignments, and increased earning capacity. The new career design means doing whatever it takes on a personal level to achieve one's established goals. If that means changing jobs—or careers, so be it. Climbing the proverbial ladder is no longer the "right" thing to do for everyone. There are alternative ways to manage one's career. The new freedoms create new paths; you can blaze your own trail.

Values Shifts among Workers

As this societal transformation proceeded and workers began to make life decisions, they now looked more closely at their values. Employers, hungry to get more work done, were pushing employees pretty hard, raising expectations of performance without corresponding appreciation for worker contributions. Many people started to ask, "Is this worth it?" "Is this all there is?" The sense that there is more to life than just work percolated through society. "Get a life" became a meaningful phrase.

────────────── **Words of Wisdom** ──────────────

People are happy to work hard for an employer. They just want a winnable game worth playing, i.e., meaningful work. They want to do good things, be measured effectively, and be rewarded appropriately.

Beyond the concept of control over one's career path, there was the more immediate desire to gain more control over present-day experiences. People wanted more time with their families, themselves, their community. They wanted to volunteer, to make a difference, to leave a personal legacy of a world a little bit better than what it was. Employers who responded to these expressions of desire for something different earned loyalty through family-centeredness, community involvement initiatives, and a higher level of personal support for employees. Initiatives included corporate involvement in causes like Habitat for Humanity, Gift of Sight, and Operation Smile; enriched individual development programs and tuition reimbursement; physical fitness facilities in the headquarters complex; and the availability of concierge services.

People are getting more involved, actively working to get their employers engaged in meeting their nonwork needs. Convenience services such as dry cleaning pick-up and delivery are becoming more common. Traditional attitudes of the-boss-is-always-right are yielding to workers joining bosses in the decision-making process.

Life-Work Balance

This trend is still in its infancy. As people examine their lives, they feel a discomfort that something is not quite right. They want something different in the balance between work, their families, their community, their faith, and their own personal development. Some have described this desire as a sort of serenity, launching us into an exploration of spirituality—in our personal lives and in our work lives. (See Richard Barrett, *Liberating the Corporate Soul: Building a Visionary Organization*, Butterworth-Heinemann, 1998).

While many commentators use the phrase "work-life balance," we suggest that the real emphasis is on having a life, with work as a secondary part of the picture. Thus, we encourage use of the phrase "life-work balance." Semantics? Perhaps. But reflect on how your thinking is prioritized. What's really more important to you . . . and to your workers?

With both parents working, the experience of raising children has become a challenge. A great many working parents will tell you that childcare is their biggest concern. Often working long hours, managing conflicting shifts, or enduring long commutes, these parents are worried about what "family" really means. There must be more to this "family thing" than just living in the same space and having the same name (although those parameters have changed, too).

Many workers are searching for balance, without quite knowing what it will look like when they find it. The uneasiness that accompanies this search, and the ever-present guilt of not having found it yet, will drive people to make some unexpected decisions about work and their careers. They will want different relationships with their employers, causing major changes in the way we employ, manage, and measure work contributions.

Telecommuting and Self-Management

Have you noticed the growth of telecommuting? What's driving this? The trend was in place long before the atrocities of September 11, 2001, changed the way we looked at having to work in the same place with coworkers. Telecommuters, and other home-based workers, enjoy a unique kind of freedom, autonomy, and self-determination. In many cases, they set their own working hours and use their uninterrupted time and independence to become substantially more productive . . . and self-satisfied. Research suggests that teleworkers are 20 percent more productive, according to the Canadian Telework Association.

Telecommuting enables employers to tap into special talent groups such as an employee who moves geographically as a trailing spouse, employees on maternity—or paternity—leave and new mothers who might not want to leave their new child right away, highly talented people who are physically constrained by disabilities, single parents who need to be home for their children, and employees who care for elderly relatives.

A survey by the *Washington Post* in 1999 revealed some insightful results from "infotechies" in the national capital area. The 3,400 respondents were asked what special privileges would be most appealing.

- 548 said telecommuting (16.1 percent)
- 396 said training/tuition (11.6 percent)
- 379 said flextime (11.1 percent)
- 375 said benefits (11.0 percent)
- 370 said bonuses (10.9 percent)
- 357 said fitness (10.5 percent)
- 334 said money (9.8 percent)
- 302 said other perks (8.9 percent)
- 227 said time off/vacation (6.7 percent)
- 109 said opportunity/growth (3.2 percent)
- 80 said recognition/security (2.4 percent)

Before you say, "that was way back in 1999," remember that we're moving into an employment environment that will be very similar to the late 1990s.

While remote workers cause managers to function differently (how many have been retrained?), this physical detachment is certainly a feature of future work relationships. With the aid of technology, remote workers can be literally anywhere in the world. This geographic expansion enables employers to hire people to work from their homes in other time zones, other countries. No longer must talent be local. New opportunities abound for employers and employees to be where they want to be, yet be productively connected.

In fact, the opportunity is so great that there is now a company, Willow CSN Incorporated that has over 1,600 agents working in the comfort (and security) of their own homes. These contract workers directly serve Willow's clients with telephonic customer service support. This unusual organization requires an investment from new agents of between $1,200 and $3,500 for the application filing fee, technology, and training. And at any given time, Willow has a waiting list of over 5,000 people who are waiting to be taken on as CyberAgent Customer Service Representatives for Willow's clients. Three to four percent of their contract workforce is physically challenged, validating that workers with special challenges—physical, mental, emotional, or family-care—can be fully employed. With this company's sophisticated Starmatic™ software, Willow CSN's teleworkers can now be located almost anywhere on the globe.

The concept of self-management is driving more people to this independent contractor status. Expect to accomplish a significant portion of your company's work through people who work for you, yet are not on your payroll. Are you ready to measure performance by results, rather than activity or promptness in showing up for work on time? Amazingly, many employers have serious problems with this approach.

Human Resources at the Strategic Table

Most companies have made the leap from "personnel" to "human resources," thought some are still bewildered and unable to discern the difference. The concept of "human resources" acknowledges that people are a vital resource to the success of the enterprise, just like capital equipment, buildings, power, materials, and financial resources. In fact, there's increasing movement toward recognizing workers as "human capital."

Lisa Aldisert, a consultant and author, puts a different spin on this definition when she suggests that it's more than the workers themselves; it's what they bring to the party. In *Valuing People* (Dearborn Publishing, 2002), she says "human capital is the collective skills and knowledge of a firm's workforce."

If the workforce is so important, for current operations and for our strategic future, then that importance suggests a leadership role for the professional(s) responsible for an employer's human resources. This function should occupy a comparable position to the chief marketing officer, the chief financial officer, the chief manufacturing officer, and the chief logistics officer, depending on the nature of the employer's business. We are beginning to see more of this elevation of the chief human resource officer, but this recognition is not universal yet.

Words of Wisdom

If your senior human resource professional isn't sitting at your company's strategic table, you will be at a serious competitive disadvantage—in the competition for the limited available business *and* in the competition for a highly competent, stable workforce. In fact, if your chief human resource officer is just *sitting* at the strategic table, you have other problems! If this vital team member isn't *actively participating* in serious strategic decisions, either the CEO or the CHRO might need to be replaced!

Strategic Staffing

As you look to the future, watching marketing trends and other influential factors in your particular environment, having the right people on-board will affect your organization's capacity to perform. Strategic staffing will become increasingly critical. Based on your company's strategic plan, what kinds of people will we need to accomplish that plan? Where will they come from? How will they be prepared? How will they be organized to get work done? How will they be led?

What will we do to encourage the right people to join us, to optimize their performance, and to persuade them stay with us for more than two to four years? What is being done *now* to prepare your organization for what it will need at some point, say five years, into the future? Are you like so many employers that are so focused on tactical and operational issues that you haven't even considered your longer-term future needs? See chapter 10 for more detail.

Personnel Strength

Concurrently, because of the expanding complexity of work to be done, employers will need to consider the intellectual bandwidth of their employees. In other words, how broad and deep are the capabilities of the people who work in your organization? Are your employees cross-trained . . . and cross-experienced? As your organization attempts to evolve into the future, what's their capacity to move beyond their current work into the jobs that will emerge?

There is a gradual movement, probably moving at too slow a pace, to move from silo organizational structure to a more open or matrix design. An increasing number of workers is demonstrating a desire for professional growth—in knowledge, skills, and experience—to avoid getting stuck in any one career rut.

Wise employers are working with employees individually, help-ing them build their personal aptitude—and compensating them based on competencies acquired.

Globalization

The globalization of just about every aspect of our lives is now a reality. Look at the clothes you're wearing, the car you drive, and the food you eat. Our business lives are similarly af-fected. It seems that the world has certainly gotten smaller. We are all much more interdependent. Given the increasing cross-border education, travel, business relationships, and understand-ings, in another generation geopolitical boundaries will have much less importance than they do today. Watch the European Union as a case study and extrapolate that cohesion interna-tionally. How will you be positioned with regard to globaliza-tion—as a leader, early adapter, or follower?

Our workforce has become global, and this phenomenon will grow in the years ahead. We've gone far beyond just sending some people from our company to work at an overseas site. Even lo-cally, people from many countries, ethnicities, and backgrounds may populate our workforce. We've seen companies with em-ployees from all over the world, and sometimes with language barriers to accompany the differences. Additionally, we are work-ing more closely with partner companies, customers, and sup-pliers in foreign lands. Some of our telecommuting or indepen-dent-contractor employees will be from other countries. This trend will expand, giving the idea of diversity new meanings and implications.

Age Factors

Today we have three generations in the workforce at the same time. Never before in history have we had such a wide range of ages—and values—in our workforce. What's the big deal? There are natural conflicts between age groups. Their values are different, their perspectives are different, their expectations are different. Even though the differences are certainly present, the mixing in the workforce and in society has also fostered similarities. Working together, people of all ages have built a productive congruence of attitudes and values. They share the positive attributes of each generation to produce a collaborative cohesiveness.

The older members of the workforce contribute a strong work ethic, maturity, wisdom, and the benefit of years of experience. The younger members contribute a high level of energy, impatience, creativity, and a tendency to challenge the status quo. For a greater understanding of the influence of generational values on the work environment, see *Generations at Work* by Ron Zemke, Claire Raines, and Bob Filipczak. Younger workers, members of Generation X, are independent, self-sufficient, and impatient with any activities that don't achieve results. Computer-literate, they seek autonomy, challenge, and accountability.

Life in the world of work is about to get even more interesting. Soon, the Millennial Generation will enter the workforce. Now four generations will be working together—that's unprecedented. Born after 1985, these self-driven young people are much more technology-oriented and are even more independent than Generation X. Having been weaned on computer games demanding mental dexterity, they will kick Generation X's high speed into overdrive, or to use Star Trek jargon, "warp speed." Problem: Many of today's business leaders will not be able to keep up with this action-oriented energy. Are there conflicts coming? How will they be addressed?

Older Workers Sticking Around

The older members of our workforce will not retire when they reach the magical age of 65. They'll remain in the workforce for several reasons: their personal values and need to be productive members of society, the vacuum effect of the jobs to be filled holding them in the workplace, and their own personal needs to generate sufficient cash to live. Consider their predicament:

- 37 percent of those saving for retirement say they are doing only a fair job of managing their retirement portfolios, and 7 percent say they are doing a poor job.
- 44 percent of those saving for retirement say they expect to live less comfortably in retirement.
- 29 percent of retirees say their standard of living has gone down in retirement

These numbers come from the Economic Policy Institute, a nonpartisan research organization based in Washington, D. C. Christian Weller, a retirement specialist with the Institute, reports that "The average American household has virtually no chance to reach an adequate retirement savings in the next 50 years." People will have to keep working.

A Faster World

Communications govern much of what we humans do. If we are to interact with each other, for whatever reasons, we must communicate. For many years, regular mail delivery was just fine. If something was more important, airmail might be worth the extra expense. If a written communication were hot-hot-hot, Special Delivery would save the day.

Then came the facsimile machine. What an innovation! We remember when they were first introduced and being adapted as a new technology. Sending and receiving important communications through the telephone lines, producing much more rapid communication, made a difference in the way a lot of companies operated.

As many corporate leaders (or their assistants) learned how to deliver important documents or sales materials within a few

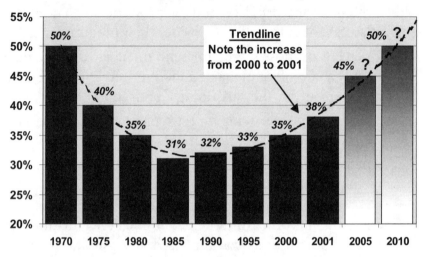

Source: BLS Research 2001

Figure 14: The Percentage of People Working at Age 65

The approximate number of people still working now from age 60 to 65 is 49%. (See figure 8.) However, with eroded pension funds, increases in living costs, and annual savings rates almost non existent, the trend for people at the benchmark age of 65 that remain working is beginning to increase at an accelerated rate. Note the trend line and increase from 1990 to 2001. It is unclear at this time what the workforce percentage rate for people ages 60 and older will eventually become, but the luxury, capability, and desire of being "completely retired" may become a lifestyle of the past.

days, or *overnight,* the overnight delivery couriers had quite an impact. In some of their service areas, couriers even delivered on the same day.

Then came e-mail and the Internet. A tremendous amount of information is available at our fingertips through the World Wide Web, instantaneously, without even asking. And these communications services are global, linking people throughout the world in real time. Instant messaging has moved into the corporate arena.

A consequence of this rapid communication is an expectation that *all* business transactions are done more quickly. Work is put off until the last possible moment, then done quickly with the use of fast communication tools. Too often, decisions are made *reactively*, without giving sufficient thought to the ramifications of the choices being made. Still, there is the uncomfortable feeling that if you do not respond immediately to the communication you have received—e-mail, courier, or telephone—you may lose an opportunity to a competitor.

Cellular telephones make us even more accessible, further reducing our time to think, to consider. Privacy is disappearing in favor of being available to anyone at any time. Speed, productivity, and quality do not necessarily go together. Faster action may mean missing some important details, a potentially high risk in today's complicated world of business.

> Information overload increases the difficulty in separating the important from the urgent.

Technology

Economic expansion will fuel a rapid growth of technology. We're not anticipating another dot-com explosion, but rather an emerging range of developing technologies that will enable employers to improve efficiency and effectiveness. Computers will, of course, play a major role, but other kinds of technologies will also be employed.

The use of technology will be focused on reducing process time to increase productivity and/or reduce the need for people. Other technologies, like anytime banking machines, will provide increased convenience for customers while reducing the need for people. Gasoline dispensing stations that are completely automatic, without even a human attendant, will achieve the same objective of providing cost-effective service 24 hours a day, seven days a week. Imagine the use of technology in science in the next ten years, in medicine, research, and bioengineering.

Computerization has instigated and supported a wide range of technologies that do more than merely increase the speed of our work. We are now able to better manage huge databases and retrieve quickly information that didn't even exist a relatively short time ago. We can model a wide range of alternatives using computers to raise our strategic planning to a whole new level. Many companies engage in deliberate strategic planning a number of times each year, instead of limiting themselves to the annual where-are-we-going approach.

Technology has enabled precision manufacturing with the use of robotics, substantially improving production and productivity, especially those operations related to small or microscopic assembly. Process innovations are changing the way workers manage their jobs. Creative invention, rapid retooling, and on-the-fly process redesign allow manufacturers to fabricate needed products on a short-run or highly customized basis. This agility will drive the role of much of the manufacturing in America, while more routine, assembly-line, large-run work will be done in less wage-intensive countries. The locus of jobs is shifting globally under the influence of technology.

We could devote an extensive amount of space in this book to the many aspects of technology. Innovations from intricate color matching to intensive patient monitoring are changing the way we work. Employers are no longer as dependent on people showing up for work to be sure the job gets done. Whatever we write here *could be* obsolete or superseded by the time you read this book.

Ever-changing technology requires a new type of worker to stay on top of the technological applications. Where will these people come from? The twenty-somethings—and even more, their counterparts still in high school or middle school—will carry this load. But they will have to be led differently, since the Technological Age is concurrent with changing values, expectations, and preferences among the people who will be needed to get this work done.

We'd like to share an interesting story with you to illustrate the challenge. The Herman Group was engaged by the U.S. Navy to consult with their senior leaders about what the navy would look like in 2015 and how they should prepare. One of the briefing officers proudly described a new destroyer under construction that would require a personnel complement of only 75 people. Technology would be applied to do the same job being done on today's destroyer with 395 people. While the need for fewer people is laudable, what *kind* of people will be needed? Will the navy be able to compete with other employers who will also need similarly qualified technologists? How does your company relate to this scenario?

Rise of Women

Women have been assuming stronger roles in business in recent years. Some of this upward movement has been stimulated by equal employment initiatives, but there's a new trend in place. Women are now seen as offering a much-needed nurturing and supportive leadership style. Part of this ability comes from the socialization of women in our culture. During their childhood, they learn nurturing, communication, and relationship-building skills. It's only natural for those talents to evolve into a highly effective leadership style for these turbulent times.

Childcare: Parents' Greatest Challenge

The increase in the number of women in the workforce has far-reaching societal implications. With mother working, rais-

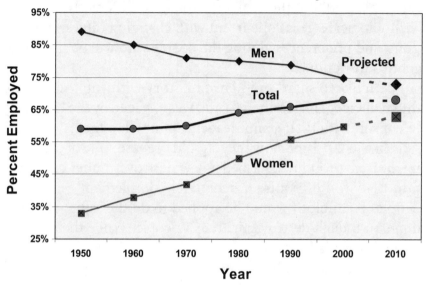

Figure 15: Increase in Number of Women in the Workforce

From 1950 to 2000, the number and percentage of women participating in the workforce has increased relative to the total number for men. In spite of the increase of women, we are still expecting to be over 10 million people short of the jobs available in 2010.

ing children presents difficult challenges. These issues affect mothers with husbands as much as they affect single moms—and dads. The biggest concern is childcare. Finding qualified and suitable providers is the first problem, followed by the need to pay for the childcare. Third, parents face the need to shuttle children back and forth before and after work. Finally, parents must make special arrangements when children are sick or when regular childcare is not available, for whatever reason. These problems are not restricted to pre-schoolers; the same, and more compli- cated, issues are obstacles to high performance for parents with children in primary, middle, and even high school. Teachers' in-service days and weather-related days off also wreak havoc with parents' schedules.

A few employers provide much-appreciated support for parent-employees. Special activities for kids, after-school programs, charter schools for employees' kids, and flexible working hours help. Some enlightened employers arrange emergency childcare for their employees' children through ChildrenFirst (*www.childrenfirst.com*). However, this service is "back-up" childcare only. Some women feel the conflict between career and child-raising so acutely they would love to get out of the workforce and go back home to be housewives and mothers. If we face a labor shortage that increases the demand for these important employees, in management or not, we'll encounter serious conflicts in social values. What will be the role of the employer? Wise employers will address this critical issue sooner rather than later.

Inadequacy of Education versus Job Skill Needs

Job requirements are no longer as simple and defined as they once were. Evolving technology, customer expectations, and ongoing process modifications have changed the rules of the game. Employers scramble to keep up their programs of required training as the turbulence roils around them. It is essential that employers keep their people well trained, prepared to serve their customers—internal and external—in ways that will meet, or exceed, expectations. To keep up or stay ahead demands a significant resource allocation—time, money, space, and more.

Some employers would rather kick-start their revolving door again and spin workers out into the street when they are no longer current with the needs of the job. Obviously, that cannot be done. If you dismiss workers because they lack the expertise you need, where will you find adequately prepared replacements? You may be forced to raid other employers who are a step or two ahead of you. That strategy will be embarrassing and probably insufficiently productive. Think about it: would you leave a good job to join a company that needs your skills because they haven't kept up? This opportunity doesn't show much promise for the future, does it?

So, we choose the option of hiring younger, perhaps first-time, workers fresh out of school. We expect these new graduates to be current with new technology, procedures, and perspectives . . . ready to leap in and save the day. Surprise! Our schools are still scrambling to prepare students for yesterday's jobs that are now obsolete. Educators are not producing graduates who are ready for today's jobs, let alone tomorrow's. Astonishingly, few educators—teachers or administrators—have a good sense of what skills employers expect their graduates to have. For the most part, dialog with business leaders or their customers simply doesn't happen. When is the last time you talked with the educators in your community?

--------------------- **Words of Wisdom** ---------------------

If employers expect schools to produce the qualified workers they need, corporate leaders must invest time and other resources to support educators in the fulfillment of that responsibility.

Our schools need more than money from the businesses in their community. They need regular briefings on what's happening in the world of work, support on curriculum design, and knowledge resources to bring the evolving designs to life. Do your employees teach classes in schools to help develop your future workers?

The problem is easy to state. While we are facing dangerous shortages of people to work, far too many of those who are available are not prepared to perform today's job duties . . . let alone the duties of the jobs that will emerge in the evolving future.

This critical shortage condition will not change, until we experience an upheaval in our educational system. Bottom line: for the foreseeable future, employers must address learning needs. And providing the necessary education, training, and personal development will be perceived as a huge expense . . . right off the company's bottom line. However, this so-called expense is actually an investment in the future that employers must make. The return on investment will be substantial.

> Some readers will believe that we can solve our labor shortage problems by bringing people into the United States from other countries. This alternative solution is not a panacea.

Immigration

Immigration is not the magic answer to the labor shortage. First, it is not feasible to absorb huge quantities of immigrants over a short period of time, regardless of their skill or education levels. Second, many of the jobs that have been performed in the United States are moving overseas. This shift in the locus of jobs means that more foreign workers will have good jobs available near home, reducing the need to move to America—on a temporary or permanent basis. Third, other jobs are being moved overseas, but with continual linkage to American companies. Two examples are computer programming that is done overseas, with coding jobs passed from country to country around the world, following the sun. Foreign companies under contract to American enterprises now perform computerized accounting and database management jobs. Sometimes, the overseas components operate as entities of U.S. employers.

Some occupations will continue to draw employees from overseas, notably healthcare and hospitality. Depending on this practice for a continuous flow of employees is risky for several reasons. First, in the aftermath of the events of September 11, 2001, immigration may become more restricted, limiting supply. With the perceived increased risk in the United States, some potential immigrants may prefer to emigrate to safer environments like Canada. Second, many immigrant workers do not bring their families, but regularly send funds home to help those left behind. The emotional tug to return to the homeland is understandably strong. Third, the economic health of the home countries will improve, creating more opportunities for indigenous workers. There will be less need to leave home to seek opportunities in the Land of Milk and Honey.

This said, we also note that the U.S. Immigration and Naturalization Service reports a massive increase in applications for United States citizenship among immigrants already in the country. In May 2002 alone, the number of applications was 121 percent larger than the number received in May 2001.

The Evolving Organizational Structure

Over the past decade, we have witnessed a streamlining of corporate structure. Layer after layer of unneeded hierarchy has been slashed from organizational charts. Depending on how well the changes were integrated into management structure, logistics, culture, and leadership development, these major changes have been a boon or a boondoggle.

Some companies have managed this "reengineering" beautifully. Others have made a shambles of the attempt, with missed opportunities littering the battlefield—internally and externally. Unfortunately, though well intentioned, an estimated 80 percent of reengineering attempts failed because they ignored the human value component. Too many of those restructuring efforts targeted cost-cutting instead of improvement.

Most executives learn from their mistakes or miscalculations, so we can fairly assume that more recent moves to shrink structure have been much more effective. Expect to see more of this reorganization to make wiser use of existing or projected resources. There is much more involved than merely reducing the workforce. Other costs must be examined and all processes and systems must be evaluated. Plans must be made ahead of time to better use remaining resources—from the initiation of the change—or losses may well exceed the benefits.

Some companies are experimenting with matrix management, creative schedules, or whole new designs that challenge organizational-chart architects to beg for mercy. Wise employers are getting their people involved with the design of the process, outcomes, and assignments of who will do what, how, and by when.

Flattening of the organizational structure actually enables the people to become clearer in their direction. It also helps reassign people that have been left out of the process somehow. The new designs will be much more responsive, fostering collaboration.

The Corporation of the Future

The design, structure, and purpose of the corporation are evolving into something very different from what they are today. The corporation of the future will be relatively small, comprised of a highly focused core team.

Mission-driven, it will be agile and nimble . . . able to shift rapidly to take advantage of changes in the marketplace, sales opportunities, and the availability of top talent. Speed and a high level of responsiveness will be the trademarks for these entities. Corporations of the future will not be overly burdened with extra people that weigh them down. Every member of the team will be highly productive and accountable.

Rather than being weighed down by huge conglomerates of divisions, subsidiaries, and the like, this agile organism will accomplish its work with an ever-changing body of contingent workers (professionals as well as functionaries), insourced and outsourced suppliers, vertical and horizontal partnerships, and strategic alliances. An increasing proportion of our working population will choose this much looser employment arrangement to suit their lifestyles, serving as term-employed project workers rather than regular employees.

The organization will expand and contract, as it needs to, based on ever-changing needs and resources. A whole new skill set will be needed by managers who must now build cooperation and collaboration, rather than managers who dictate, direct, or build empires.

The people who run this streamlined organization will need skills in leadership, collaboration, coordination, communication, persuasion, negotiation, project management, and resource allocation. They will need to be highly technologically literate and conversant and comfortable with evolving technologies. The skill bandwidth will include a keen curiosity, alertness to sense the changes, and the ability to act as a pioneer or at least an early adopter; this set of skills is poles apart from the command and control skills employed in most organizations today.

Skills for the future include interviewing, meeting management, coaching and mentoring, coordinating, supporting. How strong are your skills in these areas? How competent are your key people? Could they function in this kind of environment today? Will they be able to in the future? What must you do to get them ready for this imminent shift in the way we do business?

You'll manage a vast set of independent contractors who will sell practically anything, including their own personal services. This scenario places human resources in a whole new light. Employers will have less control, thus reemphasizing the need to be able to deal collaboratively with a wide variety of people. How does this emerging design fit with your current culture?

The problem we face here is that today's leaders, let alone

tomorrow's leaders, do not possess the polished skills necessary to succeed in the emerging environment. And very few employers are recruiting or training their high-potential people to function effectively in this new design. The focus is still too dependent on people, rather than on how people, technology, and processes must become more intensely interdependent. The message is clear: prepare to evolve more rapidly or expect your competition to leave you choking in their dust.

Closing Questions

1. How many people leave your organization to advance in their careers?
2. What are the job tenure trends for men and women in your organization?
3. How well have you explored the use of older workers to fill your employment voids?
4. Have you explored the use of foreign workers for any of your positions or have you considered outsourcing work to other locations using technology?

Opportunities for a Competitive Advantage

How do your turnover rates and other HR metrics compare to your industry averages and "front runner" competitors? Are there some experienced people who have retired (from your organization or others) that might now be available to contribute in some way? Have you employed the use of "talent scouts" to be on the lookout for good employees who leave your competitors after a short tenure?

CHAPTER FOUR

The Competency Deficit

Though in 2010 we will have a shortfall of over 10 million workers, the situation will be made even worse by the available workers' insufficient knowledge and skills. Our public schools are not doing an adequate job of preparing young people for work. Employers are dissatisfied with the level of capability of today's high school graduates. Some young people are graduating without even the basic literacy and numeracy skills. Undergraduate college education, a vital part of our system for preparing young people for careers and life, is at risk. Corporations will partner with colleges and universities for mutual benefit, enabling students to enjoy a powerful combination of academic preparation and real-world experience. Corporations may collaborate with graduate schools, helping them remain relevant, while increasing involvement in continual learning. To support increasing interest in individual development, expect to see more in-house corporate learning, including an emphasis on business literacy.

The numbers we have presented tell a chilling story. Current projections forecast a shortage of 10,033,000 people to fill the jobs that are expected to be available in 2010. A really hot economy that creates even more jobs than the Bureau of Labor Statistics anticipates could make this whole picture even worse.

But now the plot thickens. The numbers we presented are *raw* numbers of people. Warm bodies. No recognition of education, training, experience. How many unskilled jobs will be available? How many of the people you will need in 2010—or *now*— fit into that "unskilled" category?

Ooops!

There's our problem! We don't need just warm bodies. We need people who can get the job done for us. Some of our tasks might be able to be completed by unskilled labor (warm bodies), but certainly not all of them. We need people with specific skills, expertise, background, experience, training, education, and attitudes. Or we at least need people who can write a decent memo, add a column of figures, or keep careful records of quality factors in a manufacturing facility. We need people who can reason, who can think, who can solve problems, and who can communicate effectively with others.

Tall order? You wouldn't think so, until you look at some of the people who are available to hire today. If you look at who's coming down the pike, you probably won't get overly excited about prospects for the future either. While there are some wonderful people in the labor pool, there aren't enough. Why?

If we can't hire enough airport screeners, what does this forebode for your hiring during the next few years?

In July 2002 the Transportation Security Administration reported serious difficulty in hiring airport screening personnel. In New York alone, 61 percent of the applicants failed a test of English proficiency and overall aptitude skills; one-third didn't show up for their interviews. If we can't hire enough airport screeners, what does this forebode for your hiring during the next few years?

We describe our predicament as a "competency deficit." The people who are available to work today, on the whole, just don't have what they need to get today's jobs done. And as we move into the future, they'll have even less capacity to do tomorrow's jobs. The cause of this problem is simple: inadequate education and training. Plainly put, our workforce is not prepared to perform the tasks that need to be done.

Let's look at where the problems are . . . and what can—*must*—be done.

In the United States today, according to the U.S. Department of Education, we have over 90 million people whose literacy and numeracy skills are below the tenth-grade level, And that's the minimum level, points out Dr. Carol D'Amico, assistant secretary of education for vocational and adult education, where we need people to be educated to perform the jobs that need to be done. Yes, this situation means that some serious work needs to be done in our public school system to stop the flow of illiterates into our workforce, but it also means there is a job to be done by corporate America to raise these people to a level where they can be more productive and enjoy a higher self-esteem and income.

We also have an underutilized resource of what we call "obsolete workers." These are people who have training, expertise, and a solid career doing work that is no longer required in our fast-moving, ever-changing world of work. These workers need to be retrained and/or reeducated so they can be contributing members of society. Who will provide this occupational upgrading? Employers? Community colleges? Private industry?

Public Education

Public education in the United States is woefully inadequate. Compared to the needs of employers and our society, the output of the education system is substandard. Compared to achievement scores by students in other countries, the public education system in the United States is an embarrassment.

Employers are increasingly frustrated by workers' deficiencies in fundamental reading, writing, and math skills. The labor shortage is complicated by the difficulty in finding people who are qualified to work . . . or at least trainable. Insufficient basic education makes training considerably more challenging.

American Management Association studies reveal that over 38 percent of 1999 job applicants lacked the literacy and numeracy skills required to perform the jobs they applied for, according to AMA's annual survey on workplace testing. This figure is alarming when compared against the same measures in recent years: 35.5 percent in 1998 and 22.8 percent in 1997.

Several factors influence the greater numbers. First, we're reaching much further into the labor pool, hiring people with less preparation for work. This problem is exacerbated by the higher capacities demanded by computerized processes and expectations that employees will be able to perform a wider range of skill-dependent tasks. A third factor is the inadequate development of students in our public school systems.

The AMA study reported that more companies are testing for basic skills, something we'd certainly expect given requirements and exposures involved in hiring today. We learned that only 13 percent of the companies surveyed offer their employees remedial training. This remedial instruction costs an average of only $289 per trainee, according to the AMA research.

Our forecast is that more employers will invest in remedial education for their workers.

Employers will be forced into this effort; the decision won't be easy. Once committed, however, employers will strive to provide a valuable, comprehensive, and effective educational program. This venture will be expensive, but a wise investment in attracting, growing, and retaining people who sincerely want to learn and earn. Language, culture, and life-management skills will be taught along with the basics.

Teachers will be recruited from public school systems, already faced with serious staff shortages. Corporations will pay more, provide better facilities, and offer adult students motivated to learn. Some companies will collaborate with school systems to award diplomas to graduates, fostering cooperative teacher-sharing arrangements.

Public School Deficiencies

Employers are dissatisfied with the level of capability of today's high school graduates. When these entry-level workers are hired and cannot perform as expected, employers are forced to invest in company-paid training to get workers up to speed. Supervisors, unaccustomed to managing people who simply don't understand what work is all about, are challenged to the point that they force new employees to leave or quit themselves.

Current conditions cannot continue. Major reform is coming in our educational system. We see that a substantial part of this shift will come from business-driven educational models. In the future, private companies contracted by local school boards will manage more schools—and school systems. As their communities loudly and urgently express their dissatisfaction, the boards will be forced into dramatic changes for political reasons.

The parents and the employers simply will not tolerate educational systems that are not preparing youth for the lives that await them after graduation. As for-profit companies demonstrate that they can do the job—and do it better than government employees—political leaders would be foolish to turn their backs on privatization.

There are great arguments under way between educators, administrators, and politicians about students passing standardized tests at various levels of their education. Educators complain they're forced to "teach to the test." Parents bemoan that their kids can't do well on the tests. If the tests are legitimate measures of at least some of the knowledge students are expected to have, this process will be enforced. If not, the process will be modified, but the testing—the proof—must still be there. Beyond teaching to the test, educators must redesign their methods to get the job done. We will see greater investments of resources, length of school sessions, and other strategies applied to raise the standards and performance. Expect to see a lot of controversy over the next few years, resulting in substantial changes in the way we educate our children.

Vocational Education

Many Americans subscribe to the philosophy that high school graduates should go on to college. High schools even brag about what percentage of their graduates are accepted by colleges and universities. With statistical emphasis on how much more lifetime earnings can be with a college education, students are lured to the campus to begin their journey down the streets paved with gold.

Some students do very well in college. Others discover their inability—for whatever reason(s)—to perform at the academic level expected in a four-year college or university. This embarrassing revelation is perceived as socially degrading—for the student and for the student's parents. Nothing should be further from the truth!

Not every young person *should* go to college to pursue a baccalaureate, graduate, or postgraduate degree. In spite of the talk that a college education today is equivalent to what a high school diploma used to represent, college is not for everyone. A number of viable alternatives exist that may, in fact, be much better suited for many individuals. When we look at the surprisingly large number of students who drop out of college after one year or less, we are concerned that they attempt to enter the workforce with inadequate preparation . . . and perhaps self-esteem that is far lower than it should be.

There are plenty of college and noncollege alternatives for those who can't be—or don't want to be—brain surgeons. Community colleges, for example, serve as a bridge to further education and career training for over 10 million youth and adults. These locally based and governed colleges provide access to the increasing number of adults seeking postsecondary education, as a point of entry for a baccalaureate degree, and as a primary source of training and retraining for meaningful careers. Academic courses enable students wishing to continue to higher degrees to do so, but also allow those who choose to end their formal education with an associate's degree to gain valuable post–high school knowledge, understanding, appreciation, and skills. Students who were not shining stars academically in high school do have an alternative—to continue their education and/or their maturation process.

The community and technical colleges offer even more than academics; they offer opportunities for young people to gain skills, learn trades, and prepare themselves to enter the world of work better equipped than mere high school graduates. Older workers also attend these schools to pick up missed academic credits and to gain new skills. Community colleges serve a tremendous need for retraining in many communities across the country.

A wide range of skills is available at these institutions. Course offerings range from supervisory skills to boiler repair and maintenance. Community colleges offer curricula in healthcare, mechanics, computer science, food service, construction management, and much more. Some offer online courses; others have strong international programs.

Some community colleges provide unusual programs, such as the Lac Courte Oreilles Ojibwa Community College in northern Wisconsin. The college's mission is to provide, within the Native American community, a system of postsecondary and continuing education with an associate's degree and certificate granting capabilities, while maintaining an open-door policy. The Lac Courte Oreilles Ojibwa Community College curriculum reflects Ojibwa culture and tribal self-determination. The college provides opportunities for individual self-improvement in a rapidly changing technological world, while maintaining the cultural integrity of the Anishinabe (*www.lco-college.edu*).

Some trade associations partner with colleges to produce the specially prepared graduates they need. For example, The National Kitchen and Bath Association (NKBA) established an Endorsed College Program to serve the professional needs of the industry and ensure consistent, quality education for students who desire to become kitchen/bathroom design professionals. A college applying for NKBA endorsement must demonstrate that it meets NKBA's educational requirements. These requirements represent the basis of a program that the NKBA considers essential for quality education. Each student must complete classroom work and supervised internships, which will enhance and extend the classroom experiences and ensure that they have fulfilled the minimum student competencies. Industry leaders acknowledge that there are many more openings for kitchen and bath designers than the schools can possibly fill. Even with the association's professional development program, the needs cannot be met.

Other industries create their own solutions to the shortage of adequately trained workers.

In 1979, the collision industry formed I-CAR, an independent, not-for-profit, technical training organization. All I-CAR activities focus on helping the industry achieve a high level of technical training. I-CAR's ultimate goal is that every person in the collision repair industry has the knowledge and technical skills relevant to their position to achieve a safe and complete repair (*http://www.i-car.com*). Officials in this industry report that there are currently 18,500 job openings in the field, with an *average* annual income of comfortably over $46,000.

In addition to these career development opportunities, there are proprietary schools providing flight training, commercial truck driving instruction, and skills needed in ancillary healthcare occupations. These for-profit organizations offer practical training in specific fields, such as business administration, medical records technology, or diesel engine mechanics.

Words of Wisdom

There are abundant opportunities for people to learn occupational skills that will enable them to qualify for jobs they'll enjoy—and where they can earn enough money to take care of themselves and their families. College is not for everyone.

In many cases, students pay for their own education. Some financial assistance is available in the form of loans, scholarships, or grants. Increasingly, employers pay for this occupationally oriented education and training as a part of a corporate development program. Some companies reimburse graduates they hire. Others select beginning students with promise and offer to pay their education costs in return for a commitment to work for the company for a prescribed period of time. Co-op work experiences are prevalent.

Undergraduate College Education

Undergraduate college education is a vital part of our system for preparing young people for careers and life. How well is the process working? For some, it's wonderful. For others, there are major deficiencies that will stimulate significant change.

In broad generalities, there are two approaches to undergraduate education today. One is to acquire a liberal arts education, gaining an appreciation of history, philosophy, art and culture, communications skills, and an enhanced ability to think creatively to solve problems and develop new ideas. The liberal arts experience also addresses emotional intelligence—the all-important way that humans communicate and interact with each other on an emotional level. The other approach to undergraduate education is to concentrate on developing technical expertise in a particular field of study such as engineering, accounting, computer science, or business.

The years a student invests on campus should prepare the graduate for the challenges of the ensuing career. In the past, this flow has been natural and appropriate: graduates entered their field and climbed the ladder of success using the knowledge and skills gained in college. More capacity was acquired on the job, contributing to a rewarding career in that chosen endeavor.

The present—and particularly the future—suggest a much different career path. Today's graduates will change jobs many more times than their predecessors, and will change career paths a number of times as well. Our fathers each had one career and just a few jobs over their lifetimes. Each of us has had four or five career path experiences. Our children will probably have at least ten.

Many of today's students will hold jobs in their careers that don't even exist today. The employment environment is considerably more dynamic and demanding. Undergraduate curricula must change to be more responsive to the needs of the students of today and tomorrow. The traditions of the past—length of time in school, course design, teaching methods, and the requirement for face-to-face learning—will all be subject to change.

The price of attending college is still a significant obstacle for students from low- and middle-income families, but financial aid is an equalizer, to some degree. Low-income students enroll at the same rate as middle-income students if they take all the necessary steps toward enrollment, according to *Access & Persistence*, a report published by the American Council on Education (Center for Policy Analysis, 2002).

Increasing Costs of a College Education

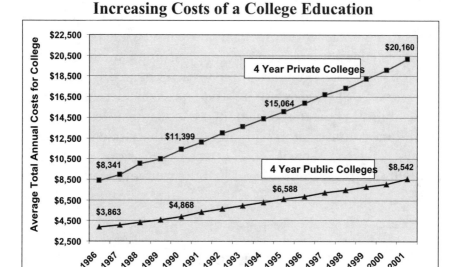

Figure 16: The Increasing Costs of College Education

The chart above illustrates the annual increases in college costs for four-year public and private colleges. The average costs include tuition, room and board, and annual fees. Note that the growth rate of approximately 7 percent is consistent for each and that the gap in cost is significant.

Students are different today than they were a generation ago . . . or even more recently. Traditionally, four-year college students have enrolled full-time immediately after high school graduation; depended on their parents to take care of most, if not all, financial responsibilities; and worked part-time or not at all. Today, only 40 percent of four-year college students fit this description, reports the American Council on Education.

Our forecast is that we'll see more emphasis on liberal arts, providing students with a broader foundation from which to manage their ever-changing careers. Students will want to be challenged, stimulated, and more deeply educated at a faster rate. While appreciating the value of learning to think, to explore, to solve problems, and communicate, students will also place emphasis on experiential learning.

We are already observing an increase in the desire for internships to gain real-world practical know-how while preparing to be knowledge leaders. The external learning gained from on-the-job work may extend the time to earn a degree. Colleges will offer a range of choices, giving students a considerable amount of flexibility in how they design their baccalaureate learning process. Some commentators will surely argue that students so young do not have the capacity to plan their educations, yet today's students are much more savvy than the students of yesterday.

─────────── Words of Wisdom ───────────

Today's high school graduates are already exposed to so much through the Internet and other media that they are far ahead of where most college curriculum designs are today. Be sure the technology in your workplace is up to speed.

Students will demand quality in their education, desiring to learn from instructors with a powerful combination of academic preparation and real-world experience. Expect to see more visiting executives, stimulating guest lecturers, and a variety of outside resources applied in the years ahead. Professors will mix their own capacity and experience with learning technologies like the Internet for a more comprehensive experience, connecting theoretical with practical.

Corporation-College Collaboration

Let's put a couple of trends together here and propose a new design for recruiting and retention in employment and education. First, we know that employers will be eager to hire bright young people . . . and hold on to them as long as possible. Remember back in the late 1990s when employers were challenged by a tight labor market? Recruiters were pursuing qualified applicants wherever they could find them—even on college campuses. As the economy heats up and the labor market tightens in this decade, recruiters again will attempt to lure students from the college campus to the corporate campus before they have graduated.

Employers will understand the value of better-educated workers, but will want them to be productively employed. The colleges will want those same young people to enroll in their educational programs and stay around for a number of years. The young people will be tugged in seemingly competing directions. These are heavy decisions for high school seniors, and college freshman or sophomores.

What strategic planning messages does this send to colleges and universities? Their students (read: revenue) may be earning money working instead of spending (or investing) money in learning. Without enough students, the very existence of colleges and universities could be at risk. Just like other kinds of organizations, these educational institutions must change the way they do business.

Our forecast is a new partnership between educators and employers. College students will work at real jobs, not just makework internships. They will earn pay at a level commensurate with their abilities as entry-level employees with various kinds of employers. Working hours will be similar to those followed by coworkers. About three-quarters of all four-year college students already earn a regular paycheck, and about one-quarter of them work full-time, according to the 2002 study by the American Council on Education.

These young people will also attend college classes, carrying a load comparable to what is measured today as a full-time complement. They will attend classes, do their homework and outside research, and participate in study teams and other activities associated with focused, aggressive learning in higher education today.

To make this happen, educators and employers will have to work closely together to schedule work and classes in ways that won't create schedule conflicts for the talented people they both need. Students who are able to take advantage of this opportunity will be thrilled. They can learn *and* earn—accumulating the funds they need to pay for their education. We could see a lot more students graduating without loans to pay back.

For a few years, perhaps as many as five or six, students will be quite willing to manage their time differently to gain the tremendous benefits. They will graduate with a degree and several solid years of meaningful work experience. The maturation and socialization process that occurs during the college years will take on a new dimension when combined with similar growth in the world of work.

The problem will be getting the educators and employers to communicate, cooperate, and collaborate. Today they hardly talk to each other. The foundations are in place, with some graduate schools of management or undergraduate schools like Hiram College (*http://143.206.107.71/www/weekendcollege/*) and Fordham University's Marymount College (*http://www.marymt.edu /weekend_college/*) offering weekend programs for working people. Innovative employers will bring more college degree programs to the corporate setting.

Graduate Schools Still Relevant?

Graduate school education is at risk. Students are questioning the value of the master's degree, particularly when the labor market is crying for them to get to work already. High-tech companies are actively recruiting on campuses across the country. A number of these employers are deliberately bypassing the traditional college placement offices to go right to the students themselves. Wise move on their part: the placement folks want to get jobs for graduates, not for current students who will drop out to pursue their careers.

While enriched academic exposure is certainly valuable in the grand scheme of life, the new drive is for practical, current knowledge. Graduate students are rebelling against being fed the same old stuff that professors dished out ten, five, or even two years ago. They want to concentrate on the leading-edge, what's-happening-now knowledge that will enable them to compete more vigorously in the world of work. As these students realize that they'll really be in control of their own careers, they're hungry for the kind of education—and training—that will keep them highly marketable. They want to be able to write their own ticket, and learning out-of-date material won't give them that power.

MBA students are already challenging their professors more aggressively. They expect their instructors to be very current, preferably leading-edge. They want more practical and applied knowledge, not just theory. In most schools, the students don't believe that's what they get. Alternatively, grad students will ask—demand—that today's captains of industry—and e-industry—be brought in as speakers and resources. An increasing number of senior corporate executives will invest part of their time teaching graduate school courses, sharpening their own skills through the experience.

The traditional on-campus time will also be up for challenge. In our digital world, why can't more instruction be done through the Internet? The shift is already underway. Live classes will be conducted online, enabling grad students to take a class break from their real-world jobs to keep learning. A learning break will be much more productive than a coffee break! Watch for more online universities to be accredited in the next few years. We expect to see more flexible course scheduling, internships, and co-op relationships established. The links between the campus and the world of work will become stronger, enhancing the value of academic, corporate, and individual benefits.

Words of Wisdom

Do you encourage—or even allow—employees to take courses online now using your company's time and computers? This support of education may be part of your future strategy to hold on to your people.

When is the last time you served as a guest speaker on a college campus, even just to a single class? Not only is this an opportunity to share your expertise and insight with young people, it's a smart way to expose those students to opportunities within your organization. One of your authors got his first job in graduate school by approaching a visiting executive after a class presentation.

Increasing Corporate Involvement in Continual Learning

Several trends and circumstances will intertwine over the next decade, motivating corporations to fund and invigorate education around the world.

Employers face increasing challenges in their efforts to hire competent workers. They need employees who can read, write, calculate, and communicate sufficiently to perform their increasingly complicated job duties. This need will become even more serious as technology develops and applications demand greater knowledge. The gap between current needs and the capacity of the existing workforce is serious, wide enough to cause costly problems for employers. Their patience is wearing thin.

Education will become increasingly important. Employers will demand better preparation of entry-level workers, and they'll ask for more help from schools to reeducate and retrain older workers. Will educators be prepared to respond? Corporate leaders have serious doubts, so they will become more involved with public education to get their needs met. They will be helping their communities, but their underlying motivations will be understandably selfish. Smart educators will welcome corporate collaboration.

Dollars and other forms of support will flow from corporations to schools. Employers will provide funds to sponsor capital expansion and technology upgrades. Corporate sponsors will put their names on public school classrooms, libraries, stadiums, and computer labs. Sure, the recognition is well deserved and appropriate. There are precedents in the university environment, churches, community centers, libraries, and similar public facilities. The advantage in this setting is that employers will place their names in front of prospective employees. Schools eager for financial support will accommodate corporate wishes as much as they can.

Corporations will lend their expertise to schools, much the way they do to United Way fund drives and other community activities. Loaned executives will work side-by-side with school administrators on financial management, curriculum design, capital projects planning and implementation, leadership development, and technology development.

Employers will provide instructors to assist certified teachers, serve as substitute teachers, and even assume part-time or full-time teaching loads—paid for by the corporations. Teachers will learn on-site from corporations, gaining specialized knowledge in science, technology, and applications of academic subjects.

Professional instructors from high schools, vocational schools, colleges, and universities will be engaged to increase the knowledge of employees. Everyone will benefit from these emerging partnerships. Where will your company be in this picture?

Career Development Gaining Momentum

Career development has, of course, been important to working people for generations. For many years, employees placed much of the control of their career in the hands of their employer. As people climbed the corporate ladder, employed by one or just a few companies during their career, this process worked well. The playing field has shifted; conditions are very different today, and these differences will intensify in the years ahead.

Today's employees, particularly younger people, are taking control of their own careers. No longer trusting employers to look out for their best interests, workers are planning and controlling their own training and development, job transfer, and engagement with mentors. Interest in career planning is at an all-time high and will become even stronger as we move into the future.

When employees get professional counseling to help keep their careers on track, they'll be more confident that they're making the right moves to advance their careers—even if they stay with the same employer.

With an increased level of support for career-sensitive employees, employers will need to be much more receptive to people transferring across departmental or divisional lines to work in other parts of the same organization. Policies will become more flexible, so workers can build their careers without having to change employers. This capacity will be an advantage for larger employers, but smaller employers will become more creative as well.

Coaching and mentoring will play an increasingly meaningful role in this arena. Coaches and mentors will counsel employees—at all levels—in career development issues. Even if there is no formal mentoring program in your organization, these communications will occur. How well prepared are your leaders and respected senior employees to deal with career development questions?

In-House Corporate Learning

With the increasing demand for training, education, and personal development, employers will invest more in formal seminars, workshops, and lectures. Traditional methods will be employed, but e-learning and computer-based instruction (CBI) will be heavily used. Distance learning will facilitate whole new approaches to how learning is accomplished for employee learners in dispersed locations. Corporate universities will blossom, with rich curricula of courses in a wide range of relevant topics.

Outside instructors will be used abundantly to supplement the in-house training staff. Professional contract trainers will bring their expertise—and an outsider's perspective—to enhance the learning—and application—experience. Guest presenters from universities and from other employers will add depth to the learning experience.

Emphasis will be placed on learning, rather than seat time or a check-off of topics on a course list. Skill building will be valued, with a focus on applying those skills. The driver will be personal and professional growth that relates to producing greater results, as well as increased satisfaction of the employees who will be hungry to learn. Workers will want to keep their skills and knowledge sharp in a rapidly changing world, but won't leave when their training is complete. Their desire will be to stay to use their learning to achieve results, to make a difference. How their supervisors regard the training—giving people an opportunity and encouragement to improve performance—will determine the intrinsic value . . . and how long people will stay to apply their knowledge.

A key to the success of your training program will be how effectively the new learning is reinforced when the employee returns to the job. Leaders should talk with their subordinates upon completion of training, to process what they have learned and how they'd like to apply their learnings. Give the graduates time, space, and support to put their newfound knowledge and skills to work, with reinforcement for the fine work they are doing.

Words of Wisdom

Don't waste your money on training and development unless your leaders—from top executives to front-line supervisors—are involved, trained, committed, and accountable to assure that the learners have an opportunity to apply what they've learned.

Training is essential to strengthen current performance and prepare your employees for the future. Training is a waste if it's not done right. If you're not going to do training and education the right way, you might as well plan your exit strategy. Your best employees will be leaving you and it will be very expensive, if not impossible, to replace them. Essentially, you're going out of business.

Business Literacy

Business literacy is the understanding of general business concepts including financial statements, cash flow, income statements, balance sheets, general pricing guidelines, basic sales, marketing and business development, the business planning process, and leadership and management fundamentals. Competency in these core learning areas for business allows for open communication with a common language.

We don't invest enough time in our schools—even colleges and universities—to help people gain a reasonable level of business literacy. As a result, employees—even supervisors, managers, and many executives—are relatively ignorant about what it takes to make a business successful. They don't understand budgets, reports, how to measure results, or the influence their work has on the organization's success.

A number of employers have counteracted business illiteracy through vigorous education programs. Sessions are taught by knowledgeable employees, accounting and finance professionals, university professors, and others with a good understanding of the quantitative aspects of business. Some organizations—public and private—have applied the tools of The Great Game of Business (*www.greatgame.com*) to help employees learn what business is all about.

When employees understand how business is managed and measured "by the numbers," the company can share actual numbers comfortably and confidently with employees. As people get to know the numbers, they take a more active role in assuring that the right results are achieved. The practice of sharing information like this is called "open-book management".

Does it work? Research has shown that employers with open-book management are able to build a different sense of participation and commitment among employees. The next graph is clear evidence that companies practicing open-book management typically enjoy longer employee tenure. And, of course, longer tenure among talented, experienced, knowledgeable employees means greater efficiency, productivity, and profit.

In companies where open-book management is practiced, it is not uncommon to see senior executives and hourly workers working shoulder-to-shoulder to watch the numbers and gently tweak manufacturing processes, supply channels, and distribution systems to maximize returns. Such close relationships inspire substantially higher levels of collaboration, rather than the nearly adversarial relationships seen in too many organizations.

For many employers, open-book management will be radical . . . even threatening. It certainly is different than the environment where numbers are kept secret. Operating with less suspicion, more knowledge, and greater personal responsibility is a different way of doing business. While we'll stop short of asserting that open-book management is some sort of panacea, we do acknowledge that, for many companies, a shift to some degree of open-book management will change the way you do business.

The Cost of Training

Over the years, executives have complained about the cost of employee training. When hard times hit, the training budget is one of the first to be cut. Some employers establish policies of hiring only people who are already trained, preferring to pay a little more for the new employee than to put money into upgrading current or future employees. The fallacy in this practice is that it assumes that the new, trained employees won't need any more training. That kind of thinking is unrealistic; more training will always be needed, if only to keep up with changes in the company's operating environment.

Open Book Business Practices versus Non-OBM

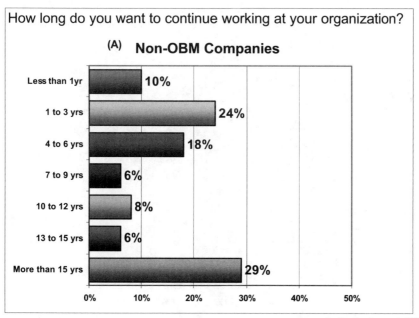

Success Profiles Inc. Research, 2000

Figure 17A: Retention and Open-Book Management Practices

Success Profiles conducted a comprehensive analysis of employees' willingness to stay in both open-book management (OBM) companies and non-OBM companies. The research demonstrated that non-OBM companies had a willingness-to-stay intent profile where 52 percent of the employees were planning to leave over the next six years and 29 percent of the employees were planning to stay over 15 years.

Open Book Business Practices versus Non-OBM

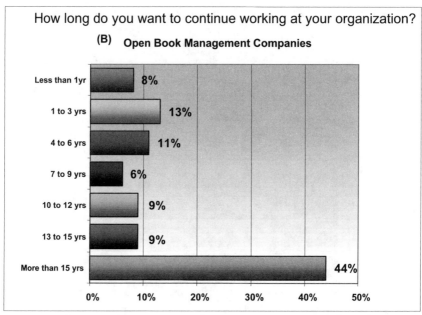

How long do you want to continue working at your organization?

(B) Open Book Management Companies

Less than 1yr	8%
1 to 3 yrs	13%
4 to 6 yrs	11%
7 to 9 yrs	6%
10 to 12 yrs	9%
13 to 15 yrs	9%
More than 15 yrs	44%

0%   10%   20%   30%   40%   50%

Success Profiles Inc. Research, 2000

Figure 17B: Retention and Open-Book Management Practices

Companies that exhibited OBM business practices (figure B, the chart on the left) had a willingness-to-stay intent profile where only 32 percent of the employees were planning to leave over the next six years and 44 percent of the employees were planning to stay over 15 years. These results were also observed by Karen Berman in her doctoral thesis, "Information and the Effectiveness of Employee Participation in Organizations."

An old adage says that if you want to measure the cost of training, measure the cost of *not* training. How well—or long—could your organization function with a poorly trained, incompetent workforce? Would you want your customers, competitors, or investors to know about your low levels of capability and capacity?

Imagine how you could win the confidence of customers and intimidate the competition if your people were highly trained, well educated, and ready for anything! While you may think investors would look askance at dollars invested in training, remember that they're looking for a return on investment—all kinds of investments. Your higher standards will attract a higher caliber of applicant, gradually raising the proficiency of your entire workforce.

In closing, let us point out that when people share learning experiences, they quite naturally become closer, more collaborative, more cooperative, and more cohesive. Just what you'd like your workforce to be. To enhance your results, take advantage of opportunities to participate in the training yourself—as a teacher and as a learner.

In today's world, a cohesive, stable workforce is a competitive advantage. Increase your employee retention rate and enjoy wondrous results. Allow your retention rate to drop and . . . . Well, we'll address that issue in the next chapter.

Closing Questions

1. Are you aware of the benefits of open book management practices and the expectations of younger employees to share information?
2. How freely is information shared in all departments of your organization?
3. Do you offer formal business or financial literacy training to engage your employees in the development of a business acumen competency?

4. How are you partnering with local colleges for the development and recruitment of your future employees?

Opportunities for a Competitive Advantage

With the costs of college increasing, are there people who could work part time as interns who would sign on for long-term employment following graduation? Are there any market research projects that could be performed by students in the marketing departments of a local university?

CHAPTER FIVE

Employee Turnover:
The Hidden Killer

Employee turnover is a ubiquitous, all-consuming problem that faces practically all employers. It is so omnipresent that many have come to believe that they can't do anything about it. There are two different kinds of attrition: Empty-chair attrition and warm-chair attrition. Empty-chair attrition occurs when an employee either voluntarily or involuntarily leaves. Warm-chair attrition occurs when the worker has made the psychological decision to leave, but has not left the organization. The decision to leave is emotional, often caused by the ineffective relationship between the employee and his/her direct supervisor. High employee turnover can induce organizational atrophy. The costs of turnover are high, however most organizations do not have a tool for measuring it. Our research suggests that the best method for calculating the cost of turnover is the new the Bliss-Gately Tool. Tenure Equity and Talent Equity help to explain that not all turnover is the same. If turnover is killing your company, it is either corporate homicide . . . or suicide.

Employee turnover has become a major topic of conversation in corporate offices, at conventions, in restaurants, and on airplanes around the world. It's a ubiquitous, all-consuming problem that faces practically all employers. Even those with relatively good retention rates (relative to their industry) are concerned that the turnover is too high for their organization. There is a common understanding that uncontrolled employee turnover is not good, placing high retention in the same category as motherhood and apple pie.

But while corporate leaders agree that too much turnover is not a good thing, too many view the problem as if it were a mosquito—a nuisance, not really critical. These leaders need to wake up and recognize that that "mosquito" is carrying a deadly virus. When you look carefully at the numbers, it becomes painfully evident that uncontrolled employee turnover can kill an organization. This "real and present danger" is a threat today and will be tomorrow. As we move through the decade, recovering from excessive turnover will be increasingly difficult and costly.

Consider this exposure. Who leaves your company as a result of dissatisfaction? Typically the workers who leave are the most competent, who become frustrated at not being able to do their job well and achieve at high levels. The more talented your employees are, the more employment options are available to them. If talented workers don't get the support they need from supervisors or top management, they feel personally devalued because they're not producing to their own personal capacity. They raise issues and try to make changes for improvement, but are often rebuffed. These highly talented workers are not bound to you; they can easily move to another employer.

Empty-Chair Attrition

During the late 1990s, we experienced unprecedented employee turnover. "If I don't like it here, I can leave," became the mantra. More employees would simply walk off the job, not even caring about collecting their paychecks. Some would quit during the first week—even the first day—on the job. Service employers such as hotels, restaurants, and service stations complained that some employees wouldn't even show up for their first day of work. Then manufacturers began reporting the same problem. Depending on people coming to work when expected became a pervasive issue.

When these employees left, their chairs—or positions—were empty. Now those jobs had to be filled . . . or eliminated. To fill the chairs, people would be transferred or promoted from within or hired from the outside. Either way, the process was time-consuming, resource-consuming, and costly to the employer in many ways. You'd think employers would get the message, but too often they just don't get that empty-chair attrition—uncontrolled employee turnover—is a major (avoidable) expense that can devastate the bottom line.

Warm-Chair Attrition

Warm-chair attrition is characterized by people who are disillusioned and are thinking of leaving. Their motivation is severely diminished; they have little or no engagement with the organization's mission or their work. With warm-chair attrition, people quit psychologically. They simply "attend" work. Their hearts are no longer in their performance. Absenteeism and tardiness are high and attitudes are negative, but they won't quit physically. Complacent, they are content to accept the income and the position they have. Their ambition has evaporated. Their "get up and go" has gotten up and gone; their motivation has been dulled by the way they have been treated by "management".

Unfortunately, many of these employees have been around for a long time, have learned how to stay out of trouble, and have become relatively incompetent compared to the job that has to be done. Consequently, employers are staffed with incompetents who cannot be terminated because we need their warm bodies in place and because there seems to be no one else to hire. Complicating the issue, supervisors do not know how to identify poor performers, let alone deal with them through discipline or development. This uncomfortable situation perpetuates itself, causing frustrated, competent employees to quit to avoid carrying the extra weight of their less productive coworkers.

When unemployment rates rise, warm-chair attrition also rises, because employees have made a mental decision to leave although they have insufficient opportunities for other employment. During the economic slowdown of 2000–2002, employers experienced high warm-chair attrition. Imagine the impact on productivity, morale, and profits. These not-really-here employees are among the first to leave as the economy heats up. Two issues to consider: First, while some managers and coworkers will be glad to see them go, the remaining load of poorly done work will be a new burden. Second, many of these workers will carry their baggage of disillusionment to their next jobs. Message to hiring employers: *caveat emptor*. Screen, test, interview, and evaluate carefully.

--------------------------- Words of Wisdom ---------------------------

Warm-chair attrition can actually be more expensive than empty-chair attrition. When people remain physically, they're taking up space—in the place of employment and on the organizational chart. The lost productivity—and opportunity—is perishable: when the less productive time has gone, it's gone.

Attrition Is Emotional

Our five years of research with 150 companies, investigating voluntary attrition, revealed that two major emotional feelings drive 80 percent of the departures:

1. **Nobody likes to feel inadequate.** When workers are put down by their supervisors, aren't trained well, don't feel supported, and don't find their work challenging or stimulating, they don't feel the intrinsic rewards. This tendency is more prevalent with less complex organizations and occupations like call centers, retailing, and hospitality.

2. **It's easier to leave than to argue.** When promises are not kept, trust is not felt, and the culture is characterized by ambiguity, employees feel like their work is a battle. When workers' expectations are thwarted, arbitrarily changed, or unfulfilled, discomfort builds. Commitments that are vague, incompatible or inconsistent, unacknowledged, or forgotten become empty and meaningless. It's much easier for employees to give up the fight and go somewhere else to work. This tendency was prevalent with more complex organizations and occupations, like healthcare, engineering, technology, and high-end manufacturing.

How many of your employees feel inadequate today? How many of your supervisors, managers, or executives recognize that part of their jobs is to help those employees overcome negative feelings? Do they care? Do they have any idea what to do to address these emotional issues and work-related concerns? If you don't have solid, confident responses to these questions, assume that some of your people are disenchanted, disgruntled, disengaged, and distinctly interested in working somewhere else.

Do you value your employees? Do they know that you value them, that you care? Every employee on your team should be valued; these are people you want to keep. Here's an interesting question: Are there some people on your payroll who you really don't want to keep? Do you not value them? If an employee isn't valued, then why was that person hired in the first place . . . or kept on the payroll?

--------------------- Words of Wisdom ---------------------

Clean out your deadwood—those people are placing a greater burden on the employees you *want* to keep. Say good-bye to the low performers and open positions to bring in the superstars.

Employee retention is a *management* responsibility, not something that can be blamed on the human resources department. The problem is that most supervisors have not been educated about employee retention or trained to retain their top talent.

Turnover-Induced Organizational Atrophy

When competent workers leave, it is with a sense of confidence that they can find a new, better job fairly quickly. Most have their next job arranged before they leave, thanks to a steady stream of recruiters knocking on their doors. Have you ever asked your top performers how many calls they get from recruiters? You might not want to; the answer may give you nightmares.

The positions vacated by the competent workers now have to be filled. Who will move into those chairs? You may promote from within; you may hire from outside. What are the chances of your replacing the departed employee with a worker with comparable competence? Let's extend "competence" to include experience, intellectual knowledge, and relationships with coworkers and customers. Let's face it: Whomever you place in the vacated position may not be as strong as the valued employee who left.

As highly competent employees leave, you are often forced to replace them with people of less competence. As the labor market tightens, finding and hiring high-level replacements will become increasingly difficult, if not impossible. Result: Your aggregate workforce gradually becomes less competent. Translate that fact into productivity, profitability, and corporate sustainability.

Over a period of time, an organization may atrophy to the extent that its functionality becomes severely diminished. Mistakes are made often. Customers are not served as they should be. Research and development becomes stale. Sales volume drops, taking cash flow along with it. Morale slides downhill. Before long, the company goes out of business. How fast this process occurs varies from one organization to another. Usually smaller companies go under first, since they don't have the capital or momentum to support them. Larger organizations continue to exist for a longer period, though many people—inside and outside—know the company is doomed . . . often before senior leaders get the message.

─────────────── **Words of Wisdom** ───────────────

The greater vulnerability for corporate demise is during an economic downturn. However, when economic conditions are wonderful, employee turnover can still be a killer.

Death by turnover comes slower, often preceded by a coma. If you reflect for a moment, you will be able to come up with a list of several organizations you deal with right now that seem to be in a coma. When voicemails are not returned, sales calls aren't made, deliveries are late, manufacturing is plagued by rework, and employees exhibit a lackadaisical attitude, you have a coma condition.

Is corporate resuscitation possible? In many cases it is . . . *if* the leader is dedicated, focused, and vigorous.

"Unemployment Is Natural"

We're confident that we'll hear this argument, so let's address it right now. Yes, it is true. We will never have a time when everyone is employed. We will, however, again reach a point that the experts in the field describe as "full employment." Under full employment conditions, everyone who wants a job will have one. Of course, we'll have the problem of matching available skills to employment needs, so truly reaching full employment may be only a theoretical concept.

> Labor economists describe full employment as the condition when unemployment in the low five percent range.

When there are not enough qualified applicants to meet the needs, there is the potential for wages to be bid up. When wages are thus inflated, without a corresponding increase in productivity, wage gain inflation results. Bid prices for new entrants to the field will drop as the need is satiated, but the grandfathered earlier entrants will still be relatively overpaid. This differential will be self-adjusting as the grandfathered workers seek to move up in their organizations. The incremental increases will be smaller until the disparity is resolved.

Four Types of Unemployment

Seasonal unemployment will always be with us, but technology has reduced the seasonality of some occupations. Concrete construction people, for instance, are able to work twelve months of the year. Technological improvements allow concrete to be poured in cold weather, so the work can now be done year-round.

Cyclical unemployment refers to the effects of the ups and downs of the business or economic cycle. We will always have this type of unemployment, though it may be localized to a geographic area or industry. Cyclical employment operates with the same sort of gyroscopic effect as airplanes that are continually going a little bit off course and correcting their flight paths.

Structural unemployment results from a mismatch between the needs and the people available to meet those needs. If we need chemical processing plant workers but have an abundance of construction machine operators, the available workers may not be able to adjust—because of education, training, experience, or intellectual bandwidth. The workers may be outstanding construction operators, and just *not able* to perform the chemical plant job responsibilities.

Frictional unemployment refers to the time it takes to find a new job when jobs are available. The work is out there, the workers are qualified; it's just a matter of getting people and jobs connected. The out-of-work time will diminish, but it may take a while. This type of unemployment is impossible to forecast accurately at this time. A measurement used in healthcare, particularly for nursing positions, is "time to fill," referring to the length of time a position is vacant before a qualified applicant is hired.

The Costs of Turnover

You may have noticed that "cost" in the subhead above is plural. That's deliberate. There are many costs associated with unexpected departures of valued employees. Our informal research, talking with hundreds of senior executives—including human resource professionals—in all kinds of organizations, reveals that few really have a grasp of what the true costs are. Even if they really care, their knowledge in this area is shallow.

We cannot emphasize strongly enough that the costs of employee turnover are serious, potentially life-threatening to an employer. Why? Those costs come right off the bottom line. They are not controllable like "cost of goods sold" or "travel and entertainment." Worse, these costs are insidious. They're often hidden in other expense categories, so you don't really see them. They are sinister, like stealth costs that can sneak up and bite you when you don't expect them.

The new people who are brought on-board are expensive. They're expensive to find, screen, hire, train, assimilate, evaluate, and sustain. If you're like most executives, you've accepted these expenses as a "cost of doing business." This kind of thinking can no longer be tolerated. Frankly, and we realize this is a bold statement, anyone who diminishes or downplays the costs of uncontrolled employee turnover is a fool, and fools should not be in positions of responsible leadership in any organization.

Why do we make such a strong statement? Let's answer our question with a question. Do you have any idea how much employee turnover costs your company each year? Do you know what it costs to replace one departed employee?

Vulnerability

Employers are increasingly vulnerable to the impact of unexpected employee turnover. In addition to the dramatic influence on the bottom line, there is the challenge of conducting business with insufficient staffing and with workers who are relatively clueless about your company. As employers realize the cost of replacing lost workers, we're seeing a rising sensitivity to the real impact of employee turnover.

Measuring the cost includes examining direct and indirect costs. Traditional accounting tools and standard reporting practices are not designed to produce accurate calculations of turnover costs. Accountants are usually not charged with monitoring those expenses. Chief financial officers desiring to serve their employers strongly in this area should work closely with their human resource counterparts to understand all the cost factors.

The list of exposures can be extensive. Consider marketing costs to attract applicants, actual costs of hiring (including an expanded human resource staff), the increase in costs of processing extra personnel files, extra costs of processing drop/add paperwork for employee benefits, and more orientation and training. Add to these concerns the cost of overtime work required from workers to carry the load of the departed employees, lost production due to slower new employees, lost production due to increased accidents and unfamiliarity with equipment, and the cost of executives' time participating in meetings about reducing turnover.

While it is valuable to calculate the cost of someone to fill in for a lost worker, find and train another, and handle the ancillary issues, it's wise to also look at annualized replacement costs. If you have to fill the same position several times during the year, with periods when the position is open, your cost of keeping the job filled multiplies.

―――――――――――――― Words of Wisdom ――――――――――――――

In many organizations, we have seen that most positions are stable, but other positions turn over much more quickly. Examine this possibility in your organization. Your statistics could be skewed by a few positions with bad job design or a couple of errant supervisors.

Some indirect costs can be even more difficult to measure. Consider the increased costs of promoting and maintaining corporate culture, difficulties in team building, and inefficiency due to people not knowing the system or procedures . . . and you really feel the heat. Tack on your growing reputation for high turnover, irritations of workers at having to carry a heavier load or work longer hours, and the stress suffered by your managerial and supervisory staff as a result. The critical loss is time; the time invested in all the activities associated with overcoming employee turnover is gone forever. That opportunity cost of time could have been invested in generating value—and profit—for the company.

Now factor in the loss of intellectual capital, corporate knowledge, and the smoothness that comes from people working together over a period of time. How much "falls through the cracks" that you never know about . . . until it comes back to bite you?

Let's consider the impacts of employee turnover:

Customers. How much is a customer worth to you? Does your company calculate the long-term economic value of a customer? How much do you lose when a customer leaves because of inferior quality or service? Customers build relationships with specific individuals at a supplier. When your employee leaves, the customer's relationship with your company is at immediate and serious risk. Have you built multiemployee depth into the relationships between your company and your customers?

Suppliers. Understandably, a key question for suppliers is whether your company is strong enough to continue paying their bills. Should they extend you credit—how much, on what terms? How much can they trust you? How well do they know you and your people? Workforce instability raises serious questions in the minds of suppliers . . . and their finance officers.

Investors. Investors watch employee turnover rates, especially among executives, sales professionals, and other key employees. They understand all too well that a company's strength is based on the people who get the work done. If there are not sufficient well-qualified people, the work may not get done and their investment is at risk. With all the competition for investment dollars today, your financial support can disappear almost overnight, if you don't have a stable, productive workforce—with enough qualified people to get the work done.

Recent indications are that bond rating companies are now looking very closely at employee turnover rates—workforce stability—in determining what rating to give a company or agency. Why is this important? The rating that the analysts assign to your organization determines your cost of capital. If your turnover is alarmingly high—in the eyes of the analysts (who are admittedly not well trained in this area), the cost of money could actually drive you out of business.

Morale. How about *internal* customers lost because of inferior quality or service? Your employees are really an internal customer group, a very important group of stakeholders. If people are leaving—unexpectedly or not—their departure has an emotional, as well as logical, impact on their friends and coworkers. When morale drops, work suffers, rumors infect, and more people leave.

Employment Candidates. People who are evaluating your company to consider working with you do check your employee turnover, formally and informally. A lot of what they pick up is anecdotal—your reputation. If you build a reputation of having a lot of turnover, it will be more difficult for you to attract new employees—especially of the caliber you desire.

Words of Wisdom

Turnover can—and should—be measured on a periodic basis. Turnover is a business metric that you should carefully monitor. It's a bottom-line issue, as well as a factor in preparing your company for its destiny, way out there on your strategic planning horizon.

The Bliss-Gately Tool

To help you, we have researched available tools to calculate employee turnover. Over the past few years, a number of consultants, universities, and trade associations have devised templates and tools to measure the cost of uncontrolled employee turnover. While each has its merits, we recommend a tool developed by William Bliss and Robert Gately. For most of our readers, the Bliss-Gately Tool will provide entirely too much information. It will take time to collect the data, though the result will be the most accurate calculation we've seen anywhere. See Appendix B.

One of the reasons we recommend this tool is the need to standardize the measurement process in this field. We are continually amazed at the variety of methods used to calculate the human-resource metrics that produce turnover rates. We recently worked with a group of 23 employers in the same field and discovered that there were 22 distinctly different methods of determining the rate of employee turnover. You can imagine why, when clients or journalists ask us for average turnover rates in an industry, we just throw up our hands. You can't produce legitimate averages when everyone is using different metrics! Now, in all fairness, we know that a lot of employers use the formulas that suit them—to look good for their publics. The danger of these homegrown tools is that senior executives don't get accurate information . . . and you know the exposure that will give you!

Few executives have the interest, frankly, in looking at turnover costs as deeply as Bliss-Gately does. Therefore, we worked with Bliss and Gately to simplify the tool so you could work with it more comfortably. The following illustrations will give you examples of three different jobs. These presentations will give you enough information to stir up some nightmares; we don't need to give you more.

Business Costs & Impacts of Turnover

Recap

Company: **ABC Hospital**

Contact: **Katherine Madison**   Title: **HR**

Job Title: **Office Administrator Hourly Rate $9.44**

Part A	$	16,187	Costs due to employee leaving
Part B	$	779	Recruitment Costs
Part C	$	4,687	Training Costs
Part D	$	2,636	Lost Productivity Costs
Part E	$	30	New Employee Costs
Parts A - E	$	24,319	Cost of Turnover (sum Parts A to E)
Annual Salary	$	19,635	Without Benefits (Line SC1.6)

Cost of Turnover (%) = Cost of Turnover ($) ÷ Annual Salary ($)

Cost of Turnover	124%	% of Annual Base Salary
Part G	$ -	Extraordinary Costs
Parts A - E + Part G	$ 24,319	Cost of Turnover (sum Parts A to E + G)
Cost of Turnover [1]	124%	of Annual Salary without benefits

[1] Includes Extraordinary Costs identified in Part G

	$0.00	Lost Sales, Top Performer
Part F1	$0.00	Lost Sales, Average Performer
	$0.00	Lost Sales, Bottom Performer
Part F2	$0.00	Lost Revenue
Part F3	$0.00	Lost Profits

-- end of Recap Worksheet --

Figure 18: Turnover Calculations for an Office Administrator of a Hospital Using the Bliss-Gately Tool

Business Costs & Impacts of Turnover

Recap

Company: **ABC Hospital**

Contact: **Katherine Madison**   Title: **HR**

Job Title: **Project Specialist Marketing Hourly Rate $27.96**

Part A	$	38,487	**Costs due to employee leaving**
Part B	$	1,118	**Recruitment Costs**
Part C	$	10,609	**Training Costs**
Part D	$	18,144	**Lost Productivity Costs**
Part E	$	92	**New Employee Costs**
Parts A - E	$	68,450	**Cost of Turnover** (sum Parts A to E)
Annual Salary	$	58,157	**Without Benefits** (Line SC1.6)

Cost of Turnover (%) = Cost of Turnover ($) ÷ Annual Salary ($)

Cost of Turnover		118%	**% of Annual Base Salary**
Part G	$	-	**Extraordinary Costs**
Parts A - E + Part G	$	68,450	**Cost of Turnover** (sum Parts A to E + G)
Cost of Turnover [1]		118%	**of Annual Salary without benefits**

[1] **Includes Extraordinary Costs identified in Part G**

	$0.00	**Lost Sales, Top Performer**
Part F1	$0.00	**Lost Sales, Average Performer**
	$0.00	**Lost Sales, Bottom Performer**
Part F2	$0.00	**Lost Revenue**
Part F3	$0.00	**Lost Profits**

-- end of Recap Worksheet --

Figure 19: Turnover Calculations for a Project Specialist in Marketing
for a Hospital Using the Bliss-Gately Tool

Business Costs & Impacts of Turnover

Recap

Company: **ABC Hospital**

Contact: **Katherine Madison**   Title: **HR**

Job Title: **Education Coordinator Hourly Rate $20.18**

Part A	$	28,362	Costs due to employee leaving
Part B	$	1,173	Recruitment Costs
Part C	$	8,962	Training Costs
Part D	$	13,089	Lost Productivity Costs
Part E	$	101	New Employee Costs
Parts A - E	$	51,687	Cost of Turnover (sum Parts A to E)
Annual Salary	$	41,974	Without Benefits (Line SC1.6)

Cost of Turnover (%) = Cost of Turnover ($) ÷ Annual Salary ($)

Cost of Turnover		123%	% of Annual Base Salary
Part G	$	-	Extraordinary Costs
Parts A - E + Part G	$	51,687	Cost of Turnover (sum Parts A to E + G)
Cost of Turnover [1]		123%	of Annual Salary without benefits

[1] Includes Extraordinary Costs identified in Part G

	$0.00	Lost Sales, Top Performer
Part F1	$0.00	Lost Sales, Average Performer
	$0.00	Lost Sales, Bottom Performer
Part F2	$0.00	Lost Revenue
Part F3	$0.00	Lost Profits

-- end of Recap Worksheet --

Figure 20: Turnover Calculations for the Education Coordinator of a Hospital Using the Bliss-Gately Tool

For a detailed description of the complete costs of turnover, please refer to Appendix B. There we provide for you an abbreviated illustration of the entire Bliss-Gately Tool.

However . . . if you or your staff want to do some calculating of turnover in your organization, you can find The Bliss-Gately Tool at *www.hermangroup.com/store/software.html*. Now, if more employers use the same measurement device, we should be able to start making some comparative sense of these vital metrics.

Trends in Tenure

Building on information about the tenure trends in chapter 2, our research has uncovered some things you probably ought to know about employee tenure and employee turnover. Here's some food for thought.

While we look at turnover rates, we should also pay attention to job tenure and longevity. A significant number of people stay on the same job for a long time, particularly people from the World War II or Traditionalist Generation (born prior to 1946). This older generation in our workforce learned the values of loyalty, stability, and not to change careers frequently. This set of values is fully understandable, when you consider the employment world as it was in their growing-up years.

More job change and career change will occur among younger people, given the conditions in the employment world when they grew up. Some younger people (and we're talking here generally about those aged perhaps 40 and below) think nothing of leaving a job after six months. Or six weeks. Or six hours. Or not even showing up on the first day after hiring or orientation.

This change in commitment to employers has caused our average job tenure in the United States to drop from 4.6 years in 1990 to 3.5 years in 2000. Our forecast is that average job tenure will drop even further—significantly further—in the 2000–2015 period, fueled by the increased number of younger and middle-aged workers who have difficulty building allegiance to any one employer or career. There will still be plenty of stable workers to balance the overall picture, but the average tenure will continue to fall overall.

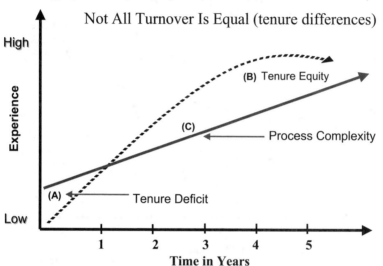

Figure 21: The Concept of Tenure Equity

All turnover should not be considered equal. As people learn their jobs over time, there is a definite learning curve. This example shows that in the first year (A), there is usually a tenure deficit. Losing an employee in the first year is nowhere near as costly as losing someone in the fourth year, because of the accumulated tenure equity or human capital value (B). Also, the more complex the process, the longer it usually takes to master the job skills (C). Unfortunately, virtually all companies measure turnover without considering tenure equity. A person in their fourth year of employment usually contributes much more than someone who is just learning their job and therefore has a much higher value. (Also see Figure 39 to observe the problem with average employee tenure based upon age.)

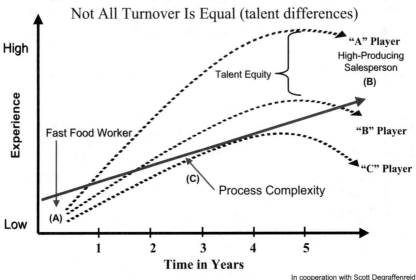

Talent Equity

The Aggregate Value of Employee *Capability* Relative to Process Complexity

Not All Turnover Is Equal (talent differences)

In cooperation with Scott Degraffenreid

Figure 22: The Concept of Talent Equity

We emphasize again that all turnover should not be considered equal. Similar to the concept of tenure equity where people become more valuable to an organization over time, there can be great differences in overall value, based upon talent. For jobs that have low process complexity (like the tasks of a fast-food worker [A], the differences between an "A" employee, a "B" employee, and a "C" employee may not be that great. With more complex jobs (like a high-performing pharmaceutical sales rep [B], an "A" employee could significantly outperform the overall value contributed by a "B" employee by a factor of five. Unfortunately, virtually all companies measure turnover without considering talent equity. When considering the loss of human capital upon an employee's departure, an "A" employee must be considered much more valuable than a "B" or a "C".

Corporate Homicide ... or Suicide

So, if uncontrolled turnover is killing your company, is this homicide or suicide? Well, maybe it depends on how much you are controlling the situation.

If the economy is hot and there are plenty of jobs available, the employment market will pull people from your organization. Even if the market is not hot, there may still be a strong demand for certain types of employees who work for you. If you are not doing enough of the right things to hold your good people, you may be an accessory to the talent theft.

When the economy is not hot and there is minimal churning in the employment market, some employers tend to treat their employees with less care. Do so, and you may abet warm-chair attrition—workers leave psychologically, but continue showing up for work physically. This condition can be considerably more expensive than if workers leave physically—empty-chair attrition.

If you treat people badly and ignore the need to consciously retain your valued people, you may be guilty of staffing suicide. You are causing your own problems, regardless of the external environment.

Assume that all of your employees are planning their next career move—right now. What plans do you want them to make? What are you doing to influence those decisions?

──────────────── Words of Wisdom ────────────────

Uncontrolled employee turnover means your bottom line is hemor-rhaging. Your company may be slowly bleeding to death. Extend your company's life by stemming the flow. Stop the loss of your valued employees by taking action that will inspire your people to stay with you. If you aren't doing what needs to be done, your leadership style may be suicidal.

If you have been neglecting your human resources, by default choosing to give this valuable resource insufficient attention, you may only be guilty of negligent corporate suicide.

The charts that complete this chapter will give you the benefit of years of research into hundreds of companies. These composite illustrations provided by Success Profiles, Inc., are self-explanatory, but should be studied carefully.

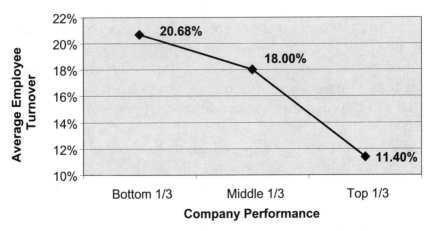

Employee Pride With Employee Turnover

Success Profiles Inc. Research, 2002

Figure 23: Employee Pride and Average Employee Turnover

The chart above illustrates the relationship between employees' pride in working for the companies and average employee turnover. The companies were classified into three categories (Bottom 1/3 performers, Middle 1/3, and Top 1/3), based upon their weighted average index score for the question: "I am proud to say I work for my company." The evidence shows that employee turnover is significantly lower for employees who feel proud to work for their companies. Also note that the most significant increase occurs when moving from the middle 1/3 group to the top 1/3 (a more difficult accomplishment).

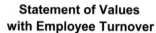

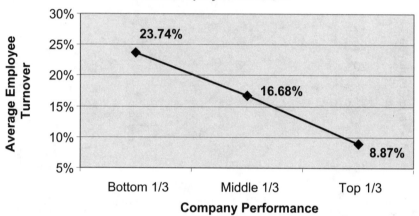

Success Profiles Inc. Research, 2002

Figure 24: Statement of Values and Employee Turnover

The chart above illustrates the relationship between organizations' effectiveness to establish and communicate their values or guiding principals and average employee turnover. The companies were classified into three categories (Bottom 1/3 performers, Middle 1/3, and Top 1/3), based upon their weighted average index score for the question: "Our company has a stated set of values or guiding principals." The evidence shows that the average employee turnover is significantly lower for organizations excelling with this practice. Also note that as the practice improves, the decrease is virtually a straight line.

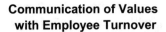

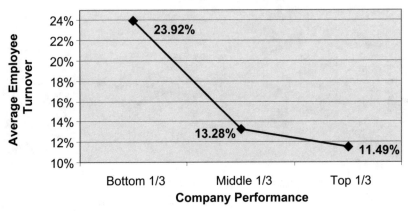

Success Profiles Inc. Research, 2002

Figure 25: Communication of Values and Employee Turnover

The chart above illustrates the relationship between organizations' communication of their core values and beliefs and average employee turnover. The companies were classified into three categories (Bottom 1/3 performers, Middle 1/3, and Top 1/3) based upon their weighted average index score for the question: "Our company has carefully articulated our core values and beliefs." The evidence shows that the average employee turnover is significantly lower for organizations excelling with this practice. Also note that the most significant increase occurs when moving from the Bottom 1/3 group to the Middle 1/3 (an easier accomplishment).

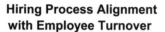

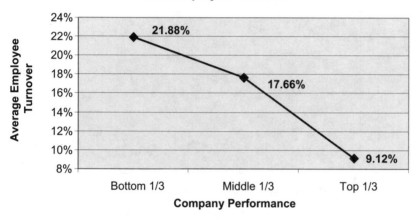

Success Profiles Inc. Research, 2002

Figure 26: Hiring Process Alignment with Employee Turnover

The chart above illustrates the relationship between organizations' hiring and selection processes and average employee turnover. The companies were classified into three categories (Bottom 1/3 performers, Middle 1/3, and Top 1/3), based upon their weighted average index score for the question: "Our hiring process evaluates if new employees will work well in our company's culture." The evidence shows that the average employee turnover is significantly lower for organizations excelling with this practice. Also note that the most significant increase occurs when moving from the Middle 1/3 group to the Top 1/3 (a more difficult accomplishment).

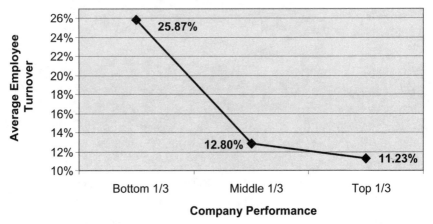

Success Profiles Inc. Research, 2002

Figure 27: Training and Average Employee Turnover

The chart above illustrates the relationship between organizations' commitment to training and development and average annual employee turnover. The companies were classified into three categories (Bottom 1/3 performers, Middle 1/3, and Top 1/3), based upon their weighted average index score for the question: "Our company places a high priority on training and development." The evidence shows that the annual turnover rate for the average group (middle performers) was reduced over 50 percent (25.87 percent to 12.8 percent) and 57 percent for the top performers. We conclude that the extent that an organization is committed to training and development is directly related to the employee retention rate and that there is an apparent "point of diminishing return" at the higher levels.

Closing Questions

1. Have you calculated the replacement costs for the more important skill positions in your organization?
2. Do you measure or evaluate both tenure and talent equity in your organization's turnover rates? Or do you consider all employee turnover to be the same?
3. Considering the high cost of turnover, do you have a formalized strategy for workforce retention?
4. Do you measure your business practices and integrate the results with your financial performance or other key performance indicators?

Opportunities for a Competitive Advantage

If you could increase the retention rate of your employees by just 6 months longer per person, how much tenure equity would that add? How much does an "A" player add to your business? Are you taking a serious stand with employees who exhibit "value subtracted," negative behavior by asking them to move on?

CHAPTER SIX

A Look Ahead: Healthcare on the Bleeding Edge

Workforce conditions in healthcare today are indicative of where most employers will be in 2006–2008. Focus on profit and loss statements and balance sheets may have a short-term positive effect on the stock price, but there are serious concerns about sustainability. When we examine the cost of employee turnover in both dollars and patient mortality, the true consequences emerge. Employee turnover has an impact on each hospital, on the industry, and on the community. With the challenging conditions present in hospitals, we might wonder why people continue to work there. The implications of the healthcare worker turnover are far-reaching. If the employee is not happy, attitude and commitment deficiencies affect performance, safety, quality, morale, and a variety of other measures. Solutions from VHA, Inc.'s white paper include developing a strong leadership platform, building healthy cultures, designing work for staff satisfaction and optimal care, creating effective human resource processes, and growing the next generation. Obstacles to successful transformation include leadership deficiency and staffing levels, neither of which is easy to overcome.

As a case study, we have selected healthcare, an industry on the "bleeding edge" of workforce and workplace trends. Based on our study of healthcare employment, facilitated by our close relationship with the VHA, Inc., we estimate that healthcare today is where most employers will be in 2006–2008.

> What's happening in healthcare is a harbinger of what is waiting for other industries in just a few short years.

There are other reasons we chose healthcare for our case study. We have served healthcare clients for more than two decades. We are familiar with how they function and with the transition they have been forced to move through in the recent past. Of the top 30 fastest-growing occupations in this decade, over half (17) are healthcare-related. (See figure 47 in chapter 9). Another reason is that healthcare is visible and affects all of us. Each of us has the potential to be engaged with the healthcare system. In time of emergency, we will expect the hospital to perform for us in a highly efficient, professional, and certainly effective manner. This expectation is not unlike the way your customers view you. You are particularly visible to your customers, and your relationship with them could be far-reaching.

Financial Issues

Much has been said about today's senior executives' misfocus of attention—in almost all fields. Their focus continues to be on profit and loss statements and balance sheets—whatever will influence the stock price in the immediate future. This concentration on short-term financials makes it difficult, if not impossible, for executives to look at the "big picture" and creatively plan their organization's future. They're forced into a reactive mode, driving a wide range of negative consequences.

Reductions in reimbursements have had a substantial impact on the healthcare industry—including both profit and not-for-profit hospitals. With a tight economy, every payor, direct and indirect, is squeezing hospitals to lower their charges. This pressure causes hospital management to concentrate on cutting costs by reducing staff, being stingy with resources (turn off lights when not in use), postponing new initiatives that might improve processes or outcomes, and insisting on lower prices from suppliers . . . sometimes with a cost-saving reduction in quality.

The next stage of this tailspin (see figure 27) is the organizational response in the area of human resources, arguably the most valuable—and the most volatile—of all resources utilized by hospitals . . . and other types of employment organizations. Tactics like layoffs, reductions in salaries, freezes on increases, reduction in training, and hiring freezes are mixed in with schedule manipulation that makes life difficult for employees who want a life outside of work.

How do people respond to the squeeze? They're certainly less motivated, resulting in less effort and lower results. Can this happen with dedicated professionals? You bet—when their job roles are changed, expecting them to do so many more tasks (often without remuneration or even appreciation) that they just buckle under the pressure. In a survey conducted by the American Nurses Association, 56 percent of respondents said their time available for direct patient care has decreased. And 75 percent feel the quality of nursing care at the facility in which they work has been compromised over the past two years. With mutterings like "this isn't what I signed on for," they leave for greener pastures. Sometimes those opportunities are in better-managed hospitals; sometimes they are out of the healthcare field entirely.

Quality suffers when staff members don't have enough time or resources to do the job that should be done. Safety exposure is a serious issue in hospitals, where disability or even death can result. When valued employees leave, they have to be replaced—often at great expense for recruiting, bonuses, training, and assimilation. Beyond the difficulties incurred by the individual hospital, the entire industry is affected.

The "Tail Spin" Effect on Healthcare Workforce Stability

1. Reimbursement Reductions
- Dominant focus on financial metrics
- Cost reduction/cutting initiatives
- Staff reductions
- Supply chain pressures
- Operational efficiency changes
  (mostly designed to cut costs)

2. Organizational Response
- Layoffs
- Salary freezes and reductions
- Flex time
- Reduce training
- Use of part time/cheaper labor
- Freeze on hiring and promotions

5. Impact on Local Markets
- Increased compensation
- Outsourced staffing for demand
- Increased overtime
- Sign on bonuses
- Decreased quality care
- Decreased patient satisfaction

3. Individual Behaviors
- Decreased motivation and effort
- Safety/quality issues
- Increased employee turnover
- Reduced job focus
- Reduced job satisfaction
- People consider changing jobs/careers

4. Impact on Health Care Industry
- Fewer people entering profession
- Labor unrest (unions)
- Reduced talent for positions
- Other diverse employment options
- Increased competition for talent (within and outside of industry)

Figure 28: The Tailspin Effect on Healthcare Workforce Stability

The healthcare industry has been in a tailspin spiral since 1990 when top-line reimbursement reductions (1) led to a negative organizational response (2) that affected individual behaviors (3) that had an impact on the healthcare industry (4), and ultimately affected the local markets (5). This spiral is extremely difficult to pull out of, because to build a base of stability requires investment. Also, the marketplace rewards the practices in #2 (It's the right behavior and a "necessary evil," but done improperly will accelerate the tailspin with crippling consequences in 3, 4, and 5).

Looking at the problems in the industry, fewer young people are encouraged to enter the healthcare professions. In fact, 40 percent of nurses surveyed in 2001 by the American Nurses Association would not feel comfortable having their loved ones cared for in the facility where they worked. Almost 55 percent of nurses surveyed actively discourage people from entering the field and 55 percent would not recommend healthcare as a career choice. This attitude is disheartening, when we remember that the best recruiters are usually your own employees.

With fewer people entering the field and more people leaving, the talent pool is dangerously reduced. The need to fill open positions forces the hospitals to allocate considerably more resources to recruit applicants in a highly competitive employment environment. Unhappy employees, having to shoulder more than their share of the load, become more receptive to union organizers; and sometimes unions, seeking to protect their members, negotiate work rules that severely restrict management's efforts to serve all their stakeholders.

The spotlight has been shining on Registered Nurses as the big shortage problem. There is no denying a nursing shortage. Recent figures report openings for 126,000 nurses in hospitals in the United States alone. Some observers suggest that we have an abundance of nurses, but they're just in the wrong place. In actuality, there may well be plenty of people trained as nurses, but they're working in a wide range of other occupations, because they were so unhappy in the hospital working environment.

The nursing shortage will continue and, in fact, actually get worse in the years ahead. There are several reasons for this condition. First, nurses are leaving the healthcare field to accept employment as administrators, teachers, flight attendants, secretaries, salespeople, and more. Second, those nurses who choose to stay in hospital employment are working for nursing employment agencies instead of hospitals. They can often earn more,

Impending Crisis in Healthcare

- *"There will be a shortfall of approximately 1 million nurses by 2010 and 1.5 million by 2020."*

    —Fitch Inc. a Wall St. Bond Rating Firm

- *"Monetary solutions alone are not enough to improve the situation. Improvements in the workplace environment, combined with aggressive and innovative recruiting efforts are paramount."*

    —Kathy Hall, MS,RN, executive director of the Maryland Nurses Association in presentation to the Senate Health, Education, Labor and Pensions Subcommittee

- *"There are three problems: Nurses are not coming into the profession, the ones who are there are not staying long enough and those who are there are not happy."*

    —George Benjamin, MD, secretary, Maryland Department of Health in presentation to the Senate Health, Education, Labor and Pensions Subcommittee 2-13-01

Figure 29: Impending Crisis in Healthcare

since they're called in when hospital employers are desperate enough to call for outside help, and they can control the hours they work. A third problem is that our schools are not graduating enough new nurses to meet the demand. Two difficulties here: An insufficient flow of new students into the schools and, second, challenges in attracting faculty, as nursing instructors retire or leave the field. In some areas of the country, there are insufficient seats in nursing schools to be able to accept new students.

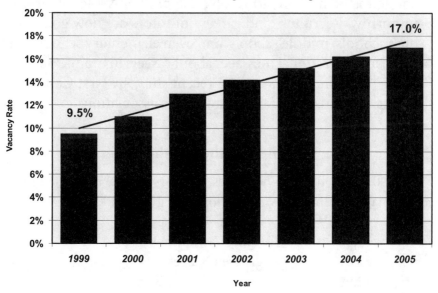

FCG Report commissioned by AHA, AAMC, NAPH,
and the Federation of American Hospitals 2001

Figure 30: Change in RN Vacancy Rate Projected to 2005

*The vacancy rate in nursing positions will grow from 9.5 percent benchmarked
in 1999 to an estimated 17 percent by 2005, according to the FCG Report.
(Note that this chart does not extend to 2010, the timeline for most of this
book.) Legitimate projections are not available, and they might be too
frightening for us to consider. By 2006 to 2008, conditions may be substantially
worse, creating even more significant problems for industry leaders. Do you
have occupations that may be affected the same way?*

Besides Registered Nurses, other healthcare occupations also have serious shortages. The associations in the industry monitor these numbers carefully, though they readily admit that not enough is being done to resolve the problems—today or even tomorrow. Recruiters and career educators are now going into high schools, middle schools, and even elementary schools with positive, inspirational messages about careers in healthcare. Look at the numbers produced by a recent study by First Consulting Group, commissioned by several of the associations in the field.

Where is there a shortage?

2001 Hospital vacancy rates for nurses, pharmacists, and imaging technicians are well over the 10% mark.

15.3%	Imaging Technicians
13.0%	Registered Nurses
12.9%	Licensed Practical Nurses
12.7%	Pharmacists
12.0%	Nursing Assistants
9.5%	Laboratory Technicians
8.5%	Billers/Coders
5.7%	IT Technologists
5.3%	Housekeeping/ Maintenance

FCG report commissioned by AHA, AAMC,
NAPH and the Federation of American Hospitals 2001

Figure 31: Where Else Is There a Shortage?

On one hand, we could say that it is good that we have so many opportunities today for people to enter the healthcare field. The new entrants could be recent high school or college graduates, retired military (and those who leave the service before retirement), and people interested in a career change into healthcare. On the other hand, inadequate staffing of hospitals inhibits service to the community. Understaffed hospitals are sometimes forced to turn away patients, even though they have the space for them.

Employee Turnover Impacts on Each Hospital

When faced with labor shortages, hospitals can be severely constrained in their capacity to meet the needs of their patients. Let's examine some of the effects to illuminate the problem.

Recruiting Costs. Vacant positions must be filled in an organization with a defined staffing requirement. Each patient requires a certain level of care, which must be provided by Registered Nurses, nurses' aides, administrative personnel, dietary workers, housekeepers, lab technicians, pharmacists, and numerous other specially trained healthcare professionals. Without sufficient staffing, the hospital cannot function as expected and service levels drop.

Qualified employees must be recruited to fill the vacant positions. This process can be quite expensive, especially if the hospital is not regarded as a preferred employer—in the community or in the industry. Included in the high costs are advertising, interviewing space, recruiting incentives, relocation costs, as well as salaries and benefits for recruiters, interviewers, and orientation personnel . . . and don't forget those *extra* supervisors to manage them.

Efficiency. Efficiency is vitally important in the hospital setting. Processes and procedures must be well coordinated by people who are familiar and comfortable with the routine. For instance, when Roger was admitted to the hospital for his heart surgery, he was moved from the emergency department to the floor where he would be monitored until he went to the operating room the next morning. Imagine what might have happened if, when the orderlies moved him from the emergency room, there was no one to receive him on the floor. What would he be fed? Would medications be administered at the right times? Anyone who has been a patient in a hospital knows the value of being cared for by a team of people who work well together so tasks can be accomplished in the right way at the right time.

Effectiveness. How well the job is done is important, but so is doing the right job. Do you know anyone who has experienced an ACL reconstruction? It's surgery on the knee to reconstruct the anterior cruciate ligament. As part of the preparation, the hospital personnel mark the knee that is to be operated on to assure the surgeon's effectiveness.

Safety. Hospitals with high turnover risk hiring people that are not familiar with all the procedures that must be followed. For instance, if patient rooms are not cleaned properly, the next patient in the room may be exposed to bacterial/infection problems. Pharmacy assistants, new on the job and not fully trained or supervised, may send the wrong medications to be given to a patient.

Output/Results. If the proper care is not delivered to a patient in a timely manner, the recovery time may be extended. This situation sometimes results when a patient has contracted an infection while in the hospital, an all-too-frequent occurrence. Not only does the patient need to spend more time than necessary in the hospital, increasing costs, but also the bed is not available for another patient who may need to be admitted. These reduced outcomes affect the productivity of the hospital and, eventually, the bottom line.

Competitiveness. Hospitals that have staffing shortages or staffing deficiencies due to unnecessarily high employee turnover often have difficulty competing in their marketplace. If we must invest more resources in staff training—and retraining—those resources are not available for other purposes. To really be competitive in today's complicated healthcare market, a hospital must control costs and deliver patient-centered performance. A stable, dedicated, and productive workforce is a leading factor in building the competitive strength that enables a hospital to keep its doors open.

Confidence Concerns. When confidence questions are raised about a hospital—in terms of mortality, unnecessarily long stays, quality of care, service time, and other factors, leaders and members of the community have reason to be concerned. Those concerns will also influence recruiting and other human resource issues.

The Impact on the Industry and the Community

How would you like to be injured in an automobile accident, picked up by an ambulance, but not able to go to the nearest hospital? According to a Special Workforce Survey conducted by the American Hospital Association, 18 percent of hospitals routinely send emergency patients to other facilities. It happens so much, there's even a term to describe this redirection: Emergency Department Diversion.

Workforce shortages also cause 30 percent of the hospitals to experience emergency department overcrowding, causing delays in service. These numbers reported in *Tomorrow's Work Force: A Strategic Approach*, published as a white paper by the VHA, Inc. in 2002, include information that 18 percent of hospitals surveyed had reduced the number of beds staffed. In 16 percent of the hospitals, surgery was delayed; 11 percent of hospitals had cancelled surgery because of insufficient staffing. The numbers were significantly higher for urban hospitals.

The shortage in so many healthcare professions forces hospital costs to rise substantially. More overtime must be paid to maintain staffing levels, while threatening to burn out the people who work the extra hours. The quality of patient care is reduced, resulting in decreased patient (and family) satisfaction. Complaints increase and the hospital earns a less-than stellar reputation. This reduced reputation makes it more difficult to recruit new employees, to attract patients and doctors, to acquire funding, and to maintain a positive position within the community. The tailspin can easily become an unstoppable downward spiral.

The funding aspect deserves a moment of special attention. Hospital expansion requires considerable funding, most often acquired through the sale of bonds. The price of the money to expand is based on the hospital's bond rating. Do bond rating agencies, and through them investors, really care about human resource issues? Investors are paying more attention to the quality and stability of the workforce and the expressed values of the organization. This attention surfaced again when Fitch, Inc., a Wall Street bond rating firm, announced that it would reduce the bond rating status of hospitals with higher turnover. This factor makes workforce stability a clear bottom-line issue. If higher employee turnover means it will cost more to borrow money, it makes sense to reduce the churn in the hospital's workforce. Your company will face the same issue.

Why Do People Continue to Work in Hospitals?

It is easy to paint a bleak picture and suggest that hospitals are doomed. They're caught in that unstoppable downward spiral, and they cannot escape. There is no hope.

However, that scenario is far from the truth, though too many hospitals are in the midst of various kinds of trauma of their own. Many are doing well, although they struggle with serious workforce challenges. They are concerned, and rightly so, because the situation they face today is critical. And tomorrow will probably be worse, unless today's efforts produce some good progress.

With all the challenges, many of which were stimulated by outside sources such as the economy and reductions in revenue, most hospitals are doing okay. A few are doing great. As they come to grips with their circumstances, savvy leaders are taking giant steps to overcome their workforce shortcomings. While we know that not all hospital CEOs and their direct reports are models of exemplary leadership, we have seen some leaders who really "get it." Their results are apparent in employee satisfaction, lower employee turnover, greater productivity, and higher patient satisfaction. These factors, of course, strengthen bottom-line performance.

As we mentioned earlier, we have had the opportunity to work directly with healthcare leaders who are striving to make a difference. As this book is written, Roger and Tom are serving as National Chair and Business Case Spokesman, respectively, for the Tomorrow's Workforce Collaborative of VHA, Inc., a member-owned and member-driven healthcare cooperative representing over 2,000 hospitals. We have found executives and managers of these hospitals eager to learn, to make improvements in the way they do business, and to strengthen their clinical and operational performance.

In the Tomorrow's Workforce project, teams of leaders from hospitals come together periodically to learn and share. They participate in data gathering by surveying their employees to assess their current situation. Using the information collected, they design and implement the solutions that will further stabilize their workforce and strengthen their present and future position in the employment market. We appreciate the opportunity to help these leaders make a difference, and to share with you some of the data collected from the participating hospitals.

Let's begin with the big picture. The following chart shows the strongest predictors of commitment, retention, and low absenteeism. Notice the similarities and differences between the managers and staff and that market-competitive benefits and wages are ranked fifth on both lists. The big rewards for working in healthcare are not compensation and benefits. These important factors have to be reasonable, but are not showing up as the most influential factors in the decisions made by healthcare employees. By the way, these data are consistent with what we have seen in non-healthcare employers.

What "Really" Contributes to Retention

The regression analyses found the following factors to be the strongest predictors of employee and management commitment, retention and low absenteeism:

Management
1. Employee involvement in change & decision-making process
2. Senior leadership active support for retention and recruitment
3. A quality-driven culture
4. Support for staff career development
5. Market-competitive benefits and wages

Employees/Staff
1. Close and supportive relationship with manager and/or supervisor
2. Senior leadership active support for retention and recruitment
3. A team-based and employee involvement culture
4. A quality-driven culture
5. Market-competitive benefits and wages

Data from VHA Research Tomorrow's Workforce Collaborative, 2001

Figure 32: What "Really" Contributes to Retention . . . Management and Employees/Staff

This research conducted by VHA, Inc. produced results consistent with those produced by Tom's company, Success Profiles, Inc., over a period of years. The input from over 600 companies corroborates what VHA, Inc. learned. The study isolated the predictive business practices that contributed to employees' intent to stay in their jobs over specific intervals of time.

The statistical analysis revealed that a few specific practices most contributed to employees' willingness to stay or leave their current employer (the hospital). We have chosen four charts to present to you, each comparing "Willingness-to-Stay Intent" to a different measure of value for the employer. This presentation will give you, the reader, an opportunity to see the powerful relationship of retention (and what employers do to encourage retention) to organizational success.

Note the satisfaction scores and consistent pattern with the slopes of the lines from low willingness to stay (less than two years) to high willingness to stay (11 years or longer).

Implications

Intent to stay with an employer is a vital measure for a couple of reasons. The first is obvious. The length of time the employee intends to stay is an indicator of satisfaction to which management must be very sensitive.

The other reason to be particularly sensitive to the intent-to-stay metric is the employee's performance. If the employee is not happy enough to intend to stay, attitude and commitment deficiencies will affect performance, safety, quality, morale, and a variety of other factors. Someone who is more interested in leaving than staying may influence other employees to seek other employment, too . . . or at least be more receptive to overtures from recruiters. And remember, recruiters will be more aggressive as the labor market gets tighter.

With the increasing importance of extending employee tenure, the more knowledge we have—from assessments and from other means such as focus groups and interviews, the more we can do to build satisfaction and longevity. The satisfaction issue will become considerably more important during the balance of the decade. More employers will seek to benchmark themselves to understand where they are and what they must do to

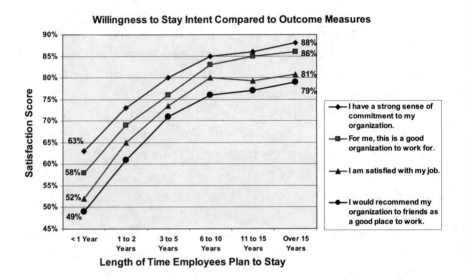

Willingness to Stay Intent Compared to Outcome Measures

Data from VHA Research
Tomorrow's Workforce Collaborative, 2001

Figure 33: Willingness-to-Stay Intent Compared to Outcome Measures

The chart above illustrates findings from a study conducted by VHA in 2002 with Tomorrow's Workforce Collaborative. The study isolated a number of predictive business practices that contributed to employees' willingness to stay in their jobs over specific intervals of time. The statistical analysis revealed that a few specific practices most reflected employees' willingness to stay with or leave their current employer (the hospital). This chart best reflects the results of the statistical analysis that quantified the relationship between the satisfaction scores of several "outcome" drivers and peoples willingness to stay or leave over time. The top four are: I have a strong sense of commitment to my organization, for me, this is a good organization to work for, I am satisfied with my job and I would recommend my organization to friends as a good place to work. Note the satisfaction scores and consistent pattern with the slopes of the lines from low willingness to stay (less than 2 years) to high willingness to stay (11 years or longer).

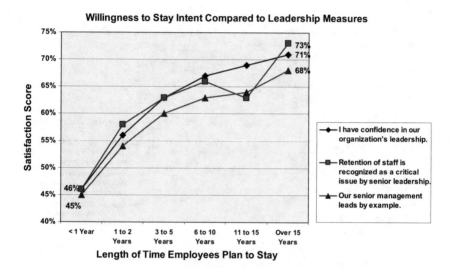

Data from VHA Research
Tomorrow's Workforce Collaborative, 2001

Figure 34: Willingness-to-Stay Intent Compared to Leadership Measures

The chart above illustrates the findings from a study of leadership practices conducted by VHA, Inc. in 2002 in connection with Tomorrow's Workforce Collaborative. This chart best reflects the results of the statistical analysis that quantified the relationship between the satisfaction scores of several "leadership" drivers and people's willingness to stay or leave over time. The top three leadership practices are: "I have confidence in our organization's leadership," "retention of staff is recognized as a critical issue by senior leadership," and "our senior management leads by example."

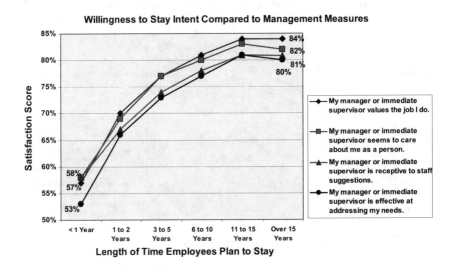

Figure 35: Willingness-to-Stay Intent Compared to Management Measures

The chart above illustrates the findings from a study of specific management practices conducted by VHA, Inc. in 2002 with the Tomorrow's Workforce Collaborative. This chart best reflects the results of the statistical analysis that quantified the relationship between the satisfaction scores of several "management" drivers and people's willingness to stay or leave over time. The top four management practices are: "My manager or immediate supervisor values the job I do," "my manager or immediate supervisor seems to care about me as a person,"" my manager or immediate supervisor is receptive to staff suggestions," and "my manager or immediate supervisor is effective at addressing my needs."

raise satisfaction scores, performance, and bottom-line results. See www.employerofchoice.net for one alternative.

To evaluate the connection between employee satisfaction (expressed as employee retention rates) and performance, consider the chart below. Here we examine the relationship between employee turnover (the opposite of retention) and patient care, based on patient mortality and how much longer patients had to remain in the hospital.

When patient mortality is up above national averages, serious questions are raised about the hospital's ability to care for patients. Obviously, that's a serious concern for the hospital's customers and the community at large. If employees are not well-trained, well-managed, and well-supported in a working environment with a stable workforce, there will always be vulnerability in the areas of work quality, efficiency, and effectiveness.

From a financial perspective, employee turnover impacts the cost of healthcare. As seen in the chart below, when turnover is higher, costs can be considerably higher. Considering average costs for patient care, the additional time a patient remains in the hospital combined with costs of efficiency, rework of lab tests, and many other factors, the lack of a stable workforce can drive costs substantially. The same kind of "cost creep" occurs in non-healthcare organizations, but is often not measured. If similar measurements were undertaken, the results would probably have a dramatic impact on the way the businesses were managed.

Solutions

What are the solutions for healthcare? The impetus and the influence lie with hospital leadership. There is a wide range of issues to be addressed . . . and soon. Leadership policies, philosophies, and behavior will determine whether their hospitals will be chosen or avoided by prospective employees . . . and patients.

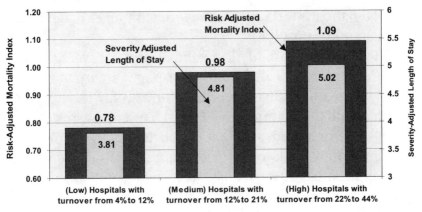

Figure 36: The Relationship between Employee Turnover and Patient Care

The chart above illustrates the results from a VHA, Inc. study that quantified the impact that high turnover has on patient care, overall costs, and profitability. The analysis revealed that high-turnover hospitals (facilities with turnover from 22 percent to 44 percent) had a higher risk-adjusted mortality index and severity-adjusted average length of stay (when compared to facilities with lower turnover). This difference in patient safety and cycle time is significant when you consider the volume of patients moving through a typical hospital in just one year.

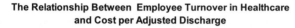

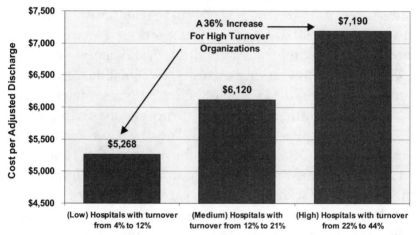

Figure 37: The Relationship between Employee Turnover in Healthcare and Cost Per Adjusted Discharge

Here are the results from a VHA, Inc. study that quantified the impact of high turnover on patient care, overall costs, and profitability. The analysis revealed that high-turnover hospitals (facilities with turnover from 22 percent to 44 percent) had a 36 percent increase in costs per adjusted discharge (when compared to facilities with lower turnover). This difference in costs is substantial when you consider the volume of patients moving through a typical hospital in just one year.

Senior executives must refocus their priorities to concentrate more on human resource issues. This shift does not reduce the importance of finances, board politics, and all the other issues that clamor for attention. The message is clear that if the workforce issues are not adequately addressed, the other issues might not matter anymore. While hospital executives express concern, we have seen too few who have really grasped the seriousness of their situation. If they did, we'd see a lot more attention given to building a stable, dedicated, and happy workforce.

To illustrate the lurking calamity, let's look at some simple math, considering the 275,000 Registered Nurses in the VHA, Inc. system. Assuming an annual turnover rate of 15 percent, 41,250 will leave member hospitals. The vacancies created mean at least 330,000 nurses will need to be recruited from 2002 until 2010. At an average replacement cost (direct and indirect expenses) of $40,000 (or 87 percent of average salary of $46,000), the total replacement costs per year will be $1,650,000,000. That's right: over $1.6 billion per year. The cost from 2002 to 2010 will reach $17,108,018,082 (that's if the problem doesn't get worse and we have 3.5 percent inflation). These figures do not consider other issues or costs that will be affected, such as patient satisfaction, patient safety, employee productivity, other employee turnover costs, administrative/overhead costs, etc. Note: We have profiled only the nursing shortage, not the similar conditions for pharmacists, coding and billing clerks, imaging technicians, and all the other professions that are currently experiencing shortages.

A reminder to our non-healthcare readers: Before you gloat and thank your lucky stars that you're not in this predicament, ask what *your* situation might be in 2006 to 2008. That is when we estimate you will encounter the same conditions that healthcare is coping with today. Don't gloat, prepare!

Worker attitudes make a big difference in changing the way things are done in healthcare, including desired longevity. And,

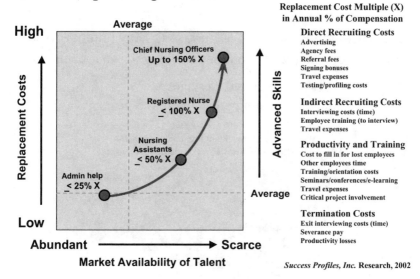

Human Capital Replacement Costs

Replacement Cost Multiple (X)
in Annual % of Compensation

Direct Recruiting Costs
Advertising
Agency fees
Referral fees
Signing bonuses
Travel expenses
Testing/profiling costs

Indirect Recruiting Costs
Interviewing costs (time)
Employee training (to interview)
Travel expenses

Productivity and Training
Cost to fill in for lost employees
Other employees time
Training/orientation costs
Seminars/conferences/e-learning
Travel expenses
Critical project involvement

Termination Costs
Exit interviewing costs (time)
Severance pay
Productivity losses

Success Profiles, Inc. Research, 2002

Figure 38: The Human Capital Replacement Cost Model

This chart represents a model for replacing key employees in a typical hospital. Replacement cost analysis was performed for several key skill positions. The total direct and indirect replacement costs were calculated for each position by examining the number of employees, average base compensation, turnover percentage, and replacement factor (the actual costs to replace skilled professionals illustrated as a percentage of their base compensation).

The Human Capital Replacement Cost Model shows the increase in replacement costs (Y1-axis), relative to market availability of talent (X-axis) and degree of advanced skills required for the position (Y2-axis). For example, the total replacement cost for administrative staff has been calculated to be less than or equal to 25 percent of their base compensation. In contrast, the total replacement costs for chief nursing officers is commonly up to 150 percent of their base compensation. The total cost of high employee turnover is extremely expensive when hospitals spend hundreds of thousands of dollars every month to replace highly skilled employees. Other studies have shown the impact that high employee turnover has on patient satisfaction, safety, and total operating costs.

VHA's Research Results – Willingness to Stay (Intent Profile)
How long do you plan to continue working for your company?

54% of the employees ages **32-39**
are only planning to stay up to 5 years

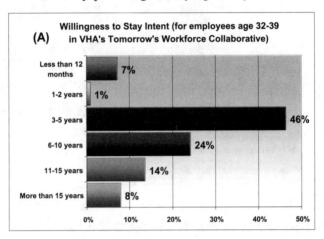

Data from VHA Research
Tomorrow's Workforce Collaborative, 2001

Figure 39A: Willingness-to-Stay Intent and Age Differences

The charts above illustrate the aggregate data from ten major hospitals (over 6,000 participants). The results from VHA, Inc.'s Tomorrow's Workforce Collaborative show two very different profiles of employees' willingness to stay based upon age group. In chart (A) to the left, 54 percent of employees ages 32 to 39 are only planning to stay up to five years.

VHA's Research Results – Willingness to Stay (Intent Profile)
How long do you plan to continue working for your company?
The employees ages **40-45**
are planning to stay longer

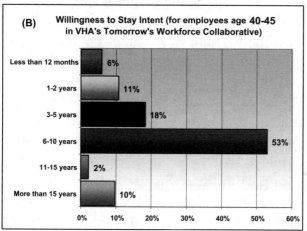

Data from VHA Research
Tomorrow's Workforce Collaborative, 2001

Figure 39B: Willingness-to-Stay Intent and Age Differences

In the same hospitals, reflected in chart (B), employees ages 40 to 45 are willing to stay longer. The trend for hospitals to not retain their younger skilled staff is an extreme challenge for the healthcare industry. Notice the marked contrast between the profile of "willingness to stay more than 15 years" and the profile of "companies that practice open-book management (OBM)."

make no mistake, their attitudes are heavily influenced by management attitudes. Yes, senior executives, mid-level managers, and frontline supervisors have a huge influence on employee dedication and tenure. This statement seems like a no-brainer. Where's the problem?

The problem is that most executives and managers are in the Clueless or Awareness Stages (Stages 1 and 2, see chapter 1 for details). They must change their thinking and change the way they are doing business. Lip service won't be sufficient; we're dealing with climatic change (see chapter 2 for more information). Executives and managers must accept that the economy will become stronger as the decade progresses—at least until 2008, from what we can see. Technology will be brought in to solve some of the problems, but that fancy technology will be useless without the people who know how to use it. A higher caliber of employee will be needed—employees who will have lots of other opportunities such as serving on the crew of high-tech navy destroyers, working on fast-emerging computer applications, applying their analytical skills in the fascinating world of finance, or teaching.

No, immigration is not the whole answer. There is a limited number of qualified people who can be brought to America from other countries, and overcoming the language and cultural barriers may not be worth the effort. In some cases, such as Canadian nurses coming to the United States to find work and to benefit from the currency exchange rate, the contributing country suffers a consequential shortage. The problems have to be solved here at home with current and future indigenous resources. As presented in the VHA, Inc. White Paper, *Tomorrow's Work Force: A Strategic Approach*, the five principal strategies for addressing healthcare's challenges are

- Develop a Strong Leadership Platform
- Build Healthy Cultures
- Design Work for Staff Satisfaction and Optimal Care

- Create Effective Human Resource Processes
- Grow the Next Generation

With education, shifting focus, and diligence, healthcare executives can indeed make a substantial difference. While their work may not change any of the external environmental factors, it can change the way the hospital does business. Every hospital is faced with the challenges of the ever-tightening labor market, costly technologies, and customers who expect high levels of service. As we move through the decade, *all* employers will face these same circumstances.

Obstacles to Successful Transformation

Overcoming these challenges has become a competitive issue. If your competitor (a nearby hospital in this case) does a better job attracting, optimizing, and retaining top talent, your hospital is in serious trouble. You're competing for limited resources—resources that can't be "bought" with big bucks. Surveys of hospital executives reveal that they're still throwing out large sign-on bonuses like bait, but find that the applicants who "bite" aren't really committed to their employers. They're committed to the highest bidder. They're fickle and will leave as someone starts a bidding war. Who wins? Who loses?

Leadership Deficiency. The major obstacle to successful transformation to be an attractive workplace is leadership deficiency. We're talking about the lack of clear corporate mission, inconsistent values, inadequate vision, and taking employees for granted. This approach just won't work anymore. The most important thing leaders can do is to internalize the core purpose and create a clear line of sight to see where they're going. If you're good at these practices, everything else is easy. If you're not, even the simplest things can be a handicap and a struggle.

——————————— Words of Wisdom ———————————

Enlightened leaders must create new corporate cultures. They must reevaluate job designs to assign appropriate duties to the right people. They must analyze schedules to accommodate lifestyle changes and preferences, even though that adjustment may require hiring more people. As with many employers, there will be an evolutionary shift to more part-time and flexible scheduling . . . something that is currently resisted by many healthcare employers.

Staffing Levels. Staffing levels will become a more critical issue, particularly if legislation like California enacted in 1999 becomes more popular. This legislation established minimum staffing levels for hospitals. Some hospitals complain loudly that the required levels are unfair, but this may not be the case. Most hospitals in California already meet the proposed staffing ratios. On medical-surgical units, for example, the state requires one nurse for six patients, a standard that about 85 percent of hospitals already meet. New proposals call for ratios to drop to one nurse for five patients, which would cause a greater impact. Similar standards may be established for other professions as legislators and regulators become more concerned about staffing, service, safety, and patient care levels.

As for the economic aspect, the California Healthcare Association estimates compliance with the 1999 requirements cost $400 million. Advocates of the higher staffing ratios characterize the amount as "a drop in the bucket" compared with the total amount spent on hospital care in the state. The bigger problem will be finding enough nurses to meet the new staffing requirements.

Hospitals have threatened to close units if they can't hire adequate staff, which would adversely affect access to care. Nurse groups argue that nurses working on well-staffed units will be less frustrated and less likely to abandon their careers, and thus will slow the high rate of attrition. These are not simple issues and there are no easy answers.

These problems must be addressed now and in the future. Healthcare, like other industries, must invest heavily in developing new talent or job growth and natural attrition will dry up an already tight supply. California unveiled an initiative to pump $60 million into training and retention programs over three years. The state hospital association had called for six times that amount, but has praised the governor for making a start. Other states are debating similar legislation, and there is support to expand nurse education loan programs on the federal level.

All these steps are necessary, yet we're still just talking about nursing. Remember that other healthcare occupations face similar conditions. Healthcare is having plenty of trouble with staffing, with far-reaching implications. The situation will get worse before it gets better, but it can get better with wise leaders who devote the necessary attention to workforce issues.

This chapter is a case study of just one industry. To reemphasize, we chose healthcare because our estimation is that their predicament is similar to what other industries will face in a disarmingly short amount of time. Perhaps now, dear reader, you will appreciate why we use such a melodramatic word as "crisis."

How would your organization cope with the kinds of challenges faced by healthcare today? Your opportunity may be right around the corner.

Closing Questions

1. How severe is the labor shortage experienced by your local hospitals? What affect will that difficulty have on your employees' healthcare benefits and quality of care?
2. Do you offer health and wellness benefits or discounts for fitness programs to help your employees be more productive and lower your healthcare costs?

3. Have you calculated with some statistical accuracy the reasons why your employees move on to other organizations or industries?
4. Do you have a "willingness to stay" element in your employee survey and have you analyzed it by position, age, or function?

Opportunities for a Competitive Advantage

What if your managers and supervisors were rewarded for (or held accountable for) an element of their performance review criteria that specifically measured the development and advancement of their subordinates? What if the concept of succession planning went all the way down to the supervisor level? How much longer would you retain your best and brightest performers?

PART 2

Solutions

CHAPTER SEVEN

The Leader's Imperative

The senior leader and his/her direct reports—the senior leadership team—set the tone and pace of the entire organization. Senior leaders, the top executives, are clearly the important messengers to distribute the messages of about the impending crisis and counteracting strategies to their direct reports and throughout the organization. By encouraging feedback, these executive messengers reinforce their positions and the importance of the messages. A champion or team of champions can help spearhead the initiative. The leadership must place major emphasis on information sharing and interdepartmental collaboration. They must communicate the appropriate recommended business practices, so that people begin to take action right away. As the result of years of measurement and benchmarking, Tom has developed what he calls The "Sweet Spot" of highly effective organizational practices. This concept is defined by the combination of critical leadership, management, business, and external practices. Measurement of key drivers is vital. Leadership must get into action?right away. Plan how you will overcome the ignorance that may get in your way.

Every organization has a senior leader. Titles include chairman, chief executive officer, president, owner, divisional vice president, and plant manager. This person is recognized as being in charge. Whatever he or she says, goes. Although many organizations run on bureaucratic energy, the senior leader still has significant influence. This strategic leader usually guides the mission, vision, values, and culture through communication with others. Role modeling and example setting also give others something to follow.

The senior leader and his/her direct reports—the senior leadership team—set the tone and pace of the organization. They are expected to stand on the top of the metaphorical mountain, looking at the full panorama of the corporate operating environment, so they can guide those below them on the mountain . . . or more specifically, the organizational chart. Their jobs are to look for opportunities and the best paths to follow. They are the people with the final decision about breaking new trails, leading the organization into uncharted waters in pursuit of success. Part of their jobs is also to watch for danger, to alert subordinates to risks and offer guidance about how to avoid or mitigate those threats.

─────────────── **Words of Wisdom** ───────────────

With the knowledge gained from this book, and the considerable experience and insight held by senior leaders, all key people in the organization must be alerted to the Impending Crisis. Strategies must be developed to begin to change the way business is done. Priorities must be set, action must be initiated, and measurement systems must be put in place.

You're reading the book. You understand the problem and the need to generate solutions in a timely manner. Wherever you are in your organization, know that other people are also concerned. They may not have read the book yet, but they're sensitive, they're thinking, and they're exploring ways to address various aspects of the crisis.

A Tale of Two Leaders

Ned Albee, senior vice president of human resources of Lancaster General Hospital in Lancaster, Pennsylvania, tells a story about how he and his boss were on the same frequency without realizing it. Ned purchased a copy of Roger's book, *Keeping Good People*, after hearing him speak at an industry conference. Excited about what he found in the book, he turned down page corners and did a lot of highlighting as he moved eagerly from chapter to chapter. As soon as he finished the book, he went to the office of Mike Young, his CEO, to give him the book to read. Sitting on Mike's desk, highlighted and dog-eared was another copy of *Keeping Good People*, ready to be delivered to Ned! Needless to say, a lot of the recommendations in that book have been applied at Lancaster General!

Messengers and Messages

Senior leaders, the top executives, are clearly important messengers in these circumstances. But what messages should they carry, and to whom? From a hierarchical perspective, we might suggest that these key people should convey the messages about the Impending Crisis and counteracting strategies specifically to their subordinates, to their direct reports. That's their job. No argument here. However, since these senior leaders are, we assume, highly respected by everyone else in the organization, they have a greater role to play.

The message needs to reach all stakeholders within your organization. That message is that there is a crisis looming and that the company will take steps to manage the impacts of the crisis. This challenge presents an opportunity for teamwork, cohesiveness, and collaboration. The message should be serious— a clear warning, but also full of hope—that leadership is investing time, thought, energy, and gradually more resources into attacking the problem. There is no reason to panic or abandon ship. Your people need to see that you have your act together. They need to have confidence in you.

The message from the top must stimulate strategic thinking, intentional movement, purposeful planning, and deliberate action. But there should also be a sense that senior executives cannot—and will not—do it all. The responsibility for response and crisis management belongs to everyone in the organization. Leaders lead the troops, but everyone does the work.

Get other "messengers" involved. Depending on the size and structure of the organization, this next wave could include middle managers, supervisors, junior executives, and team leaders. This group must now work together at their level(s), and with their subordinates, to examine the risks to their organization. The time focus should probably be from now until the end of the decade, though most of the concentration will be on the next few years.

It should go without saying, but we'll say it anyway for emphasis: your human resource professionals must be involved very early in this process. All of them, not just the senior HR executives. These are go-to people for many employees seeking "real" answers. Be sure they're fully informed, involved, and consulted for their ideas.

These messengers will carry messages to others who need to be involved. Included in this group are hiring managers, sales professionals, purchasing managers. The tasks now are to design and begin to implement the changes that are needed. One task might be to strengthen the hiring process. Another might be to train supervisors and managers in the fine art of employee retention. Setting up better measurements might be another focus. Still another group may be challenged to upgrade the employee evaluation process.

Feedback

The power of communication comes when messages travel more than just one way. You need feedback. If you don't have a good system already in place, establish ways that your people—at all levels—can communicate with you. The open communication will enable you to be closer to what's happening in your organization, and that will be essential during the crisis period.

If your organization is small enough, schedule regular get-togethers where you and your people can talk with each other. A little bit larger, and your company may need to arrange a series of regular gatherings. If you are larger yet and/or have multiple locations, install a hot line in the office of the CEO or a direct report. This phone can be answered personally when the executive is in, but most times will be set to accept recorded messages. Encourage callers to leave their name and number so you can call back. Can you imagine the sense of importance that will be conveyed when a top executive calls an "ordinary" employee to thank that person for valuable input? Thank-you notes can be almost as effective.

From his experience as a coach, Tom emphasizes the importance of giving instant feedback and responding promptly to feedback received. When we are "in the moment" is the best time to achieve the results you desire—and deserve—from the feedback process.

―――――――――――――――― **Words of Wisdom** ――――――――――――――――

Listen carefully to feedback, then act on it. The employment crisis, the need to change the way you're doing business, will not go away. Band-Aid® treatments will not work. You must find out "where it hurts" and solve the problems. Symptoms are good to know about, but you and others must search for the causes. Your management of this crisis in your organization must be action-oriented. Be sure action is part of your message.

Champions

When some sort of change effort is undertaken in an organization, someone is usually appointed to be the person to make it all work, to get people inspired, to make it happer. his person is often described as the "champion." This person is the advocate of the program, the leader and the driver of the campaign. We encourage you to name a highly responsible, well-respected senior leader to be your champion. In larger or more complex organizations, you may ask your champion to build a *team* of champions to keep the crisis management campaign alive and well.

The champion should be very visible, working directly with all employees in designing and implementing your organization's response to the crisis. Part of the champion's role is to keep the crisis management project "top of mind" for every executive, manager, and supervisor. Find ways to get everyone involved, to build his or her sense of ownership of the problem and the solutions.

The champion(s) will organize and encourage the crisis management process, but will not necessarily be the specific people in charge of the effort. The actual role of the champion will be determined uniquely in each organization. In some cases, the champion will be more of a coordinator, a facilitator, bringing together the people who will actually manage the various components of the ongoing response.

Create your own model. There is no one right way of responding to this crisis. What fits for your culture? The key is to maintain awareness and work toward solutions to strengthen your organization's positioning for future success—however you define it.

If you knew there was a flood coming, would you jump up and down in the middle of the street wailing, "Where's Noah when we need him?"

Leadership and Management

Back in 1980, Roger wrote a book titled *Disaster Planning for Local Government*. It was a specialized book, to be sure, drawn from his work as coordinator of disaster services for an urban county in Ohio. As a public administrator, Roger discovered that guidelines for the work were confusing, written in "Federalese," and practically impossible to work with. So, he simplified the process, wrote the book, and began teaching federal, state, and local officials how to plan for and manage disasters. Sound familiar? That's what must done in the corporate environment: sharing, collaboration.

If you knew there was a flood coming, would you jump up and down in the middle of the street wailing, "Where's Noah when we need him?" Of course not! What would you do? Think. Assess your situation. Focus on your objectives. Gather the information you need to make decisions. Consider alternatives for addressing the problem. Plan what must be done, by whom, in what sequence, and with what coordination. Assign resources. Begin the work. Monitor progress. Be alert for problems, exceptions to plan, respond as needed.

Stay focused on your objectives while remaining alert to other risks. Maintain calm. As much as possible, continue with normal activities.

You can use the same concepts to manage your crisis. What's your objective? It's probably to fortify your position in your marketplace by strengthening and solidifying your ability to perform profitably.

> Know what to measure, how to measure it, and how often to measure progress. Most importantly, know what to do with the measurement information you collect.

You'll get started, but will you continue the crisis management work? One way to sustain your effort is to keep people informed of your progress. And that means measurement. Tom gained years of experience as a highly effective coach of athletes, particularly swimmers and divers. While still in college, Tom was twice recognized as an NCAA All-American Athlete in the sport of springboard diving. In 1986, the National Collegiate Athletic Association recognized him as Coach of the Year. Tom cites benchmarking and measurement as important competencies to build successful athletes . . . and successful companies.

As a fine example, we note that Lance Armstrong, international bicycle racing champion, has mastered measurement to improve his performance, distancing himself from every other cyclist in the world. He knows precisely what his pedal cadence, watts of energy, and pulse rate is throughout every segment of his training and racing. For his nutrition, he weighs his pasta to the gram for every meal to get the precise amount of protein, carbohydrates, and fat that his body requires.

Know what to measure, how to measure it, and how often to measure progress. Most importantly, know what to do with the measurement information you collect.

Effective measurement is a powerful tool for leaders to improve results. In profit-making organizations, and even in some not-for-profits, revenue growth is imperative. While top-line (sales) growth and achievement is important, and a valuable indicator, the real focus must be on bottom-line (profit) growth and achievement.

─────────── **Words of Wisdom** ───────────

Leadership effectiveness does make a difference in results. The right leaders—in place and fully engaged, vertically and horizontally, with clear vision of their goals—can produce gratifying outcomes. The right leaders, leading the right people, for the right reasons, make a tremendous difference.

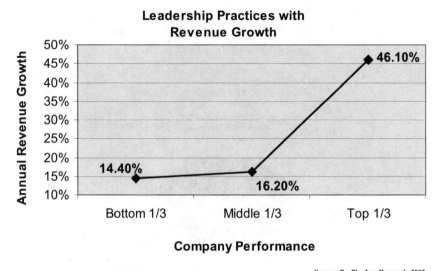

Success Profiles Inc. Research, 2002

Figure 40: Leadership Practices and Revenue Growth

This chart illustrates the relationship between organizations' leadership effectiveness and compounded annual revenue growth. The companies were classified into three categories (Bottom 1/3 performers, Middle 1/3, and Top 1/3), based upon their weighted average index score for the questions measuring leadership effectiveness. The evidence shows that the annual growth rate is significantly higher for organizations with exceptional leadership. Also note that again the most significant increase occurs when moving from the Middle 1/3 group to the Top 1/3 (a more difficult accomplishment).

Recommended Business Practices

In years of research, Tom has discovered that certain business practices are consistent with longer employee tenure. His data link with Roger and Joyce's research into the same areas. There are solid connections between these practices and organizational success. How well does your management team perform in these critical areas? In the assessment process that is part of the Employer of Choice[SM] evaluation, we have confirmed the power of these practices.

The "Sweet Spot" of Highly Effective
Organizational Practices

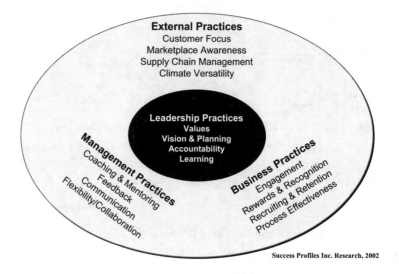

Success Profiles Inc. Research, 2002

Figure 41: The "Sweet Spot" of Highly Effective Organizational Practices

Over an 11-year period, Success Profiles has measured the performance of over 600 major companies and has collected data on over 5,000 individual business units. Our collective research reveals that there is a "Sweet Spot" of highly effective practices that consists of 16 disciplines in four major categories (leadership practices, management practices, business practices, and external practices).

These practices not only correlated with the business outcomes of growth, profits, and retention; the evidence demonstrates that these practices drive results. There are dozens of other practices that consultants suggest are important, but the evidence shows that they are insignificant drivers of business results. Therefore, before an organization is performing well in these practices, most improvement efforts are well intentioned but often result in a waste of time and money.

Leadership Practices

Values: James Collins, author of *Built to Last*, asserts that core values are the essential and enduring doctrine of an organization. A small set of timeless guiding principles, core values require no external justification. They have intrinsic value and importance to those inside the organization. Values-driven leaders articulate the company's "reason for being" at every opportunity. They convey the company's fundamental aspirations and why they are important. The primary way values-driven leaders promote the dream and define organizational success is through their own behavior. They live out the values in their daily lives, serving as inspirational role models.

Vision and Planning: Vision is essential to explicitly define an organization's long-term ambitious future. It provides constancy in a changing world; it is motivating and should pull people forward instead of pushing them. The competency of planning connects an organization's vision to its core purpose, goals, strategies, and tactics. In simple terms, this competency conveys a consistent message of "a clear line of sight, as to where the organization is headed, what needs to be accomplished and how things will be done." For deeper insight into this concept, we recommend reading *Built to Last* by James Collins.

Accountability: Leaders have always been held accountable for results. Accountability can be defined as a personal acceptance of the consequences of making a commitment and taking action. However, the best accountability comes when everyone feels the same concern and the same high investment in the outcomes of decisions. They hold each other accountable for contributing their best. They fully share all relevant information, and they use sound decision-making processes. Sharing responsibility this way cannot prevent all failures, but it does increase the probability of success. Practices that demand high accountability include fiscal responsibility, quality, and performance measurement.

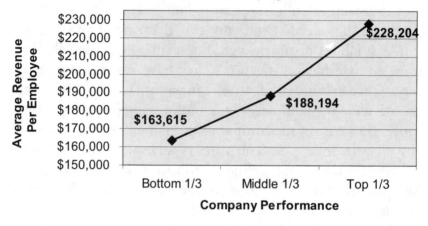

Defined Organizational Values with Average Revenue Per Employee

Figure 42: Statement of Values and Revenue per Employee

The chart above illustrates the relationship between organizations' effectiveness to establish and communicate their values or guiding principles and average revenue per employee. The companies were classified into three categories (Bottom 1/3 performers, Middle 1/3, and Top 1/3), based upon their weighted average index score for the question: "Our company has a stated set of values or guiding principles." The evidence shows that the average revenue per employee is significantly higher for organizations excelling with this practice.

Learning: Knowledge is power. Gaining more knowledge builds more power: a competitive advantage, particularly if the knowledge is managed well to produce results. Mistakenly, many companies have viewed knowledge management as a computer initiative. Knowledge management is first a people issue. Accelerated learning is critical to this initiative. If individual learners can become more effective in their ability to learn (create new knowledge) and communicate with others (exchange new knowledge), the business will become more innovative and flexible. Key learning activities also include competency (skills) training, career path development, and succession planning and preparation.

Management Practices

Coaching and Mentoring: We wish that we could change all the titles of "managers" today to "coaches." Unfortunately, the old industrial model of micromanaging what people do still lives in the word and concept of management. In business today, coaches and mentors have become the role models of choice. Many research studies have quantified that employees will leave "working for" their immediate manager or supervisor more than they will leave "their job" or "their company."

On a daily basis, the toughest job a "coach" has is confronting poor performance and encouraging behavior change. Great coaches have not only acquired certain knowledge, skills, and competence to coach, but they have a distinct attitude, a deep and genuine concern for the *coaching relationship*. This coaching attitude is true in sports, in business, and in world-class performances of all kinds. Coaching is developing people on purpose, and everyday work conversations offer coaching opportunities.

Feedback: It's been said many times that "feedback is the breakfast of champions." Our research demonstrates that the process of eliciting and acting on feedback is a competency that significantly differentiates high-performance organizations from average ones. "Measured feedback" combines the competency/process of compiling the information/data with the creation of *actionable knowledge* that can be used to develop a business case for meaningful change.

Feedback is also providing information in all directions, up, down, and across. As a business practice, a culture of open feedback contributes the greatest impact to overall performance when it is directed upward, truly valued, and acted upon. Feedback as a competency is most closely linked to exceptional leadership and high employee engagement.

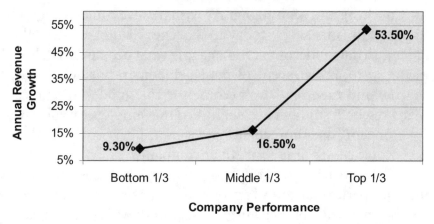

Figure 43: Feedback and Engagement with Revenue Growth

The chart above illustrates the relationship between organizations' feedback and engagement effectiveness and annual revenue growth. The companies were classified into three categories (Bottom 1/3 performers, Middle 1/3, and Top 1/3), based upon their weighted average index score for the questions measuring feedback and engagement. The evidence shows that the annual growth rate is significantly higher for organizations excelling in this practice. Also note that the most significant increase occurs when moving from the Middle 1/3 group to the Top 1/3 (a more difficult accomplishment).

Communication: Consistently, all organizations will score lower on "communication" as a business practice than any other competency. That having been established, what are the attitudes that cause the wide variation in perception between organizations that share information in an "open environment" and those that don't? The words that most often come up are: "trust and high values" versus "fear and insecurity." Organizations with a "low trust" environment cite communication as their greatest weakness or poorest performance area. Organizations with established, explicit, and demonstrated values score significantly higher in communication and information sharing. If you want high productivity, company leadership must be open, honest, and confident with information sharing and communication. Regardless of whether information is good or bad, today's expectation is that it's best to communicate it early and frequently.

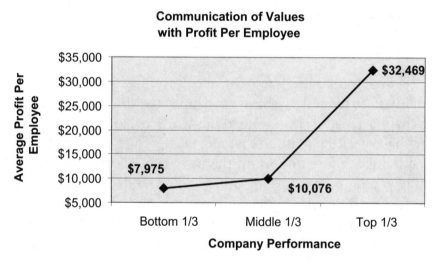

Success Profiles Inc. Research, 2002

Figure 44: Articulation of Values and Beliefs with Profit per Employee

This chart illustrates the relationship between organizations' communication of their core values and beliefs and average profit per employee. The companies were classified into three categories (Bottom 1/3 performers, Middle 1/3, and Top 1/3), based on their weighted average index score for the question: "Our company has carefully articulated our core values and beliefs." The evidence shows that the average profit per employee is significantly higher for organizations excelling with this practice. Also note that the most significant increase once again occurs when moving from the Middle 1/3 group to the Top 1/3 (a more difficult accomplishment).

Flexibility and Collaboration: "Command and control" management styles and equitable practices (treating everyone the same regardless of performance) are guaranteed to drive away high achievers faster than any other behaviors.

──────────────── Words of Wisdom ────────────────

Words of Wisdom: You cannot treat your best performers the same as your average performers . . . unless you want your best performers to leave. Equitable business practices drive away the highest-performing talent.

People want a less hierarchical culture that encourages creativity, diversity, and psychic ownership. As we discussed at length in chapter 1, people now want a "life-work" balance not a "work-life" balance; keep in mind that most people age 22 to 35 believe that living is more important than working. Working is something you do to live, not the other way around. This value is in conflict with the messages heard by some of their elders.

Organizations that create flexible and collaborative workplaces grow faster, are more productive, and create higher human capital value by retaining their employees longer. Flexible practices, including telecommuting, flextime, and job sharing, also reflect a high-trust environment where leadership is respected and higher results are achieved.

Business Practices

Engagement: We hope that "engagement" doesn't become another consultant-speak buzzword that ends up in Dilbert® comics. But alas, it's probably too late. As a business practice, engagement can be defined as the degree to which people come to work every day with a compelling, active, and passionate interest in their work. They come into work every day eager to get things done. Engaged workers demonstrate "psychic ownership," a sense of being highly accountable, and a tendency to think and act like business owners. They are much different than employees who are not engaged, who simply "attend work." Our research confirms that people with high engagement are significantly more productive than their coworkers. The most important practice to ensure high engagement is to select the right people for the right job.

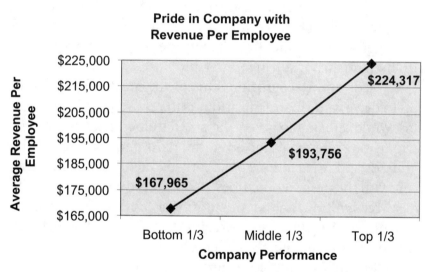

Pride in Company with Revenue Per Employee

Success Profiles Inc. Research, 2002

Figure 45: Employee Pride and Revenue per Employee

This illustration describes the relationship between employees' pride in working for their companies and average revenue per employee. The companies were classified into three categories (Bottom 1/3 performers, Middle 1/3, and Top 1/3), based on their weighted average index score for the question: "I am proud to say I work for my company." The evidence shows that the average revenue per employee is significantly higher for employees who feel pride in their companies. Also again, note the straight-line relationship.

High engagement cannot be artificially created with rewards or bonuses. At best, the effect of buying high engagement (extrinsic motivation) is short-term with disappointing long-term results. The more effective motivation is intrinsic. The ultimate demonstration of engagement is observed when people passionately come to work every day, knowing exactly how and why their work adds value to their customers, their company, their coworkers, and to themselves (in the form of compensation).

Contrary to popular belief, high engagement and psychic ownership don't require an equity position or stock options. To illustrate, many people are highly engaged in their work with not-for-profit ventures. Also, many people with significant money invested in their company's 401(k) plan are not engaged at all. Engagement comes from having the right people on board, with high quality, inspiring leadership.

Rewards and Recognition: One of the most effective practices to drive value in organizations is to reward people for good work while refusing to accept substandard performance. Mediocrity is not tolerated, nor is substandard performance. If the standards and expectations are clearly defined, and are in alignment with the desired outcomes, people receive the appropriate praise, recognition, and compensation as a result of their performance. This formula supports productivity, employment attractiveness, and a high level of employee retention.

Far too often, people are rewarded and recognized based upon an "equitable" process that in the long term will backfire. Tenure-based compensation and equitable compensation tend to reward low performers and penalize high performers. These forms of compensation are by-products of the "stone age" industrial business model, where the value of human capital wasn't recognized or measured. It assumes that people become more valuable solely based upon their tenure. While this value may appear true on the surface, it is often an invalid assumption (see the concepts of tenure equity, talent equity, and warm-chair attrition in chapter 5). We've all heard the expression about a 20-year employee having one year of experience twenty times.

Tenure-based compensation can create a condition where people cannot connect what they do every day to the value they add and, ultimately, the amount they are compensated. This antiquated compensation design can also create a culture of entitlement and an illusion of job security.

Does performance-based compensation produce the greatest business outcomes and financial results? It depends. Rewards (artificial incentives), like punishments, are often effective at producing one thing, temporary compliance. Carrots and sticks are both strikingly ineffective at producing lasting change in attitudes or even in behaviors. They do not create "psychic ownership" or an enduring commitment to any value or action. Performance rewards only work well when they are aligned with the employee's connection to the company mission, values, and goals. The right kind of charismatic leadership can inspire an employee to energize the intrinsic drive that will produce results . . . that can then be rewarded.

Recruitment and Retention: In previous chapters, we discussed in detail the cost to replace skilled people. It is expensive and can range from 30 percent to 200 percent of their annual salary.

Words of Wisdom

If employers spend less on hiring and enjoy a more stable workforce, they can achieve a serious competitive advantage. If recruiting is viewed as a "strategic investment," rather than a "tactical expense," and the process and outcomes are measured and tracked, the result can be a terrific return on investment.

Smart corporate leaders will adopt Employer of Choice^SM practices as strategic initiatives, woven into the fabric of the entire organization. Successful recruiting and retention cannot be perceived as merely "an HR issue." These are management responsibilities, with human resource professionals in advisory and support roles.

It has been proven time and time again that the most effective method of attracting and retaining quality people is through employee referrals. The number of quality referrals that reflect the values and quality peer-to-peer relationships of coworkers is a good indicator of a healthy culture with high morale. High morale (attitudes) will most often translate into higher productivity (behaviors). Imagine the power of "community" when the people who work together are comfortable together and want to stay together.

Process Effectiveness: High-quality business practices that benefit from continuous improvement initiatives will always produce work environments where ease of work translates into high productivity. In the mid-1990s, many consulting firms encouraged companies to engage in "reengineering" efforts primarily focused on cutting costs and eliminating people. In terms of building productivity and results, these initiatives had approximately an 80 percent failure rate. The successful initiatives engaged the workers in seeking ways to improve processes to enhance performance. Before any major process change can be implemented, the following "7 Habits" or guidelines are essential:

1. Overall quality must improve.
2. Overall time must be reduced.
3. The number of steps must be reduced.
4. The end-result process must be easier (more user friendly).
5. The new process must utilize people more effectively, not just eliminate jobs.

6. Costs should be reduced or at least stay the same; if everything else improves and costs stay the same, the initiative may still be worth the effort.
7. The improvements must add value to stakeholders (customers, employees, suppliers, etc.).

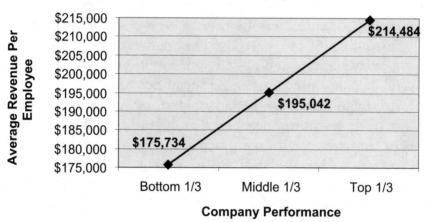

Figure 46: Recommend Company to Friends and Revenue per Employee

The chart above illustrates the relationship between employees' willingness to recommend their company to their friends and average revenue per employee. The companies were classified into three categories (Bottom 1/3 performers, Middle 1/3, and Top 1/3), based upon their weighted average index score for the question: "I would recommend my company to friends as a great place to work." The evidence shows that the average revenue per employee is significantly higher for employees who feel pride in their companies. Also, once again, note the straight-line relationship.

Our research demonstrates that organizations that develop successful process-effectiveness initiatives *as habits* also perform other essential business practices extremely well.

External Practices

Customer Focus: Accurate and in-depth customer information helps the organization focus its business practices on customer expectations, rather than insiders' perceptions. Being customer-focused means your organization is going beyond understanding your customers' basic levels of needs and satisfaction. It means forming a "connective link" between your customers' wants, expectations, and satisfaction as well as the organization's overall business processes and strategic activities.

An organization can maximize performance with minimal waste of time and resources by aligning business strategy, processes, and service efforts to focus on its customers. When an organization knows who its customers are, what its customers expect, and what's most important to them, the organization is obviously better equipped to satisfy and retain its customers. When an organization fully internalizes these concepts, it will experience an increase in loyal customers and improvement in financial performance.

Marketplace Awareness: The term "market awareness" represents the *entire* market for an industry or business segment. "Market*place* awareness" defines the portion of the market that a business services. Included in marketplace awareness is all the important information related to those who buy within the boundaries of a company's primary market: Customer intelligence, competitive intelligence, and the business dynamics that create demand among the most loyal/profitable customers.

Our research shows that one of the top 15 weaknesses of small and mid-size organizations (with less than 500 employees) is a lack of marketplace and customer awareness. The primary reasons that companies are poor at this essential practice are lack of resources and lack of competence. Too many businesses treat all customers the same. They don't understand the degree of profitability or long-term economic value that differentiate one segment of customers from another.

It's common to see businesses that have 20 percent of their customers produce a profit, 50 percent that break even, and 30 percent that lose money. The best organizations align marketing and business development initiatives with strategies and tactics that demonstrate an intense focus on the most valuable customers. Companies with high marketplace awareness realize that "the customer is not always right and not all customers are created equal."

Supply Chain Management: As a business practice, supply chain management ties suppliers and customers together in one concurrent business process focused on the ultimate "end use" customer. By striving for a "seamless" process, a company is able to lower costs, eliminate duplicate functions, and quickly respond to market changes and opportunities.

It is very common for organizations represented in a typical supply chain to have very different goals and measures of what is considered success. Companies do not readily share information with their customers and suppliers, because in an attempt to be more profitable, they are driven to gain a competitive advantage over their trading partners. Each stakeholder in the chain makes decisions about its business that are hidden from its customers and suppliers. This secrecy creates inefficient disconnects in the supply chain that add costs and time at every step in the delivery of products and services. We describe this ineffectiveness as "value-subtracted" service.

─────────────── Words of Wisdom ───────────────

Use of technology and ease of information sharing will be two of the most important competitive advantages of the future. This area includes sharing information with all stakeholders, especially employees. Wise employers will take full advantage of the technology while changing the way they do business with supply chain partners.

───────────────────────────────────

Climate Versatility: Success often depends on the ability to understand, forecast, and adapt to external climatic changes occurring throughout the business marketplace. Climatic events often move too slowly for people to perceive them as a real threat, though climate (in general) has produced more extinctions than any other natural event.

As we discussed in chapter 1, organisms and companies that succeed over the long term are those that adapt the earliest to climatic-type changes. Their senior leaders sense changes coming, strategically watching long-term trends. Senior leaders are responsible for guiding companies through climatic change, staying ahead of the change to take advantage of trends and not be victimized by them. Remember, if you succeed a little less by not adapting to climatic issues, you may eventually become extinct.

Leadership in Action

Leaders lead. They set the pace. They take action. They use proven techniques that inspire people to follow them . . . and enforce the principles that empower them to lead effectively. Some of our readers will already be familiar with these concepts, but others will gain some insight. These maxims are wise to remember . . . and to be reminded of.

Mission, Vision, and Guiding Principles

We recommend getting everyone involved in designing the vital statements of who you are, where you're going, and why. The process we've found most effective is to create draft statements at the senior levels of the organization. This sketch can be very open, perhaps with alternative wording or various ideas of what might be included. Next, share this initial work with middle managers and ask them to share it with their team members.

Get lots of ideas about what to include—or not include. Roll this input back to the top of the organization for construction of proposed statements. Then distribute this work again for people to comment. As Roger is fond of saying in some of his speeches, "Remember the proverb by the ancient philosopher, Anonymous: 'People support what they help to create.'" You're building psychic ownership.

Completing the statements is not enough. Post them where they can be seen throughout your facilities. Give copies to employees—current, new, and future. Send them to your customers, suppliers, and investors. Proclaim "This is who we are, this is what we stand for!" If you want to be connected with us, you should know where we're coming from. If this philosophy doesn't feel comfortable, go somewhere else.

Keep People Informed. Management professors and consultants like to talk about "mushroom management." Defined, this approach is likened to growing mushrooms: "keep them in the dark and throw a lot of fertilizer on them." People don't like to be kept in the dark, and they certainly don't need "fertilizer" from management!

When workers are given plenty of information about the company's strategies, strengths, needs, progress, and challenges, they feel more a part of what's happening. They enjoy that warm feeling of belonging. Does it make a difference? Let's measure information sharing against average revenue per employee.

Often someone on the frontline, let's say in sales or customer service, has a much better finger on the pulse of what's happening in the marketplace than someone in management.

Embrace Change. Let's face it. Change is inevitable in today's world. Don't fight it. And you can't manage it. Embrace it. Ride with it. Enjoy it. Relish it! And keep everyone informed about changes that are contemplated. Ask for their input. Often someone on the frontline, let's say in sales or customer service, has a much better finger on the pulse of what's happening in the marketplace than someone in management.

Empowerment. Some commentators argue that "empowerment" is an overused buzzword from the 1990s. We believe that it's a descriptor of a highly influential practice that attracts top talent, enables people to feel more productive and meaningful, and drives a sense of accountability that generates substantially higher results. Want some evidence? See Figure 40.

The impact on average revenue growth tells a story. Note that this empowerment must be *real*. Mere lip service, with continued aggressive monitoring and controlling by superiors, will not produce these results. To make this approach work well, invest in training and education, clarify desired results, accept risk, establish comfortable boundaries, and reinforce positive behavior. When people are empowered, they take more initiative. They accept higher levels of accountability. And they're justifiably proud of their results.

Another benefit of this leadership style, which is sincerely appreciated by workers of all ages and degrees of experience, is that people tend to stay around longer. Turnover is considerably lower when people are highly engaged in their work, making their own decisions, and driving their own results. They can see the difference they make and understand that they're valued.

Selection. Insist that your human resource professionals and your managers exercise careful judgment in hiring. Be highly selective, using tools like CheckStart™. (See more about this tool at *www.hermangroup.com.*) Heed the warning that Roger sounds frequently in his speeches: "No More Warm Bodies." Recruit only top talent. The consequences will be higher productivity and fewer problems.

Personal and Professional Growth. We've already talked about the high value of education, training, development, coaching, and mentoring. Here's the evidence that investment in employee growth can have a positive impact on reducing employee turnover. Bonus: you're retaining better-trained employees who will have even more capacity to get things done!

Build Pride. As a leader, you have an opportunity—an obligation—to send a clear message of enthusiasm, optimism, excitement, and pride to all your people. Corporate life is like a pep rally, and there's always a game to play. Are you proud of your people? Tell 'em! Are they proud to be part of your team? Thank 'em! Do you want them to stick around and keep up the great work? Tell 'em!

Our friend Bob Nelson, best-selling author of books like *1001 Ways to Reward Employees*, reminds us constantly that when people are recognized for their contribution and feel good about their work and "community," they stay.

Words of Wisdom

Your best recruiters are the people who work for you. If they are top-caliber people, empowered and appreciated, they will attract others of at least equal quality. If you want to grow a corporate community of the fine people all your competitors would love to have, this method is the way to do it. You don't even have to pay those recruiting bonuses; people love to be surrounded by coworkers they can respect and admire.

Overcome Ignorance

Your employees—including your executives, managers, and supervisors—are ignorant. Now before you get defensive, recognize that "ignorance" means lack of knowledge, not stupidity. Your people have insufficient knowledge about the issues in this book. They just may not realize the seriousness of your situation. They don't know what should be done to overcome the predicament. They don't know where to start . . . what each member of your team can and should do.

Your job is to overcome this ignorance. Recognize that ignorance can breed arrogance. Without knowledge and appreciation of what's going on around them, employees (even leaders) can build what we call the "Arrogance of Ignorance." These people get their knowledge from their own press releases. They think they're wonderful?without having any legitimate comparison to any other organization. Like pride in the proverb, "arrogance goeth before the fall."

Educate your workforce. Start with the leaders at the top of the organization. Teach them so well that they are able to teach their direct reports. Then those people pass the word along to their team members, continuing the process until everyone is informed. Carrying the message initially is part of the messaging process we described earlier in this chapter, but there's more.

Overcome ignorance about leadership techniques. Overcome ignorance about good management. Overcome ignorance about how to collaborate, how to work together to achieve desired results. Help people understand how to accomplish their shared vision. Education. Training. Experience. Reinforcement. Recognition. Continuously.

We can't emphasize enough the importance of learning. Not just skills and technical information, but learning how to function in your organizational community.

This section could also be called "Overcome Complacency." It is so easy to atrophy and just slide back to where it's comfortable . . . to a nice, snug cocoon of mediocrity. We'd wager that too many of your employees are mediocre—in their knowledge, their attitude, their performance, and their contribution to your future.

———————————— **Words of Wisdom** ————————————

Reach every single employee on your team with a clear message: "There is no room for mediocrity anymore." Imagine the difference you could make, if each and every employee vowed to stamp out mediocrity and reach toward full potential!

You can read more about overcoming mediocrity at www.impendingcrisis.com. Meanwhile, focus on helping everyone do just a little bit better.

Closing Questions

1. How do you measure the effectiveness of your organizations' leadership practices?
2. Have you established and communicated a respected statement of values or guiding principles to all employees—and applicants?
3. Have you created an employee pride index and correlated it in any way with your employee turnover or other human capital metric?
4. How successful are you at recruiting new hires through employee referrals?
5. Do you have equitable business practices that may be driving away your high achievers and future leaders?

Opportunities for a Competitive Advantage

How many elements/practices mentioned in the concept of the "Sweet Spot" are you really good at? If everyone in your organization would recommend just one "excellent" person to your organization, how much would that help your recruiting and retention efforts? If one of your younger employees were attending a social function with friends, what do you think that individual would say about your organization?

CHAPTER EIGHT

Change the Way You Function

In order to survive this impending labor crisis, organizations must change the way they function. Tomorrow's high-performing, selective employees will not tolerate antiquated management practices; they will look for companies offering employee-centered working environments. Technology cannot solve the problem of too few people. The solution is an evolution of the business model to include systems and processes that are more efficient. Now is the time for your organization to challenge everything about the way it functions. Examine all the strategic perspectives, then build business efficiency by recognizing it's not how many or how few people you have working for you, but how effectively they are able to accomplish the work to be done.

If you always do what you've always done, you'll always get what you've always gotten.

Source Unknown

We cannot become what we want to be by remaining what we are.

Max DePree

Change is necessary. If you do not change, you become stagnant. And who wants to work for a stagnant organization?

Can you be successful tomorrow using yesterday's practices? Or can you become more attractive as an employer by carefully examining and challenging your current practices?

Watching the trends in workforce values and attitudes, it's easy to see that the "A" players (and those who consciously aspire to be top performers) are not highly motivated to work for employers who are shackled to the traditions, practices, and cultures of yesterday. They're looking—sometimes aggressively—for the employers who demonstrate that they have the courage to break out of the mold.

Business as Usual

The employees you want to attract—and hold—in an intensely competitive employment market are special. They want a work environment that is substantially different from what they perceive as "traditional." The "traditional" things that employees usually expect in an average organization are:

- Senior executives who stay in their corner offices.
- Closed communication—only those who "need to know" get information.
- Hiring of "warm bodies" just to keep the jobs filled.
- Tolerating employees who don't get the job done or have lousy attitudes.
- Taking customers for granted.
- Taking employees for granted.
- Upper management that makes all important decisions.
- Everyone doing the same job gets the same compensation.
- Emphasis is on individual performance.
- Training and education restricted to managers and salespeople.
- Trust is low—among employees and management.

- The focus is all-business; fun is not compatible with business.
- Performance appraisals done at the same time for all employees.
- Mediocrity and "get-by" attitudes are prevalent.
- Reserved parking spaces near the front door for executives.
- Insecurity among managers to hire people more talented than they are.

And the list goes on. These practices are changing in "enlightened" organizations where leaders understand that things must be done differently. In some companies, the changes come slowly, too often blocked by vice presidents, directors, or senior managers who want to keep things just the way they've always been. They're reluctant to lose their perceived status and control. These resistant people, blocking progress, haven't yet learned that they can be considerably more effective by not worrying about their status and collaborating with others. They haven't yet learned that yielding "control" through the empowerment process is actually much more productive. They're still protective of their position, of their space, because the top leader(s) have not helped them shift their mindset. It's a new world, and with the impending labor crisis, new world thinking is essential.

Organizations Doing It Right

In this new world, enlightened organizations are doing it right. Let's briefly explore alternatives to the bullet-point typical expectations listed above.

- Senior executives who stay in their corner offices.

    The Chief Executive Officer of Baptist Pensacola Hospital in Pensacola, Florida, works in an office on the first floor. He's located just off the main lobby and has big windows so people never feel he's hiding something. This office is completely separate from the administrative suite—and is accessible to employees, visitors—everyone. Being so up-front is extremely rare today, but will be more prevalent in the future.

- Closed communication—only those who "need to know" get information.

Wise organizations now share all sorts of information with their people. The concept of openness is becoming more popular, to one extent or another. Again at Baptist Pensacola, corkboards outside the CEO's office display the latest results in measurement of performance in their five pillars: Service, Finance, People, Growth, and Quality. Anyone—employee or not—can walk into the reception area at any time and look at current information. All employees receive a newsletter—not monthly, *daily*. The operating philosophy of this organization is "no secrets, no excuses."

- Hiring of "warm bodies" just to keep the jobs filled.

A chain of casual dining restaurants known as Texas Steakhouse and Saloon, headquartered in Rocky Mount, North Carolina, prides itself in highly selective hiring. Even their web site emphasizes their desire for "positive people who like to work hard and have fun." At Baptist Pensacola the message is clear, too: they are uncompromising about only hiring people who fit their culture, regardless of how talented and experienced they may be. With over 120 technical recruiters, Microsoft Corporation, Redmond, Washington, has earned a reputation of working aggressively to acquire the top talent.

- Tolerating employees who don't get the job done or have lousy attitudes.

  Wise employers are becoming firmer in their discipline, saying "good-bye" to people don't fit, don't perform, or don't want to be there. At Met-Life, employees who do not meet their high performance standards know that they need to finds jobs elsewhere. Low performance is simply not tolerated.

- Taking customers for granted.

  All the employees at Fresno Surgery Center, Fresno, California, bend over backward to serve patients *and* their loved ones. Trained by Ritz Carlton, these caring healthcare workers share a warm family feeling. By the way, those employees enjoy a free lunch every day. People are very well treated there, which is why this healthcare organization enjoys minimal employee turnover.

- Taking employees for granted.

  Employers who really care about their employees—what they think, how they feel, what kind of support they need, how well-balanced their lives are, etc., will be most competitive in the employment marketplace. Bank of Marin, Novato, California, is one that emphasizes life-work balance. While many employees are afraid to survey their employees, organizations like Baptist Pensacola will survey employees as many as seven times a year.

- All important decisions made by upper management.

  Open Book Management companies like Commercial Casework, Inc., Fremont, California, share decisions with their employees. Front line workers (union members) have a say in what the company does, how that work gets done, and how productive the company is. Employees have access to all sorts of company measurements, including financials, and are trained in business literacy.

- Everyone doing the same job gets the same compensation.

  A number of organizations—public and private—are shifting to compensation systems based on an employee's competencies. Performance-based pay is even more popular. The concept of internal equity will be passé in many organizations. At Platinum Coast, a premium quality dry cleaner in Naples, Florida, the finishers can earn $1 more per hour for exceeding the production standard. The company also gives bonuses to its customer service representatives for high performance.

- Emphasis is on individual performance.

  Teamwork makes a big difference today. Companies like Jackson-Hewitt, Parsippany, New Jersey, emphasize team performance and pride. When people feel pride in current performance and connection with a sense of history, they are more attached to the company.

- Training and education restricted to managers and salespeople.

  In today's world, all employees need to be trained. The accounting firm of Blum, Shapiro & Company, PC, West Hartford, Connecticut, strives to help *all* employees stay current in their fields. Everyone is expected to continually grow. Baptist Pensacola requires that all employees complete a minimum of 60 hours of training and development each year.

- Trust is low—among employees and management.

  At Motek, Inc, a software developer in Beverly Hills, California, trust is so strong that employees work closely to help each other complete personal projects to be sure everyone succeeds for the benefit of the company.

- The focus is all-business; fun is not compatible with business.

    Employees at Stratus Technologies, Maynard, Massachusetts, enjoy company parties on the lawn adjacent to their facilities. At the headquarters of Gymboree Corporation, Burlingame, California, employees take afternoon recesses—usually outside for games or relaxation if the weather is good. The Home Depot Corporation in Atlanta, Georgia, is one of many companies with a large, fully equipped health club in its headquarters.

- Performance appraisals done at the same time for all employees.

    An amazing number of employers still ask their managers and supervisors to conduct performance appraisals at a specified time of the year. This practice forces appraisers to compare—at least unconsciously—one employee against another, instead of fairly evaluating each person. The more effective approach is to conduct appraisals during the anniversary month of the employee's hire. Some companies, like General Electric, deliberately compare employees, periodically weeding out the lower ten percent of performers. While there's a value to cleaning our low performers, this practice can place a lot of stress on supervisors.

- Mediocrity and "get-by" attitudes are prevalent.

    Continuous improvement has gotten a lot of attention over the past few years. At Baptist Pensacola, 6,717 bright ideas were implemented in 2001 that produced a cost savings of $2.9 million. Toyota and American Airlines have promoted this practice for years.

- Reserved parking spaces near the front door for executives.

  Wise employers have stopped this practice. The only reserved parking spots are for visitors, the mail car if there is one, pregnant employees, and perhaps an Employee of the Month. If executives want good parking spaces, they just need to arrive early.

- Insecurity among managers to hire people more talented than they are.

  At Springfield Remanufacturing Company, Springfield, Missouri, the succession system is designed so that anyone with talent can rise to high levels in the organization, from wherever they start. There are no obstacles, only encouragement. We've observed that their succession planning isn't a program or initiative, but a way of life.

Employers acquire and allocate resources to operate, including human resources. Since we know that the same human resources will not be available to you in the years ahead, it is *imperative* that you change your methods, procedures, systems, policies, and other aspects of the way you operate. The way you operate is tightly linked with the number—and type—of people you need to employ . . . and keep. Baptist Pensacola Hospital reduced their employee turnover by 50 percent from 1997 to 2002. This organization is winning awards, impressive bottom-line achievement, and pride, as the focused and dedicated leaders build a high quality, compatible, cohesive, stable workforce.

The employers we have listed are representative of those applying good employee practices. There are many more. We emphasized Baptist Pensacola Hospital (*www.bhcpns.org*), because we have observed them doing so many good things—and achieving enviable results as a direct consequence. Such strategies will be required of all successful companies during the balance of this turbulent decade.

Let us tell you a few other things that happen at Baptist Pensacola before we go on. You may gain some ideas that will work in your organization.

Every department at this hospital (just under 1500 employees) has a 90-day written action plan. Doesn't sound like a big deal? Do *your* departments each have written 90-day plans? In our consulting, we've encountered substantial corporations that don't have 90-day plans.

No one is hired at this organization without having gone through at least one peer interview. No one. Initial screening interviews are done by human resources and department heads, but then the employees who would work with the applicant take over. A peer panel usually consists of two to three employees, but could be larger. Many applicants are interviewed by more than one panel. A recent applicant, who would fill a job that interacts with a number of departments, actually went through four peer interview sessions.

Each of the facilities in the Baptist Health Care Corporation in Pensacola holds a quarterly Employee Forum. In this process, 16-20 sessions are held around the clock over a two-week period. To reach all shifts, sessions are scheduled at 5:00 Saturday morning, Sunday evening, 2:00 o'clock in the morning during the week, and at other times convenient for employees of the 24/7 organization. The president of the hospital gives a report of goals, results achieved, and where help is needed. This presentation is followed by a question-answer session with top executives, rewards, and recognition. Each quarterly series is themed, with the CEO, COO, and facility president wearing theme logo tee shirts. Drawings are held for more tee shirts, dinners for two, logo items, and more. Attendees get a blue "I attended Employee Forum" button to wear for 24 hours. The button is then turned into the cafeteria for a soft drink or a dessert. Attendance? An average of 90 percent of the employees participate.

The Role of Technology

We've heard stories *ad nauseum* about how technology will solve all of our problems. Better technology equals fewer people. Forget it. Technology cannot possibly solve *all* the problems we have—and will have—over the next decade. Technology is applied against problems we face today, with mixed results. Sometimes outcomes are terrific. In other cases, attempts to use technology complicate things so badly that we h   ̣ to manage the negative consequences. Many technologies require employees with specialized skills, and those people may not be so readily available. Without people, you may not be able to operate the technology. Can you imagine a fire department investing a couple hundred thousand dollars in a brand new super pumper, then not training or hiring the people who can use it to fight fires?

Over the past twenty years, business has focused on doing what it has always done, but applying less expensive methods, devising approaches to produce higher quality, and installing very expensive information technology. The objective has been to find better ways to do what we've always done instead to creating new business models that could take us quantum leaps ahead. Costcutting, process redesign, and technical innovation have robbed resources from exploring whole new ways of doing things. In explaining this problem, Don Mitchell and Carol Coles, co-authors of *The Ultimate Competitive Advantage: Secrets of Continually Developing a More Profitable Business Model* (Berrett-Kohler, 2003), cite the example of "the relative ease with which Federal Express succeeded with hub-and-spoke overnight envelope delivery while the delivery time for first class letters [by the U.S. Postal Service] was growing ever slower."

The largest technology club to beat down business problems is the computer. There is no question that computers have had a tremendous positive influence on business. We can now do more and do it faster than ever before. Does that mean that computer technology is applied and available all the way down to the front-line operational level? No. If you strive to hire young people who are highly savvy technologically, this deficiency can be a problem. If they don't see new technology being used, they may choose not to join you.

Efficient, effective, and full use of computer technology—today and certainly tomorrow—requires a workforce that is very comfortable with computers and all they can do. Members of Generation X (born 1965 to 1985) have gradually become computer-proficient. The next generation (the Millennials) is significantly more proficient than even the Xers. These young people, now in middle school and high school, will inject an exciting—and daunting—new dimension into the use of computers to accomplish work. For the most part, they are totally comfortable with this technology and easily stay current with changes and new developments. The computer is practically an extension of the "Self" among these young people.

> Are you prepared for the social upheaval that will occur, as young people join your workforce with a set of expectations that differs from your current culture?

As they move into the workforce, Millennials will quickly become one with the technology they find in the workplace, pushing the use of computers to amazing new heights. Older colleagues will have to scramble to keep up, unless those older folks are allowed to maintain a status quo. These young folks will not be content with the status quo and will be much happier driving change. Constant (rapid) evolution, speed, and tremendous amounts of data won't seem like much to these young adults, but they may drive their older counterparts nuts. Are you prepared for the social upheaval that will occur, as young people join your workforce with a set of expectations that differs from your current culture? How will you prepare to maximize your benefit from this new wave of expertise, while harnessing their power to produce your desired results?

Exploring other technologies, robotics will play an increasing role in changing the way we manufacture goods—in the United States and overseas. Nanotechnology is just beginning, and genetic research will produce whole new industries in fields we can hardly even dream about today. This l... could go on and on, but the important issue is how relevant technologies will affect your organization. How will these developments change the way you do business?

Technology is already changing the petroleum retailing business. We have seen well-staffed service stations with mechanical services and products to serve the motoring public shift to convenience stores with gasoline as one of the products. The next step in this evolution will be gasoline-dispensing facilities that are completely automated with no attendants actually on duty. This design is already operational in Malta and other countries around the world.

Technology can be used to support significant business model changes. Another example from Mitchell and Coles' book: Ecolab was in the business of selling cleaning chemicals to manufacturers, institutions, restaurants, and others. Ecolab learned, probably through their network of astute sales professionals, that it was more important for restaurants to keep good relations with health inspectors than to simply have good cleaning supplies. Business Model Change: "Ecolab expanded its offerings to include the chemicals to *sanitize* everything in a restaurant. With its knowledge of the chemicals, Ecolab also added ways to improve and maintain the equipment to make better use of the chemicals. Later the firm also defined itself as being in the pest elimination, janitorial, floor care, water treatment, and management advice businesses. . .the company can show a customer how to save lots of money, get better results, and still pay normal prices for its chemicals and services." They've focused on maintaining the high health grades in the restaurants they serve, building such a close relationship that no local provider or new entrant in the field can break into their business.

You can't do business tomorrow using yesterday's techniques.

Business Model Evolution

Now is the time to closely examine your current business model. How long have you been operating with the same philosophy, design, structure, tools, processes, techniques, and results? If you have not concentrated on continually innovating and changing your business model, chances are your competitive advantage may have evaporated. Business model management is a rapidly moving, evolutionary process that demands constant attention. Again, we repeat: "You can't do business tomorrow using yesterday's techniques."

The most successful employers of this decade—and beyond—will be constantly alert to opportunities for change . . . not just for the sake of change, but for the specific purpose of continually transforming their organizations into highly responsive organisms. The advantage will go to the agile corporations—more to the smaller than the larger. Larger organizations take longer to innovate and to change. Their cultures will continue to get in their way until boards of directors and senior executives comprehend their vulnerability and aggressively drive innovation.

How's your business model? Changing business models can keep you in an enviable position, driving the kind of organization that attracts "A" players who want to work with leading edge people and companies.

Small-step evolutionary changes in business models can be more comfortable and less risky. Extending the current model with subtle shifts can be effective in some operating environments. Gradual improvement can produce results. Leaders who seek dramatic, revolutionary changes, however, can generate greater impact by looking for opportunities to make large gains while taking calculated risks. The secret is to make revolutionary moves feel like more comfortable evolutionary moves, though the pace may be rapid.

Mitchell and Coles emphasize the importance of measuring your performance and trends relative to your competitors and potential competitors. Applying good business intelligence, learn what business models your competitors are using and have used in the past. A databank of this kind of information about other companies—and your own organization—can provide a powerful foundation for ongoing collaborative creativity by your team. We emphasize the same approach, with a concentration on people practices. Treating good people well means that your good customers will be treated well, too.

Corporate leaders must "escort" their team members through a different kind of strategic exercise. We say "escort," because you should guide them, but encourage them to think independently of you. The worst thing that can happen is for everyone to sit back and wait for you to make decisions or pronouncements. Where is your organization going? Why? How is that different from where you are and where you've been? What's driving the changes? What are you doing to attract, optimize, and hold top talent? How will you respond to internal and external changes and, more importantly, how will you place your company clearly in the leadership role in your industry? Industry leadership will enable you to attract the "A" players. Remember the old Eskimo adage: "If you're not the lead dog, the scenery never changes."

Operating environments will be considerably different in the future than they were yesterday or are today. What will your organization's operating environment look like? Now is the time to sit down with your top executives, advisors, and the people in your organization who are most familiar with what's happening. Those experts with their fingers on the pulse of real and potential shifts are probably your people who are closest to the customer.

──────────── **Words of Wisdom** ────────────

We urge you to tap the expertise of your sales professionals and customer service representatives. Bringing them together with top executives will probably establish a new—and refreshing—collaborative dynamic. As people start looking seriously at what the future will hold, such collaboration will make a lot of sense.

Senior leaders must set a new direction for their organization. For many of them, this assignment will be particularly difficult. First, they won't be sure which way to go, or where they want to be when they arrive. Those who see strategic movement as a journey won't be confident of which direction to go. The frustrating problem for them is that they won't fully understand their starting point. Even if you know, for instance, that you want to go to Bozeman, Montana, you must first know if you are in Greensboro, North Carolina, or San Diego, California.

Even when you know your starting point and have begun your journey, you must frequently measure to be sure you are staying on course . . . and that the course is still the right one to follow. Beware of momentum that can carry you swiftly and powerfully in the wrong direction. Remembering the sage advice, "Measure twice, cut once."

Strategic Perspectives

What markets will you be in? Who will your customers be? Where will they be located? What will they expect from you? How is that different from today? How will you manage the transition? What kinds of people will you need on your team and where will they come from?

What facilities will you need five or 10 years from now? How will they be designed? Where will they be located? What will your distribution channels be? How will that logistics picture differ from today's?

Your resources will probably be much different in the future. Engage your purchasing agents in this future-thinking process. Should you be working with the same suppliers? How many? In several industries, we have seen a sharp reduction in the number of suppliers used by manufacturers. This sort of strategic shift reduces paperwork and other bureaucratic hassles and places remaining suppliers in a stronger and more collaborative role. Be sure to zero-base your thinking. What supplies or suppliers will you even need in the future? What about your channels of distribution?

Who do you need to partner with now to make your emerging strategies work in the years ahead? Big changes involving strategic alliance partners and other outside entities don't happen overnight. These issues are calling for your attention *now*, so you can be ready for the future when it arrives. To stay competitive in our fast-moving world, the future is not years away, but may be weeks, days, or even hours away. Stay alert . . . and nimble. Do you hear our sense of urgency to get started? With fewer people available in the years ahead, now is the time to get alternative systems designed and connected.

Now is the time for your organization to challenge everything about the way it functions. Discover new models that fit more for your evolving circumstances. If any aspect of your operations isn't exactly what you'll need for a high level of success in the near-, mid-range, and long-term future, you must start making changes now. Your leadership will be crucial. You will inspire and drive the challenge, while encouraging and moderating the change process.

Beware of making change just for the sake of change—or worse?to make the boss happy. In your challenging process, evaluate what changes need to be made incrementally to reach the place you'd like to be at end-game, at that target period in the future. Accept that as you get into the process, your target date may well change, perhaps moving to an earlier time, or later. Be flexible. Be agile. Be responsive.

Pay careful attention to how any change you foresee might affect other aspects of the organization. Are those other aspects ready to function with the change in place, or do they need to make some of their own changes before they can integrate with the initial changes? This process is more complicated than it may seem on the surface. Business model innovation and implementation will be a competitive strength—or weakness—for your organization.

Building Efficiency

How efficient is your organization today? And what impact does efficiency have on your staffing needs? What happens to your bottom line if your workers, their systems, and their processes are more efficient? All sorts of reengineering efforts have been undertaken to reduce staffing levels, but that "rightsizing" is not the answer. The question is not how many or how few people you have working for you, but how efficiently they are able to accomplish the work to be done.

Words of Wisdom

Where most employers made their mistake in all of their downsizing, rightsizing, and tightsizing was to ignore reducing costs and improving efficiencies in *all* areas of the operation. This oversight is what we mean when we emphasize changing the way you do business. Change means more than just reducing the number of employees.

It's stupid to simply cut payroll and believe that everything will be all right. You may reduce personnel costs, but without taking further steps, you haven't upgraded the way you're doing business. The people who remain are not able to run the system the way it was intended (with a larger number of workers), so productivity plummets. All you have done is remove some people; you haven't changed the process. You're trying to use a system designed to be run by a complement of X people with, say, .75X people.

You will not solve the Impending Crisis for your organization by simply cutting people or reducing the number of positions on your organizational chart. You must find new ways of doing things that eliminate steps, reduce the need for space, and/or optimize the use of technology. If you were to start all over again to design what you do today, what would it look like? What is in the way of your doing your work in that idealistic way?

The solution is to change the way you do business, the way work gets done, the way results are achieved. You must even challenge and confirm that your targeted results are congruent with where you want to be, now and in the future. Find ways to achieve your objectives by using fewer people better. It's the human resource equivalent of "working smarter, not harder."

Concentrate on the people who are part of your organization today. Support them in continually challenging the way you do business, exploring ways to change your business model, systems, processes, and every other aspect of the way you function. The more involved your people are—all your people, the stronger will be your results. As you bring new people into the organization, be sure they understand this vital component of your corporate culture. Static organizations will face limited futures and possible extinction.

Closing Questions

1. How well does your organization respond to changes in your business practices?
2. Is there a genuine awareness that you need to change the way you approach and managing your human capital?
3. Do you perform any formal benchmarking to learn about better employee retention practices from other organizations (both within your industry and outside)?

Opportunities for a Competitive Advantage

If every one of your managers went on just one benchmarking "field trip" a year and was responsible to report back to their peers and present a formal accounting of their learning, how many improvement efforts could be implemented? How many of the "outdated," traditional practices listed (in the beginning of this chapter) are habits in your organization? How many of the "best practices" mentioned *could* you adopt? If everyone "knew the score" of the critical numbers, how much could you improve the productivity of your business?

CHAPTER NINE

Human Resources: A Strategic Investment

Since people are clearly our most valuable resource, the Human Resources department must play a strategic role in your preparation for the Impending Crisis. The triangle of influence, the CEO, CFO, and CHRO need to work together, engaging others in the processes of planning and implementation. Part of the problem is the shortage of HR executives who understand business strategy. Corporations must begin now to "grow their own" through career pathing and coaching. A stable workforce is a strategic advantage. Workforce stability strengthens corporate capability, while it drives bottom line profits. Determine what human resources you will need to get the job done in the future. Evaluate your current staff then begin the planning process to insure you'll have the people you will need.

Your most valuable—and most volatile—resource is your human resource. As you read in the first section of this book, we will be over 10 million workers short—in the United States alone—by 2010. Note: Don't wait until 2010. This crisis presents real dangers *right now*. Remember, we were already 4,731,000 people short in 2000. While this critical labor shortage will certainly affect some industries more than others, remember "the rising tide lifts *all* boats."

A slowed economy spreads a fog over the reality of the labor situation. When business slows down and we reduce the number of people working for us, workforce shortages are quickly forgotten. However, as business picks up again with economic growth, many employers will be startled to discover that they *cannot* acquire the human resources to expand again. Yes, indeed, they will not be *able to*. As you can imagine, not having enough people to fill the jobs can be devastating. Recruitment and retention will take on a new importance, becoming even more important than in the beginning of the decade.

Directly or indirectly, practically every employer will be affected by the stark reality of not having enough people. Smaller employers will be at greater risk, from one standpoint, because they don't have as many employees. They're more vulnerable; losing one employee could be devastating. From another standpoint, smaller companies have an advantage because their leaders can have more direct influence on the factors that attract and hold top-quality employees. And, a sign of the times, a lot of "A" players want to work for smaller companies, where they can see firsthand the difference they make. Smaller companies need more versatile people; "A" players are quite often more versatile . . . and looking for opportunities to utilize that versatility.

We will see considerable growth in the occupations that will design, operate, and maintain high technology. The Bureau of Labor Statistics groups these occupations into two categories: Computer and mathematical. These occupations are projected to add the most jobs, 2 million, and grow the fastest among the eight professional and related occupational subgroups. As a result of ongoing advances in computer technology and the continuing demand for new computer applications, the demand for computer-related occupations will continue to increase.

> **Three out of five new jobs will be in the rapidly growing business services industries, primarily in computer and data processing services.**

Not all the people with high technical competence will be employed by the larger corporations or agencies. Three out of five new jobs will be in the rapidly growing business services industries, primarily in computer and data processing services. In this segment, employment of computer and mathematical occupations is projected to more than double. In addition, in almost all industries, employment of these workers is projected to grow significantly faster than the average for all occupations. A large proportion of these technology workers, particularly on the service side of the field, will be self-employed people working from home. They will not be available for regular employment by companies that need them; they'll be quite content to operate on their own.

―――――――――――――― Words of Wisdom ――――――――――――――

If your people are such a vital asset, you need to be sure that your human capital support process is strong. Very strong. Attracting and hiring top talent will differentiate your organization from all those who would compete with you—for business or for people.

While the optimization of that workforce rests heavily with line management, a number of highly important roles rest with the company's department of human resources. These professionals are responsible for acquisition of the people who are qualified to do the job—and fit with the company's culture. The human resources function is responsible for acquisition and

Fastest growing occupations, 2000-2010

		Employment	
Rank	Occupation	2000	2010
1	Computer software engineers, applications	380	760
2	Computer support specialists	506	996
3	Computer software engineers, systems software	317	601
4	Network and computer systems administrators	229	416
5	Network systems and data communications analysts	119	211
6	Desktop publishers	38	63
7	Database administrators	106	176
8	Personal and home care aides	414	672
9	Computer systems analysts	431	689
10	Medical assistants	329	516
11	Social and human service assistants	271	418
12	Physician assistants	58	89
13	Medical records and health information technicians	136	202
14	Computer and information systems managers	313	463
15	Home health aides	615	907
16	Physical therapist aides	36	53
17	Occupational therapist aides	9	12
18	Physical therapist assistants	44	64
19	Audiologists	13	19
20	Fitness trainers and aerobics instructors	158	222
21	Computer and information scientists, research	28	39
22	Veterinary assistants and laboratory animal caretakers	55	77
23	Occupational therapist assistants	17	23
24	Veterinary technologists and technicians	49	69
25	Speech-language pathologists	88	122
26	Mental health and substance abuse social workers	88	116
27	Dental assistants	247	339
28	Dental hygienists	147	201
29	Teachers, preschool, kindergarten, & elementary school	234	320
30	Pharmacy technicians	190	259

The quartile rankings of Occupational Employment Statistics annual earnings data are presented in the following categories:

1=very high ($39,700 and over), 2=high ($25,760 to $39,660), 3=low ($18,500 to $25,760), and 4=very low (up to $18,490).

The rankings were based on quartiles using one-fourth of total employment to define each quartile. Earnings are for wage and salary workers.

(Numbers in thousands of jobs)

Change

Number	Percent	Quartile rank by 2000 median annual earnings	Most significant source of education or training
380	100	1	Bachelor's degree
490	97	2	Associate degree
284	90	1	Bachelor's degree
187	82	1	Bachelor's degree
92	77	1	Bachelor's degree
25	67	2	Postsecondary vocational award
70	66	1	Bachelor's degree
258	62	4	Short-term on-the-job training
258	60	1	Bachelor's degree
187	57	3	Moderate-term on-the-job training
147	54	3	Moderate-term on-the-job training
31	53	1	Bachelor's degree
66	49	3	Associate degree
150	48	1	Bachelor's degree
291	47	4	Short-term on-the-job training
17	46	3	Short-term on-the-job training
4	45	3	Short-term on-the-job training
20	45	2	Associate degree
6	45	1	Master's degree
64	40	3	Postsecondary vocational award
11	40	1	Doctoral degree
22	40	4	Short-term on-the-job training
7	40	2	Associate degree
19	39	3	Associate degree
34	39	1	Master's degree
33	39	2	Master's degree
92	37	2	Moderate-term on-the-job training
54	37	1	Associate degree
86	37	1	Bachelor's degree
69	36	3	Moderate-term on-the-job training

Figure 47: Fastest-Growing Occupations

This table lists the fastest-growing occupations between 2000 and 2010. Seventeen of the top 30 are healthcare related. Also, 19 of the top 30 involve degree programs.

Occupations with the largest job growth, 2000-2010

Rank	Occupation	Employment 2000	Employment 2010
1	Combined food preparation and serving workers	2,206	2,879
2	Customer service representatives	1,946	2,577
3	Registered nurses	2,194	2,755
4	Retail salespersons	4,109	4,619
5	Computer support specialists	506	996
6	Cashiers, except gaming	3,325	3,799
7	Office clerks, general	2,705	3,135
8	Security guards	1,106	1,497
9	Computer software engineers, applications	380	760
10	Waiters and waitresses	1,983	2,347
11	General and operations managers	2,398	2,761
12	Truck drivers, heavy and tractor-trailer	1,749	2,095
13	Nursing aides, orderlies, and attendants	1,373	1,697
14	Janitors and cleaners, except maids and housekeeping	2,348	2,665
15	Postsecondary teachers	1,344	1,659
16	Teacher assistants	1,262	1,562
17	Home health aides	615	907
18	Laborers and freight, stock, and material movers	2,084	2,373
19	Computer software engineers, systems software	317	601
20	Landscaping and groundskeeping workers	894	1,154
21	Personal and home care aides	414	672
22	Computer systems analysts	431	689
23	Receptionists and information clerks	1,078	1,334
24	Truck drivers, light or delivery services	1,117	1,331
25	Packers and packagers, hand	1,091	1,300
26	Elementary school teachers, except special education	1,532	1,734
27	Medical assistants	329	516
28	Network and computer systems administrators	229	416
29	Secondary school teachers, except special & vocational	1,004	1,190
30	Accountants and auditors	976	1,157

The quartile rankings of Occupational Employment Statistics annual earnings data are presented in the following categories:

1=very high ($39,700 and over), 2=high ($25,760 to $39,660), 3=low ($18,500 to $25,760), and 4=very low (up to $18,490).

The rankings were based on quartiles using one-fourth of total employment to define each quartile. Earnings are for wage and salary workers.

(Numbers in thousands of jobs)

Change		Quartile rank by 2000 median annual earnings	Most significant source of education or training
Number	Percent		
673	30	4	Short-term on-the-job training
631	32	3	Moderate-term on-the-job training
561	26	1	Associate degree
510	12	4	Short-term on-the-job training
490	97	2	Associate degree
474	14	4	Short-term on-the-job training
430	16	3	Short-term on-the-job training
391	35	4	Short-term on-the-job training
380	100	1	Bachelor's degree
364	18	4	Short-term on-the-job training
363	15	1	Bachelor's degree or higher
346	20	2	Moderate-term on-the-job training
323	24	3	Short-term on-the-job training
317	13	4	Short-term on-the-job training
315	23	1	Doctoral degree
301	24	4	Short-term on-the-job training
291	47	4	Short-term on-the-job training
289	14	3	Short-term on-the-job training
284	90	1	Bachelor's degree or higher
260	29	4	Short-term on-the-job training
258	62	4	Short-term on-the-job training
258	60	1	Bachelor's degree
256	24	3	Short-term on-the-job training
215	19	3	Short-term on-the-job training
210	19	4	Short-term on-the-job training
202	13	1	Bachelor's degree
187	57	3	Moderate-term on-the-job training
187	82	1	Bachelor's degree
187	19	1	Bachelor's degree
181	19	1	Bachelor's degree

Figure 48: Occupations with the Largest Job Growth

This table lists the occupations with the largest job growth between 2000 and 2010. Nineteen of these top 30 only involve "on the job" training.

Occupations with the largest job decline, 2000-2010

Rank	Occupation	Employment 2000	2010
1	Farmers and ranchers	1,294	965
2	Order clerks	348	277
3	Tellers	499	440
4	Insurance claims and policy processing clerks	289	231
5	Word processors and typists	297	240
6	Sewing machine operators	399	348
7	Dishwashers	525	483
8	Switchboard operators, including answering service	259	218
9	Loan interviewers and clerks	139	101
10	Computer operators	194	161
11	Dining room and cafeteria attendants and bartender help	431	402
12	Electrical and electronic equipment assemblers	379	355
13	Machine feeders and offbearers	182	159
14	Telephone operators	54	35
15	Secretaries, except legal, medical, and executive	1,864	1,846
16	Prepress technicians and workers	107	90
17	Office machine operators, except computer	84	68
18	Cutting, punching, and press machine setters, operators	372	357
19	Postal service mail sorters, processors, and processing	289	275
20	Railroad brake, signal, and switch operators	22	9
21	Wholesale and retail buyers, except farm products	148	135
22	Meter readers, utilities	49	36
23	Butchers and meat cutters	141	128
24	Parts salespersons	260	248
25	Inspectors, testers, sorters, samplers, and weighers	602	591
26	Eligibility interviewers, government programs	117	106
27	Door-to-door sales workers, news and street vendors	166	156
28	Procurement clerks	76	67
29	Railroad conductors and yardmasters	45	36
30	Barbers	73	64

The quartile rankings of Occupational Employment Statistics annual earnings data are presented in the following categories:

1=very high ($39,700 and over), 2=high ($25,760 to $39,660), 3=low ($18,500 to $25,760), and 4=very low (up to $18,490).

The rankings were based on quartiles using one-fourth of total employment to define each quartile. Earnings are for wage and salary workers.

(Numbers in thousands of jobs)

Change		Quartile rank by 2000 median annual earnings	Most significant source of education or training
Number	Percent		
-328	-25	2	Long-term on-the-job training
-71	-20	3	Short-term on-the-job training
-59	-12	3	Short-term on-the-job training
-58	-20	2	Moderate-term on-the-job training
-57	-19	3	Moderate-term on-the-job training
-51	-13	4	Moderate-term on-the-job training
-42	-8	4	Short-term on-the-job training
-41	-16	3	Short-term on-the-job training
-38	-28	2	Short-term on-the-job training
-33	-17	2	Moderate-term on-the-job training
-29	-7	4	Short-term on-the-job training
-24	-6	3	Short-term on-the-job training
-22	-12	3	Short-term on-the-job training
-19	-35	2	Short-term on-the-job training
-18	-1	3	Moderate-term on-the-job training
-17	-16	2	Long-term on-the-job training
-16	-19	3	Short-term on-the-job training
-15	-4	3	Moderate-term on-the-job training
-14	-5	2	Short-term on-the-job training
-13	-61	2	Work experience/related occupation
-13	-9	2	Bachelor's degree
-13	-26	2	Short-term on-the-job training
-13	-9	3	Long-term on-the-job training
-12	-4	3	Moderate-term on-the-job training
-11	-2	3	Moderate-term on-the-job training
-11	-9	2	Moderate-term on-the-job training
-10	-6	3	Short-term on-the-job training
-9	-12	2	Short-term on-the-job training
-8	-19	2	Work experience/related occupation
-8	-12	4	Postsecondary vocational award

Figure 49: Occupations with the Largest Job Declines

This table lists the occupations with the largest job declines between 2000 and 2010. Twenty-nine of the top 30 primarily involve "on the job" or work-related training.

development of human capital. Included are non-value-added tasks such as benefits management, payroll systems, and records administration. Increasing emphasis will be placed on value-added services such as performance management, training and development, and succession planning/preparation. How strong—in capacity and proficiency—is your human resources department?

Has your company's leadership consciously and deliberately identified human resources as a vital part of the organization? We're not just talking about lip service, but clearly demonstrating how important people are to your success? Fad titles like "vice president of people" aren't the answer . . . unless they are accompanied by a highest-level commitment to treating the human resource as a valuable asset.

Acid-test question: Is human resources important enough that the senior human resource officer is an active participant at the strategic table? There has been a lot of talk in recent years about HR sitting at the strategic table. The time has passed for just *sitting*; it's time for action. Senior human resource officers—whatever their official title—should be *active* participants in sculpting the organization's strategy. Their compensation and influence should be on par with other senior executives, with bonuses based on human-capital metrics.

A substantial proportion of your strategic decisions will involve your workforce in some way, so human resource executives should be in continual strategic communication with colleagues. Do *your* senior human resource professionals speak "business"? Do your senior executives in other fields speak "HR"? How well is human resource strategy woven into your corporate strategy? Are human resources implications considered in each major strategic decision? Is a human resources report presented at board meetings on an even par with the company's financial report?

Triangle of Influence

All the senior executives of an organization have roles to play. Each has an area of responsibility that is vitally important to the success of the company. Results are all measurable and, in a number of companies, people at this level derive at least part of their compensation in the form of bonuses or incentives based on their group's performance.

These executives need resources to get their missions accomplished. They need capital resources and they need human resources. Those two elements are essential to the achievement of objectives.

Successful organizations in the future will be led by what we call a "Triangle of Influence." This strategic advantage is an offense team at the top of the organization. Members of the team, coordinating very closely together, will be the chief executive officer, the chief financial officer, and the chief human resource officer.

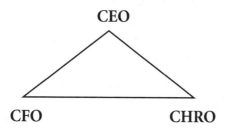

Together they will act offensively, rather than defensively, to drive the success of the organization. Leading and serving (other executives), they will assure that the company has sufficient financial and human capital to perform. They will demonstrate a powerful balance between focused assessment metrics and bold strategic actions.

An example of this success story is the leadership team at

Boddie-Noell Enterprises. Boddie-Noell is not a household name, but the Rocky Mount, North Carolina, company accomplishes great things. They run the largest franchisee of the Hardee's restaurant chain (over 325 units); a chain of over two dozen Texas Steak Houses in Virginia, West Virginia, and North Carolina; a land development company; a motel; a conference center; and other emerging restaurant concepts.

Chief Executive Officer Bill Boddie, Senior Vice President of Personnel Services Bob Crumley, and Chief Financial Officer Craig Worthy enjoy a high degree of respect and admiration for each other, describing their relationship as "extremely close." The three officers jointly manage many corporate responsibilities including wage and salary administration, payroll administration, all insurances, risk management, legal, and others. They believe these shared responsibilities, working in tandem on most issues, balanced with a respect for each others' "specific areas," are critical to focused, strategic direction and unhampered corporate success.

In the healthcare field, Chief Executive Officer Mike Young at Lancaster Health System in Lancaster, Pennsylvania, is continually "on the same wave length" as Senior Vice President of Human Resources Ned Albee and Chief Financial Officer Joe Byorick. They work very closely together, but because of the nature of the enterprise, they add a fourth player as well. Chief Operating Officer Marion McGowan represents all the health system's clinical services, a vital function in a healthcare environment. Her teammates value her process orientation and her ability to listen, analyze, and relate issues to systems.

Human Resources Labor Shortage

Part of the problem today is that not enough human resource professionals have sufficient understanding of what makes an organization "tick" to move into those upper slots. Greg Hessel, an experienced recruiter with Heidrick & Struggles, specializes

in executive searches for top-level human resource professionals. He laments that there are precious few people in the field
who can effectively perform at the very senior level. With an insufficient supply of highly competent, multifaceted human resource generalists, CEOs are limited in their effectiveness.

The truly great top executives are constantly searching for
highly proficient professionals. And with the exodus of many
senior human resource professionals into practice as consultants or retirement to the golf course, the "A-Player" talent pool
has been significantly depleted. There is a strong "class" of people
at the number-two level in human resources who have great
potential to move into the number-one positions and be highly
successful, but many of them are not quite ready yet. To be more
effective in the future, these leaders must become significantly
more proficient in business and financial literacy.

Without highly competent human resource professionals at
their sides, top executives are handicapped. There are so many
critical things to be done on the people side of the house, but
the strongly talented senior human resource executives just aren't
plentiful enough. Our schools, and organizations like the Society for Human Resource Management, still have some work to
do to help people grow into this vital role. Hessel observes that
the conditions of the 2000–2002 period threw the human resource function backward, pushing practitioners into tactical,
rather than strategic, initiatives. If this tactical attitude is allowed
to prevail, organizations will find themselves crippled without
effective, strategic HR leadership.

———————————— Words of Wisdom ————————————

Chief executive officers should bolster their present and strengthen their future by investing in the development of human resource professionals. They must build their "bench strength"—future members of that Triangle of Influence. Up and coming managers in this specialty should be exposed to other aspects of the organization's operations to broaden their perspectives and knowledge base. A considerable amount of professional growth must be accomplished on a grow-your-own-from-within basis. This practice may be considered to be part of your succession planning process to prepare for your company's future. Include development in the ever-changing field of human resources, but also include a good dose of business management, sales and marketing, finance, and other disciplines.

A few side comments are appropriate here. First, a clarification of terms. The phrase "personnel management" has come to refer to the administrative aspects of human resources. "Human resource management" has a much broader context, encompassing strategic, tactical, and operational aspects of people as a major resource. While the term "personnel" may be outdated, we have not yet fully recognized the power, depth, and breadth of "human resources" in the organizational governance context in many places. The term "human capital" is also used today, particularly when talking about workers being an asset of the organization.

A second comment addresses career pathing. We have seen a number of companies assign executives or managers from other functions, like manufacturing, to assume responsibility for human resources. Such an assignment is viewed as a rung on the upward career ladder. While future leaders may gain exposure to human resources this way, the practice can be damaging to the employer. Human resource challenges call for professionals who are educated, trained, and experienced in the details and nuances of this field. It's a lot more complicated than most non-HR executives realize. That said, we encourage *rotation* through the human resource department as part of management and executive development programs—just not in the leadership role. At the same time, human resource executives should be exposed to other leadership roles to build their proficiency as business leaders.

Third, take a look at succession planning and preparation in your organization. Does it exist? Is it flourishing throughout the organization, or does "lip service" get the job done?

Have you identified high-potential talent, the "A" players who can lead your company in the future?

Evaluate all your employees, particularly those who may have potential for key positions in the years ahead. Who are the "A" players? How do you recognize, reward, and challenge them? Who are the "B" players? How are they treated and what are you doing to develop their potential? What's being done to help the "C" players step up or step out? Have you purged the "D" players from your organization, so they don't drag you down and consume your resources? Evaluate your team members in terms of their:

- Attitude
- Willingness
- Work Ethic
- Confidence
- Leadership
- Alignment
- Engagement
- Intellectual Bandwidth
- Accountability
- Ownership Thinking
- Commitment and Intention to Stay

For more information and insight into this vital area, we recommend that you read *The War for Talent* by McKinsey consultants Ed Michaels, Helen Handfield-Jones, and Beth Axelrod.

A Stable Workforce: Strategic Advantage

In these turbulent times, a stable, productive workforce is clearly a competitive advantage. When your organization is competing for customers, distribution channels, investor attention, and supplier support, the stability and continuity of a highly competent workforce is an enviable strategic strength.

--- Words of Wisdom ---

Stability in a workforce doesn't just happen. It is driven—and sustained—by senior leadership. Top executives achieve this worthy objective by supporting their human resource professionals, by becoming personally involved with the people and people processes, and by exercising the leadership that assures a vibrant, forward-focused, engaged community of dedicated and delighted employees.

The quality of worker your company needs, whether current employee or targeted applicant, is determined by the quality of leadership. We know that "A" players are attracted to organizations already populated, at least at the top, by other recognized "A" players. These most desirable employees are also attracted to companies with supportive cultures, encouraging environments, and well-tuned systems. A company's senior executives influence these factors, often very directly.

Your human resources department is arguably the most influential department in determining the quality, diversity, and suitability of the people your company hires. These are the people at the forefront of employment marketing, recruiting, screening, and interviewing. These are the people who will "sell" your opportunities to the prospective employees you want to join your organization.

What kind of a message do your human resource professionals get from you? Whether you are the chief executive officer, president, vice president of sales and marketing, chief financial officer, senior vice president of manufacturing, or anyone else in the leadership ranks, have you visited your human resource department lately? Do these important support people understand what you, as their customer, need from them? Do you understand how to best use their expertise, their services, their support?

How involved are you and the managers of your departments in the employment process? Do you volunteer to join recruiters on trips to college campuses or career fairs? How strong—and effective—is your presence? Do you join with employment staff members in conducting professional interviews (there are techniques like behavioral interviewing that can even strengthen your day-to-day work with your subordinates)?

Are you visible at employee orientations? We recommend that as a top executive, you should be involved in welcoming every new employee to your team—through the orientation program or in some other way. As the old adage goes, "People don't care how much you know until they know how much you care." Personal relationships make a big difference in employee tenure. And those relationships help in day-to-day operations and during those times when everyone must closely examine what they're doing, and why.

Toward a Healthy Bottom Line

Uncontrolled employee turnover generates a tremendous expense that drains resources from a company's bottom line.

Every dollar that must be invested in unnecessary recruiting, hiring, orientation, training, and assimilation of new employees is a dollar stolen from profit. For example, JoAnn Kozeny, vice president of human resources for Omaha Steaks, Omaha, Nebraska, returned $348,000 to the bottom line of her company last year. How? By concentrating on careful hiring and strong employee retention, she saved that much in recruiting, hiring, and training costs.

Can you imagine how much money is spent—wasted—by employers that must keep replacing people who leave? A well-known automobile manufacturer, which declined to be named, conducted a study of the turnover cost in their dealerships. Then, recognizing that the extra replacement costs for departing technicians, service people, and salespeople were coming off the bottom line, they did an interesting analysis. Using their margin (that generates the profit of the dealerships), they calculated how much more revenue they would have to generate to cover the unnecessary replacement costs. The numbers were *huge*, demonstrating vividly that an investment in employee retention would pay big dividends.

IHS Support Solutions, a division of Leveraged Technology, Inc., in New York, was plagued by uncontrolled employee turnover. Admitting that he's a real numbers guy, President Eric Rabinowitz concluded that their over 300 percent staff turnover was costing his company some serious dollars . . . and was severely limiting the company's capacity to grow. Without a stable workforce, he couldn't confidently go after new business. Working with Joyce, IHS dropped turnover to under 25 percent in less than five months. It's easy to see why IHS is now considered a leader in the helpdesk industry.

When The Herman Group served as a consultant to Opryland Hotel in Nashville, now part of the Gaylord Hospitality Group, employee turnover was reduced in one year from 131 percent to 93 percent. Based on Opryland's calculated value of $1,200-

per-person cost of turnover, the first year's savings drove $2,300,000 straight to cash flow. Attention to retention produces financial results.

—————————— Words of Wisdom ——————————

The Impending Crisis means that workforce issues will be hitting hard on the bottom line. The more that can be done to stabilize your workforce now and bond with the people you have, the less cost you will incur to replace people later.

Note that we're talking about the unexpected, premature, sudden loss of valued employees. That's what hurts, because of the high emergency-response costs to get the vacant positions filled quickly. It's *much* less expensive to engage in the controlled recruiting expenses of finding the right people to fill new positions as the company grows.

Determine Your Staffing Needs

What kind of human resources do you need to get the ob done in the future? As you move through this transformation—from where you are today to where you want to be tomorrow—what talent will you need, where, and for how long?

To properly answer these questions, look to your organization's strategic plan. Your plan projects where your company will be in terms of growth or status quo stability, in terms of new products or markets, and in terms of organizational structure and design. Just as you plan the acquisition and upgrade of capital, equipment, and facilities, you must plan the acquisition and upgrade of people to do the human work of the organization. Does your plan include human-capital metrics along with metrics related to market share, revenue projections, cost of money, and other measures that are mission-critical to your business?

As you look down the road into the future, what will your workforce look like? How many people will you need—on the payroll and under outside labor contracts? What will be their capacity—competency, skills, experience, and knowledge? Take a snapshot of what your workforce will look like in, say, three or five years. That picture is your strategic staffing goal. That goal must be realized, if your company is to meet its other objectives.

How many of these people are onboard now? Can they be developed so they will have the capacities you need in the future? You should be able to draw a fairly accurate picture of both your needs and your evolving capabilities at interim periods into the future. What kinds of people need to be hired, when, where? How do you need to train and develop them to be ready for their assignments in the years ahead? What kind of attrition should you anticipate? How many of those employee departures will be at your volition and how much will be voluntary turnover? How vulnerable will you be, and what impact might those unexpected departures have on your organization?

Remember that strategic planning can't really meet the organization's needs without good data and actionable knowledge.

Strategic human resource planning, also known as "strategic workforce planning," should be initiated as soon as possible. This concept is not new. In fact, there's a 3,000-member organization of professionals devoted to the practice: The Human Resource Planning Society (*www.hrps.org/home/index.shtml*). As an integral part of the comprehensive organizational plan, your company's human resource professionals, in concert with those responsible for long-term strategic planning, should work hand-in-hand to develop and implement a legitimate strategic workforce plan.

Remember that strategic planning can't really meet the organization's needs without good data and actionable knowledge. The time has passed when we can "fly blind" or rely on anecdotal information to drive our future. Tom has marveled at the amazing effectiveness of planning activities of corporate leadership teams when they use the results of the research he does for them. The phrase "Knowledge is power" is taking on new meaning.

In the next chapter, we explore in detail the issue of strategic *workforce* planning, arguably the most vital aspect of comprehensive corporate strategic planning.

Closing Questions

1. Is there a projected shortage of labor for any of your key positions? (See figures 47 and 48.)
2. Do you have any jobs that will be eliminated, freeing up incumbent employees you could utilize elsewhere? How well prepared are those people to move successfully into new positions?
3. Have you examined the present and future learning needs of your employees by position?
4. Do you have formalized programs in place to "grow the next generation" of workers for your organization? At the high school level? At the post secondary level?
5. What is the relationship between the CEO, CFO, and CHRO in your organization? Do they really work as an effective team?

Opportunities for a Competitive Advantage

What would be the benefits of having your Senior HR person better understand the financial or operational metrics of your organization? What would be the benefits of having your CFO better understand the Human Capital and replacement cost metrics of your organization? Are there any occupations that are diminishing over the next few years that could provide a pool of potential future employees?

CHAPTER TEN

Strategic Workforce Planning

We cannot emphasize enough the need for strategic staffing, sometimes called strategic workforce planning. Engaging in this process will insure that when tomorrow or next year comes, you will have the right people in the right jobs to support your corporate success. Begin by assessing who's already on staff that could handle the position. Now look at your plans for the future. What kind(s) of person(s) do you need to hire? Then work to close the gaps between who you have (or can grow) and who you need. Smart companies will involve marketing executives to market the firm to prospective candidates. Your positioning in the labor marketplace as an Employer of Choice^{SM} will be critical to your success. Be sure to pay close attention to selection and hiring, orientation, and the supervisor's influence. Be mindful of the roles played by organizational culture, engagement and recognition, employee retention, and succession planning. As you continue your planning, be sure to implement and maintain your strategic workforce plan. It is an integral part of any strategic picture.

It is tempting to start this chapter with quotations like "if you don't know where you're going, any road will take you there."[1] There are all sorts of quotes and stories that tout the value and

---

[1] Lao-Tsu, the father of Taoism.

importance of planning. Most organizations prepare strategic plans, even if they only focus a year ahead. Most plans, from what we've seen cover a 3-5 year period. They should be reviewed frequently, with the recognition that operating environments are changing a lot faster than they did in the past.

Corporate strategic plans typically look at markets, product lines, customer bases, manufacturing or service capacity, logistics and distribution, research and development, and financial issues. All too frequently these plans do not adequately address people requirements. However, no corporate strategic plan is really complete without a comprehensive workforce component. To be viable, a strategic plan must explore staffing implications. Without people, the plan cannot be implemented. Just as a company must plan for its financial capital needs and equipment capital needs, attention must be given to human capital needs as well.

There are a couple of different ways to approach formal strategic staffing—actually developing an action plan and putting it in writing. One is to create a separate strategic staffing plan; the other is to prepare a staffing plan that is integrated into the comprehensive corporate plan. Some might suggest a third approach is to build a workforce component in the corporate plan, but also manage an ever-changing, flexible plan in the human resources department. We would look at the third option as being a very useful tactical plan, but would argue that a strategic perspective, tightly linked with the corporate plan, is essential in a well-run organization.

The terms "strategic workforce planning" and "strategic staffing" are interchangeable. The success factor is to assure that both *what* and *how* are addressed in your planning. You will find that the *when* element will be ever-present, since circumstances may shift your plan into a higher speed, may slow it down, or may steer it in a whole new direction overnight. At least with a written plan, you will have a starting point from which to move.

Align the Plans

The strategic staffing plan must be based on the overall corporate design. With a clear understanding of the corporate direction and goals, what kind of people will be needed? There must be tight alignment between the human resource plan and the corporate plan or there is a risk of serious mismatch. As you read this section, you may think we're getting too basic in our discussion. However, as consultants, we have seen far too many corporate plans that don't even address human resource issues—applicant recruiting or succession preparation, that we mention it here to be sure the words are said. *Without congruency, you're in a fantasy world of dangerous disconnectedness.*

Let's start with the element of time. What time frame do you use for your strategic planning? Do you look three years into the future? Five years? Ten years? Consider the workforce implications of each element of your comprehensive plan, over time, then be sure that those people requirements will be fulfilled by your workforce plan. It's important to look at your long-range targets, but also pay close attention to the interim periods. Workforce development and shifting to meet corporate objectives is usually an evolutionary process, except when/if outside factors cause you to add—or remove—a lot of people at once.

Let's look at the long-range picture. Let's assume your planning period is five years into the future. According to your plan, what will your organization look like in five years? What kinds of people will be required to manage and operate the company? Where will they be? How many of them will be needed? What qualifications and experience will these workers have? What kind of organizational structure will you use? What people will work directly for the company and what people will be contracted on a temporary or project basis? What roles will insourcing and outsourcing play in your future plans? Answers to these questions will help you develop your targets. These issues should be carefully discussed with your senior executives responsible for the various aspects of the business, though it may not be that easy for them to forecast their needs.

The most effective approach is to design organizational charts for what the future company will look like in order to accomplish the goals at a given point of time in the years ahead. What kinds of people will be needed in each of the positions shown? What qualifications and experience will they need to get the job done?

Assess Your Current Circumstances

To hit those targets—what your workforce must be in, say, five years, you have to know where you're starting. So, what is your position today? How many people do you have? What are their qualifications? How big is the gap between where you are and where you want to be in five years? In many organizations, the question may be how to address the gap between *present* needs and fulfillment. If you are not meeting current requirements, you may need to make some substantial changes to prepare for the future.

The achievement of your long-range human resource objectives simply won't happen overnight or with the snap of your fingers. Anticipating that you'll be able to quickly handle whatever comes in the years ahead won't work either. Given the projected labor shortage, even throwing a lot of money at the hiring challenge at the last minute won't work. Strategic staffing is an ongoing process that requires planning, careful preparation, and continual monitoring. You're working with a fluid situation: people you counted as being with you in the future may well leave before you expected.

Begin by assessing your current workforce. How many people are on the payroll? How many are actually working for you? Those two questions may seem similar, but they're not necessarily the same. Considering warm chair attrition (see chapter 5) and lack of competencies (chapter 4), you may well have people on the payroll who are not sufficiently productive. Now is the time to identify your low performers and either bring them up to standard or give them "creative career redirection opportunities."

Your assessment should be as objective as possible. Various kinds of tests, legitimate performance appraisals, and achievement measures should be applied to create a realistic profile of each employee. Evaluate their talents, education, skills, experience, and attitudes. What are their capabilities? How well are they performing? Are their jobs getting done? How well? If you are not getting satisfactory performance—find out why? Once you've identified the barriers to high performance, concentrate on overcoming them as soon as possible.

Words of Wisdom

Carefully evaluate your leaders, managers, and supervisors. How's their performance . . . particularly compared to what you need from them in these challenging times? If you don't feel "warm fuzzies" about every one of your key people who guide others, you've got some work to do. Hunt down your pockets of mediocrity and eliminate them. Or you'll have serious difficulty moving forward.

It will be tempting to engage in some subjective, informal evaluations of your current organization structure and the people who occupy spaces on your organizational chart and in your buildings. We prefer the approach taken by employers like National Commercial Bank in Jeddah, Saudi Arabia. Under the effective leadership of a seasoned human resource professional, Oscar Maril, the 4200-employee bank conducted a highly structured People Assessment. Each division head prepared a detailed study of the human resources in his division and presented the report in a formal meeting chaired personally by Abdulhadi A. Shayif, the bank's most senior executive. The reports objectively evaluated current conditions—including gaps between needs and capacity to meet corporate objectives. Each division head then presented his initial plans of what would be done to overcome the deficiencies, based on present-day and future timelines.

The objectives of their People Assessment process are to:

- Understand the present and future match between the organization's business strategy and the staff it has to execute it.

- Assess the company's talent pipeline and through dialogue (focused on performance, potential, and development) decide how the talent may be best managed to meet the interests of the bank and its people.

- Define the actions and priorities to fortify the organization and retain/develop high-performing , "A" players.

This kind of in-depth, critical evaluation can create a powerful advantage for an employer, particularly if it is conducted on a regular basis.

Close the Gaps

An important part of your strategic staffing will be to close the gap between your current needs and your current capacity. Why do we emphasize getting your house in order before engaging in heavy long-term planning? Simple. If you don't have a good starting point, your ending point is unlikely to be much better. Without competent, effective people, your fancy planning will be like rearranging the deck chairs on the *Titanic*. We are beyond the times of cosmetic improvements. These are times for measurable accomplishment.

Considering carefully the people you decide to keep, create education, training, and development plans to strengthen their current capacity and prepare them for future responsibility. Formal classroom learning, on-the-job training, and sending people to off-site programs will all be helpful approaches to growing your people. Look to community colleges and professional contract trainers to help you get the job done.

The learning and growth component of human resource development is an essential part of building the workforce you want in the future. People want to grow, to keep up in their field. Give them the opportunity and you will increase their longevity. Ignore their needs for growth and be prepared to watch them walk out the door. Losing people with future potential means you'll have to hire replacements or find other people within the organization to move into those positions.

Definitions. Training is the process of skill building. Trainers help people learn and apply new skills, how to do things. Education is the process of gaining knowledge and understanding. Educators help people appreciate the world around them, how things interact with each other, and how to think, plan, organize to develop ideas and put them into action. Development is usually more personalized, driven by coaches or human resource development professionals. Special assignments, internships, apprenticeships, and other experiential learning opportunities fit into this category.

Your strategic workforce plan should include a strong emphasis on building people into more proficient members of the team . . . for the future. From our experience, our strong recommendation is to create an individualized development plan for every employee. The plan designs what growth will take place— from instruction, experience, coaching, mentoring, special assignments, and more. The plan details how to move the employee from the present level of capability to where that employee needs to be each year. The employee, the employee's immediate supervisor, and a qualified specialist from the human resource development department all work together to construct the plan. The supervisor is responsible for assuring that the plan is properly implemented and for supporting the employee in the strategic growth process.

_____ Words of Wisdom _____

As we move further into the decade, coaching will become much more important than simply managing people. As part of your preparation for the future, invest now in efforts to build the coaching skills of your executives, managers, and supervisors.

Construct a written development plan for each employee. Not only will this give the employee a greater sense of value, it will help build your overall program of how you are preparing current employees for future opportunities.

Marketing and Recruiting

As you build your comfort with your current workforce, compare what you have today with what you will need in a year, two years, and so forth to your target point. Chances are, even if you're not anticipating significant growth, you will need to bring new people on board. What kind of people will they be? What capabilities will they have? Will these new workers be recruited to backfill lower-level positions and work their way up as current employees are trained and promoted? Or will you need to hire people in at higher levels to build skill levels and leadership strength? To achieve your long-range target, what kinds of people need to be hired in year one, year two, etc.?

Consider attrition. You're probably going to lose some people. Accept it. Some will find better jobs—for them—somewhere else. You may encourage and support their departure in some cases. Other employees will leave to accompany their spouses to new job locations. Some may leave to care for their aging parents, to start their own businesses, or to spend their lottery winnings. Where is your vulnerability? You can measure that risk, you know. We have performed this service for a number of our clients. Know where your holes *might be* and have plans for filling them with people who will fit your culture and the job—today and tomorrow. Yes, those decisions can be made scientifically, too.

Words of Wisdom

Be very deliberate about how you build your organization. Look for people who will stay. Your objective is to achieve a *stable* workforce with a high level of competency and productivity. Strive to attract, hire, and hold "A" and "B" players. As previously stated, they will stay longer, if they are challenged and if they feel they are really making a difference. Having top performers—highly competent people—will be a magnet to attract others of equal caliber.

Your workforce plan and its supporting documents should describe—in writing—the kind of people you want to attract. Now the big question: *Why should these people work for you?* Remember they will have plenty of other opportunities. Why should they choose to work for you? What makes—or will make—your organization attractive to your targeted prospective employees? Next, how will you reach these specific kinds of people with your recruiting message, your invitation?

Just as you use marketing strategies to reach prospective customers, you will use marketing strategies to reach prospective employees. The employment market will be changing over the coming years. How will you penetrate it effectively to reach your targets? We suggest that it's time for your human resource department and your marketing department to put their heads together. While you're getting people together, plan to provide some sales training to your employment interviewers and hiring managers; they'll need it.

Your human resource employment team should not be doing the recruiting alone or in a vacuum. The hiring managers should be involved in this process. They should be attending job fairs, visiting college campuses, and participating in trade or professional associations. Teach them what to look for and how to make the right approach. Remember the proven fact that your current employees are your best recruiters. Former employees can also be good recruiters for you. Consider putting together an information and guidance packet for your "talent scouts" to help them identify those "A" players you're looking for. Talent scouts always perform better when they're informed and educated.

Positioning in the Employment Marketplace

To differentiate yourself in the employment marketplace, deliberately position your company where you want to be. Position yourself to be attractive to the people *you* want, so they will choose to work with you. Note: This effort includes sending the message to your current employees as well as future team members.

Roger and Joyce conducted research a few years ago into what criteria desirable employees were using to select their preferred employers. Joyce and Roger came up with eight categories defining the principal categories people used to choose their employers. This information is included, with about 200 examples of what leading-edge companies are already doing, in *How to Become an Employer of Choice* (Oakhill Press).

1. **The Company.** An Employer of Choice^SM is stable, has a solid history, and a fine reputation in the community and in the industry. The company is recognized and respected. The company's products and services are "worthy"—they deliver a positive value for society. They are produced well— quality is valued. The company is socially conscious and environmentally sensitive. Finally, their facilities and working environments are compatible with what the desired workers seek.

2. **The Culture.** There's a lot to be said for organizational culture. Some may say it's hard to define and is really not that influential. Our position is just the opposite. People want to work for a company with high values and standards. They want a culture that provides a much-needed sense of community. Today's workers are not interested in status barriers—everyone works together. Traditions, rituals, and history are all important as threads that weave together the working community.

3. **Enlightened Leadership.** Even though the most influential relationship in any company is usually between the worker and the worker's immediate supervisor, people want to be led well from the top of the organization. They want their senior leaders to have a clear sense of where they're taking the organization in the future. They expect their senior leaders to think and operate strategically, looking to the future. Senior executives in Employer of Choice^SM companies will be sure the chief human resource officer sits at the strategic table, recognizing the vital importance of people. Leaders will be visible and accessible, reaching out to others. They'll embrace change and make continual change and improvement comfortable for all.

4. **Care of People.** Quality-of-life issues are increasingly important to workers in today's fast-moving, highly active world. A homelike, safe, healthy environment makes an employer

more attractive; it's practically expected today. People want good working conditions, flexibility, and lots of recognition. They want their families valued and involved. They want to know what's going on; a good internal communications system is a common characteristic of Employers of Choice[SM]. Contact with alumni is more commonplace, encouraging more people to become "boomerang" employees and return to the fold.

5. **Growth and Opportunity.** Personal and professional growth are strong motivators today, as employees concentrate on their future marketability. Whether they stay in one place or move around, people want to be able to choose their own circumstances. Staying current makes that choice possible. Supervisors are advocates for employee growth, encouraging their people to take training, gain new experience, and participate in the company's mentoring program. Fast-track opportunities abound, as people grow in a wide range of experiences.

6. **Meaningful Work.** People want to do something "meaningful" in their work today; "just a job" doesn't feel right for many workers. They want work that "makes a difference," either for the public, customers, or internal customers. They want to see the value of their work. People want to stretch, to reach their full potential, expanding and enriching their jobs, enjoying stimulating opportunities. Many Employer of Choice[SM]–qualified companies provide ways for their employees to be involved in the design of their work, so they really feel a part of what's happening.

7. **Compensation and Benefits.** Today's workers seek a package of compensation; they're looking at a bigger picture than just cash in their pockets. While concerned about fair and competitive pay, they're also looking for profit sharing, stock options, domestic partner benefits, direct deposit of paychecks, a wide range of insurance coverage options, wellness

programs, adoption coverage, time off, discount pricing (for big-ticket items), and childcare. Some are even asking for petcare benefits.

8. **Making a Difference.** Social values are increasingly important—what are we doing to improve the world around us? Savvy employers are involved in their local communities and in broader interests that serve humanity. They lend their support—financial, in-kind, and human—to United Way, community theatre, Habitat for Humanity, Operation Smile, youth programs, and clean-up/fix-up projects.

Employers eager to attract and hold top talent must become much more responsive to what desired employees are looking for. The corporate design and approach will change with the times, creating new relationships between workers and their employers. Successful employers will continually evaluate their shifting conditions to more closely link their culture and opportunity with the workers who are looking for what the employer offers. The result will be employees who feel so comfortable, like hand-in-glove, that they never want to leave. This stability will enable employers to plan more confidently for the future.

Any employer who would like to be formally recognized as an Employer of Choice[SM] can apply for that recognition through a process managed by Employer of Choice, Inc. Information is available at *www.employerofchoice.net.*

Employer of Choice[SM] positioning significantly strengthens a company's recruiting posture to attract desired applicants. Working for a company that has earned this kind of third-party recognition also bonds current employees, substantially reducing employee turnover. You can imagine how investors feel about financially supporting a designated company. Suppliers have better feelings about getting paid—and offering special arrangements—when they're dealing with a recognized company. Customers like to be associated with a winner.

An interesting question: If you're not an Employer of Choice^{SM}, what are you? Whether or not you apply for the formal recognition, be sensitive to how your organization is positioned in the employment marketplace.

Selection and Hiring

Attracting the most desirable people to your employment office is just the beginning of the process to bring top quality employees on-board. Wise employers will be considerably more selective as they build their future workforce. Pay particular attention to what is called "job fit." To quote Chuck Russell, a recognized guru in the field of selection assessments, "You can't train your way out of a bad hiring decision." As Russell observes, "The cost of hiring one poor employee is far greater than the cost of having an effective selection process."

Assure that your organization is using the latest assessment technology in your selection process. Assessments will dependably screen out people who cannot do the job, though they do not dependably identify star performers. The good news is that you make money with average employees who are led well. It is the poor performers who destroy profits.

Use the least expensive and most accurate screen first. For example, if a 10-minute assessment that costs $10-$15 will screen out poor performers, do that before spending valuable interview time with someone who is unlikely to be able to succeed at the job anyway. If employees interact with customers, use machinery, use tools, or drive vehicles on company business, cover your potential liability by testing for drugs. If employees handle money or valuable tools and material, use honesty/integrity testing. After your screening process has been completed, you can invest in the high cost of interviewing.

———————————— Words of Wisdom ————————————

Employers who are most successful in hiring—and keeping—top talent advise that consistency and speed in the hiring process make a profound difference. If you have a fine candidate on the line, reel that applicant in quickly. If you don't move smoothly and deliberately in a timely manner, that great catch will get away.

Anticipate negotiating individual compensation arrangements with each new employee. Even though we'll hear the hue and cry from those who insist we must maintain internal equity with our compensation systems, creativity, responsiveness, and sensitivity to discrete needs will drive future negotiations. Expect to see more attention invested in competency-based pay and performance-based rewards for people in all kinds of jobs.

We'll see increased emphasis on performance and results—which is why we encouraged you to start strategic workforce planning by getting current employees up to snuff. This new flexibility in employee-employer relationships will include pay, benefits, perks, and personalized awards for achievement.

Orientation

Why are we talking about orientation as we discuss the strategic workforce planning process? Working with a wide range of consulting clients, we have discovered that when an orientation program is done well, new employees feel more bonded to the organization and tend to remain with the employer for a longer period of time. When orientation is done poorly, people leave sooner . . . and those who stay are continually confused about the value of their work, expectations, and motivation. Essentially, they're low performers—particularly compared to what they could be.

———————————— Words of Wisdom ————————————

The people you hire today are, potentially, your greatest resource for corporate success in the years ahead. As a senior leader, your participation in new employee orientation sends a vital cultural and leadership message: "We're all involved here in the drive toward what we want to be in the future." Everyone—even the newest employee—has value. Share your perspectives about your organization's mission, values, and vision. Tell people where you're taking the company—and why. Explain why you want them along with you. Reinforce the sense that each one of them was handpicked for the contribution he or she needs to make as an essential member of your team.

Let's take this orientation issue just a little bit further. Are your current employees on-board the way they need to be? Chances are that some of your more tenured people would learn quite a bit from your orientation process. They would also benefit from learning other information that is shared during the course of bringing new people into the fold. You're expecting these key people to support and reinforce your messages to new folks, so you'd better be sure they understand it. You can imagine how strategically important it will be for you to have everyone singing the same tune.

Organizational Culture

Every workplace has a culture. It's easily defined as "what it feels like around here." Are people happy to be part of your environment? Are they committed, or is it just a job? When people simply "attend work," you have robots instead of a team of dedicated professionals. Do you expect—and respect—professionalism among all employees? Are administrative assistants, custodians, salespeople, customer service representatives, managers, executives, receptionists, production workers, and delivery people—to name some representative job titles—all recognized as professionals in what they do? You don't need to hold a doctorate or a license to be a "professional" in today's vernacular.

Organization cultures include degrees of hierarchy, autonomy, accountability, and openness. Cultural norms include how people communicate, how much initiative they take, and how they are rewarded. Quality, urgency, and even whether you have assigned spaces in the parking lot flow from your culture. Plenty has been written about corporate culture, so we do not need to dwell on the topic in this book.

Does your culture need to change to strengthen your success? What changes may be needed? Why? Part of your strategic workforce planning involves examining your culture. Is your current culture getting in your way? Is it enhancing the way you do business? If changes are recommended, how might they be accomplished? Assuming that it's your job to lead the charge, how will you do it? How will you measure your results on the path to constructive and deliberate culture change during your strategic planning and implementation process?

Cultures are multifaceted and far-reaching. They come into being over a long period of time. They were built through an evolutionary process and can't be changed overnight. Can leaders influence cultures? You bet! Just don't expect instant miracles. Change is often subtle and takes time.

Engagement and Recognition

How well engaged are your employees? It's not enough that they show up for work each day, even if they're freshly scrubbed and have eaten a good breakfast. Are they excited? Are they enthusiastic about their work and the difference they can make each day? That difference doesn't have to be world changing, but it must be positive for their work group, product, company, customer, or other stakeholders. Do your people go home at the end of their work period with a sense of satisfaction that they've accomplished something worthwhile? If not, how long do you think they'll stay with you in an increasingly competitive job market? One key is to engage new employees on their first day of work.

--- **Words of Wisdom** ---

Build psychic ownership among employees and you will increase job tenure. Create and feed a feeling of personal connection with the work of the organization and the results that are achieved. Build pride in the "ownership" of those results, the intrinsic reward for a job well done. Continual intrinsic rewards build a sense of psychic ownership that's hard to break, and that attracts others internally and externally.

Senior executives can be influential in getting people to feel more engaged; frontline managers can be even more effective. However, your odds of those managers doing their jobs depend on the leadership they receive from above. What are the messages around the topics of engagement and recognition in your organization? Are attitudes positive? Are people turned on about what they are doing? Do colleagues, coworkers, and peers know that you really appreciate them? When was the last time you said "thank you" to an employee?

Why is this platform important for strategic workforce planning? The higher your level of engagement, the stronger your results will be. If your people are not sufficiently engaged, you need to help them get more motivated to perform well. If your people perform well because they *want* to, your company could be considerably different tomorrow than it is today. Remember, we're looking at introducing new technologies, new systems, and different organizational structures. If your workers are not receptive and inspired to find better ways to do things, you're in trouble. Strategic workforce development goes far beyond some number crunching to see how many people you'll need. The quality of your workforce is vitally important.

Recognition is powerful. If you merely give mediocre recognition, it's practically meaningless. However, when you convey strong recognition, appreciation, and gratitude in appropriate doses, that support goes a long, long way towards reinforcing the desired behaviors. When leaders are personally involved in delivering that recognition and reward, the bonds between employer and employee are strengthened. As you promote higher cohesiveness among your people, those bonds will be quite meaningful.

As you build for the future, include a number of different types of rewards in your recognition program. A letter from the senior executive of an organization can carry as much—or more—weight than a fancy trophy or a night at dinner and the theatre. Get creative—it will become part of your culture—how you salute those who do well. Not only will you inspire higher performance, but also people who are sincerely appreciated tend to stay with you longer.

Employee Retention

A strong employee retention program is an important part of the Strategic Workforce Plan. Once you've hired the people you want, it's essential to hold on to them. An effective retention program means a greater return on each of those valued employees. A stable workforce means higher efficiency, continuity, productivity, and customer service. Morale is stronger, as is your reputation in the community as a good place to work. That reputation will help attract more people of the caliber you want.

An employee-centered retention philosophy, driven by senior leaders, is a critical first step. If other leaders, managers, and supervisors know that their superiors believe in a strong retention program, the rest is easy. Well, easier. Without clear and demonstrated support from the top, retention results simply won't be that good.

Research and understand why people leave your organization. While exit interviews are valuable in some situations, we emphasize ongoing re-recruiting. Know how your people feel; conduct frequent surveys to discover where you might have problems. Concentrate on the people who stay with you to learn what makes them happy . . . then give them more of it!

The Supervisor's Influence

As we discussed in chapter 2, the most influential factor in how long an employee stays is the relationship between the employee and the employee's immediate supervisor. So, how well trained are your supervisors—at all levels—in the principles and techniques of employee retention? Do they see retention as part of their jobs? Do they feel your reinforcement through recognition and reward . . . or negative consequences, if their behavior is chasing away your needed employees?

Unenlightened supervisors believe that employee retention is only something for human resources to worry about. Quite the contrary. As we emphasized earlier in this book, employee retention is a *management* responsibility; human resource professionals are merely there to advise, support, guide, and provide resources. Human resource personnel cannot work with employees on a day-to-day basis, providing them with the support, training, care, and coaching that inspire people to stay with an employer. The employee's supervisor is responsible for this kind of relationship building.

The problem is that too few companies emphasize retention as part of the supervisor's role, and even fewer offer any kind of incentives to encourage the investment of time and energy in the people side of enterprise. The labor shortage of this decade will no doubt stimulate more companies to clarify for their managers and supervisors that retention *is* an important aspect of their jobs, not something that can be delegated or abdicated. Your managers may need some shifts in their thinking and priorities, then they may need training to help them do the job that will be expected of them.

Succession Planning

Your strategic workforce plan should include a succession plan. There should be at least one person in line for every key position in your organization. In most cases, that backup person will already be on the payroll, but there's no requirement for that. Some backups could be working for other companies, though you know who they are and where to find them when you need them. You might have even completed testing and interviewing, so the person can be brought on board quickly in an emergency.

It will be tempting to engage in succession planning for just the top people in the company. The "chiefs"—chief executive officer, chief financial officer, chief operating officer, chief human resource officer, chief manufacturing officer, and on and on. Yes, planning at that level is important to do. But you should place *equal weight* on succession planning for frontline supervisors, for production operators, for drivers, for salespeople.

Consider this: If a vice president doesn't come in tomorrow, will anyone really miss that executive's presence? If an assembly-line worker or a restaurant server or retail cashier didn't show up, how would the impact be different? The risk would probably be greater: if a frontline worker doesn't show up, who is going to carry the burden of assuring that the ultimate customer is well-served? How strong is your succession planning for the people you depend on every day? Do you have a prescreened list of people who could be transferred or hired from the outside to get the job done?

Place your emphasis on "A" players with talent equity. Your people who know their job well may be "at risk." If their learning and productivity value curves drop off, they're becoming psychologically ready to move to another company.

Watch the talent equity curves for each of your people (see figure 22). When the line starts a downward trend, you are vulnerable to losing that valued employee and must take action. If appropriate, identify that individual as a candidate for movement, either laterally or in some other direction (like an outside learning or work experience) to rekindle the worker's interest in a career with your organization.

———————— **Words of Wisdom** ————————

Do not stop at succession planning. That's just part of the picture. Invest in succession preparation, too.

Invest in cross-training, job shadowing, coaching, mentoring, and cross-experience. You should be as ready as you can be, in case you have an unexpected need. The advantage is that you'll be preparing people to move up, so their superiors—the people they're backing up, can also move up, too. If your company is growing, this process will become even more valuable for you. There are no guarantees, of course, but high levels of readiness build a comforting level of strength and potential into the organization.

Implement and Sustain

As your strategic workforce plan comes together, start putting it to work. Once you measure your progress, you'll discover that human resource planning makes a lot of sense. Validate your support for preparing tomorrow's workforce by including those reports of progress in staff meetings and planning meetings.

As you continue your short-, medium-, and long-range planning, be sure that strategic workforce planning is part of the picture. When there are changes to be made in what your organization does and how it does it, check the human resource component. Every important decision about direction, new products, new markets, new facilities, and all other movement should include a review of the impact on human resources . . . or the human resource impact on the success of the decision.

Keep in mind that your greatest concern, realistically, will be the functioning and contribution of your human resources, your people, today. At the same time, keep looking toward tomorrow.

Closing Questions

1. Does your strategic plan include a comprehensive program for workforce development, based on current and future needs related to strategic goals?
2. What would it take to become an Employer of Choice^{SM} to gain the marketplace branding advantages and economic benefits?
3. Are the key members of your leadership team involved in your employee orientation initiatives to convey the vision, core purpose, and values of your organization?
4. How well do you understand and quantify the reasons why employees leave or stay with your organization?

Opportunities for a Competitive Advantage

If every one of your leaders read this book prior to your next strategic planning session, how much more attention would your workforce stability initiatives receive? Is one of your top three strategic initiatives: Creating and maintaining a more talented and stable workforce? What would be the economic benefits/ outcomes five years from now if it were?

CHAPTER ELEVEN

Call to Action

Don't wait to begin your preparation, because it seems like too much work. Use our handy checklist as a starting point and begin now to take action. This Impending Crisis that we forecast is coming. The impact of waiting is too high a cost to pay. You can't afford to wait.

Professional speakers are encouraged to end their presentations with a call for action. Salespeople are taught to go for the close. Athletes are trained to win their competitions. The common theme: *Do Something. Achieve Results.*

We want to send that message to you, the leaders and potential leaders who read this book. As you might have suspected in the preceding pages, we wrote this manuscript with a mission— a passionate mission to focus attention on what is clearly an imminent crisis facing practically all employers.

When will this crisis affect you? Each industry, each community, each business is different. We cannot legitimately forecast when you will be affected or how serious the impact will be. You are unique. What we do know, unequivocally, is that you *will* be affected. Some will already be feeling the effects of the labor and leadership crisis as you read this book. Others will be hit in a month, a few months, or even a couple of years from now.

Working with our publisher, we released the first edition of this book before the crisis conditions were really felt, in an effort to give ample warning to as many organizational leaders as we could. Forewarned is forearmed. We reasoned: The earlier you knew, the better positioned you could be.

Now it's your turn. We have shared with you the cold, hard, indisputable facts of what is—and what will be. The revelation is over; it's time for action. What will you do? In our role as management consultants, we've offered a lot of advice. We've challenged you with questions. We've provoked your thinking. All these activities have been in your mind. Now it's time to move these ideas from your head to your hands—with heart.

In a spirit of caring, begin your strategic planning and preparation to respond to the crisis—to manage your organization differently, based on the information and insight you've gained from this book. Start to make things happen.

Checklist to Get Started

Here is a checklist of suggestions to get you moving.

✓ Arrange for everyone on your strategic team to read this book. You need to get everyone on the same page. To assure that all your key players fully understand your predicament, have them learn the facts firsthand for themselves.

✓ Take inventory of whether you are at Stage 1, Stage 2, Stage 3, or Stage 4. Evaluate how much time it will take you and your organization to become competent. Possible time line:

- Small Companies: 18 months
- Medium-Sized Companies: 2–3 years
- Large Companies: 3–5 years

✓ Schedule a meeting soon to discuss seriously what you have learned and how the evolving crisis will affect your organization. This date should not be far off. Remember the value of urgency. You may want to hold this strategic meeting away from your place of business, in a setting that will allow you to work intensely without interruption.

✓ In this strategic meeting and subsequent gatherings, creatively examine every aspect of the way you do business. Challenge everything. If you find that this process is difficult, perhaps because each participant has an understandable personal agenda, you would be wise to bring in an outside facilitator to help you dig beneath the surface. In Roger's experience as a consultant and facilitator, he has seen leadership teams very effectively get out of their "boxes" with some objective assistance.

✓ Now it's time for each strategic-level player to bring his/her management team into the game. You might make it a sort of game—a challenging, thrilling, invigorating experience of reinvention. Start with a clean slate—anything goes—and re-create your organization. Re-create your processes. Explore vigorously what you do, why you do it, and how else the same objectives could be accomplished. Don't be afraid to question whether the objective itself is even worthwhile! Dig deep! Stretch your thinking! Be sensitive to the fact that your managers, while they are probably quite good, are traditionally focused on a relatively short-term perspective. You may need to have them read this book, as well as provide them some education and training on strategic thinking and out-of-the-box conceptual thinking.

✓ Begin to engage the rest of your employees. Make this engagement really positive. In no way should anyone associate this process with the infamous reengineering fad. Too many people viewed reengineering as a euphemism for cutting jobs and people. Gradually, you will make changes, hopefully striving to hold on to your valued employees. Anticipate some serious retraining as the process continues. Do not expect this transformation to happen overnight. It won't. It shouldn't. It took a long time to build the structure and system you have now; it will take a long time to change it, to replace it with something substantially different.

Sounds like a lot of work, doesn't it? We surely won't deny that perception. This process won't be easy, but nothing worthwhile ever is, we're told. Perhaps that's why we have to use a word like "crisis" to describe what's coming—and what must be done to prepare for it.

To keep things in perspective, we must also tell you that you can't stop or eliminate this crisis. It *is* coming, just as sure as the sun will come up tomorrow morning. Your job is to manage the crisis and its fallout. Your mission is to fight it, to reduce or neutralize its impacts on your organization. Remember, other employers will be joining the battle to protect their own positions. You're fighting the crisis and its potential impacts in your organization; others—including your competitors—will also be seeking ways to mitigate the impacts of having too much work and too few workers.

Too Much Work

Some of our readers will conclude that what we're suggesting must be done is simply too much work. Maybe the crisis isn't as serious as Roger, Tom, and Joyce say it is. So, ignore us. Don't do anything to change the way you do business. Don't make any changes in the ways you attract, optimize, and retain employees.

If you take this attitude, we encourage you to still spend some time talking together as a strategic leadership team. What are the risks of inaction? If you don't believe you will be affected by the crisis we describe, how might you respond when your customers and suppliers are? How will you monitor what's happening to your organization, what's happening inside your organization, so you have some warning signals if we're right?

We're reminded of the stories about the canaries in the coalmines. Miners would take a caged canary down into the mine with them. Being more sensitive to the lack of oxygen and the presence of toxic gases, the canary would pass out and perhaps die before the miners themselves were affected. When the canary stopped singing, the ever-alert miners would scramble out of the mine to the fresh air on the surface. Many lives were saved by those sacrificial canaries!

What's your canary? Do you need more than one? How will you know when the chirping stops? Tom's experience in measurement of business performance shows that there are numerous factors that, when measured well—and frequently enough will sound warning signals. Watch out for negative values on

- Leadership practices
- Management practices
- Business practices
- External practices

For more insight into these practices, see chapter 7.

The Impact of Waiting

The further we move into the first decade of the 21st century, the more critical the crisis will become. No, it's certainly not necessary to get started right away, but the problem won't go away. It will become more serious as time passes. More importantly, your competitors can buy this book just as you did. If they take action before you do, what will the impact be on your organization? Remember, we're talking about organizations that compete with you for customers *and* those that compete with you for workers.

We don't mean to sound dramatic with the preceding statement about your competitors, but we can't downplay your vulnerability.

Closing Questions

1. Who in your organization would benefit from reading and understanding the major learning elements in this book?
2. Recognizing the Impending Crisis that will eventually affect us, how long will it take your organization to adapt? (Is it one year, two, three, five?)
3. What can you do personally to take this message to the most influential people in your organization?
4. What external support do you need to successfully prepare for the Impending Crisis?

Opportunities for a Competitive Advantage

What if you could personally be the catalyst to accelerate the workforce stability initiatives in your organization? How would that help you personally in your career path advancement? How many other people could you affect or positively impact by improving your workplace and becoming more of an Employer of Choice^{SM}? What is holding you back?

Good luck! And let us know if we can help.

Roger E. Herman, CSP, CMC, FIMC
roger@impendingcrisis.com

Tom Olivo, CPCM
tom@impendingcrisis.com

Joyce L. Gioia, CMC
joyce@impendingcrisis.com

ENDNOTE

After writing over 70,000 words to communicate our vital message to you, how should we end this book? Well, we can tell you that it has been an exciting, invigorating, and highly educational project. But our concurrent research and client service work have been frightening. The more we learn about the critical need for strategic action, the more we become concerned because we see so little of it. During the writing process, practically every day we encountered situations that reinforced our work and reenergized us to finish this important book as soon as possible.

Our clear closing message is simple:

1. Please understand how serious the Impending Crisis is and how it will affect your organization.
2. You can't do this work alone. Have your associates read this book, talk about it, and strategize about what you must do together as a leadership team.
3. Start now. We can't emphasize enough the need for a sense of urgency about this work.

> This situation is not merely an opportunity to gain another strategic advantage over your competition. This work is necessary for you to stay in business as a viable entity in the years ahead.

More Thought-Provoking Information

As we've written this book for you, we've uncovered or bumped into more information than we could possibly include in these pages. While a book must be thorough, it must also be thin enough to be read by its intended consumers. Even after we put this manuscript to bed—publishers insist on some sort of an end point so they can print—we found more to share with you. That is the authors' dilemma.

So, we're going to take advantage of technology. We will share information, commentary, and advice electronically, as well as through the printed word. You are invited to join our ongoing exploration of the Impending Crisis at *www.impendingcrisis.com*.

CONCEPTS ADDRESSED IN *IMPENDING CRISIS*

The overall value of employees increases with the development of their competencies and raw talent.

The overall value of employees increases with their time on the job.

The chief executive officer, chief financial officer, and chief human resource officer must work together as a cohesive team, making full use of human resource metrics.

Four separate categories of unemployment indicate different conditions; unemployment isn't just unemployment anymore.

Employees who have left psychologically and emotionally, but not physically, actually cost the employer much more than people who quit.

The degree to which people are willing to stay with their current employers linked to satisfaction and other business practices.

The profile and relative quantity of people available in the workplace, based upon birth rates and immigration. The actual wave itself is caused by the Baby Boom generation. The years ahead will see significant changes in the numbers of workers in various age ranges.

APPENDIX A

Valuing a Business: The Human Capital Metrics

Traditionally, businesses have been valued by several methods—all of which revolve around financial measures. Profit has certainly been important, understandably, and the price/earnings ratio has been important to Wall Street. ROI—Return on Investment—is a powerful view, challenging whether we're getting enough benefit from what we put into the company.

From our perspective, one of the downfalls of the inordinately heavy emphasis on financial measurements, other yardsticks are not adequately considered. For-profit corporations, particularly those whose stock is publicly traded, laser focus almost all of their attention on what the numbers will be at the end of the quarter or the next reporting period. In the drive to make those numbers look good, corporate leaders too often ignore the human side of enterprise. They push their numbers at the expense of their people. Unfortunately, such decisions risk sacrificing long-term achievement for short-term financial showings.

We would suggest that, while these are important measures and should not be ignored, there are some other measures that are moving into a strong position. They will be somewhat difficult to quantify, so we've suggested some approaches. We readily accept that these ratios will be challenged, as they should be.

This methodology is an evolving process that will have a number of subtle differences in the way it is applied by various employers . . . for various reasons. We offer these yardsticks as a starting point, raising issues more than concentrating on fine-point accuracy at this stage.

As more light shines on the proportionally rising cost of *human capital*—as opposed to other types of capital such as machinery, buildings, or dollars—executives will pay more attention to human resource metrics. In this chapter, to give you some insight into the field, we'll present a selection of commonly accepted metrics in the human capital arena.

1. The Revenue Factor. This metric relates the total revenue earned by the company to the number of people employed to earn the revenue.

Revenue per Employee = Total Revenue ÷ number of FTEs

This is the basic measure most understood by managers. The number of Full-Time Equivalent employees should include both regular and contingent labor.

2. Voluntary Separation Rate. This metric divides the number of voluntary separations by the number of employees (headcount).

Voluntary Separation Rate = Voluntary Separations / Headcount

Along with time to fill jobs, this number represents potential lost opportunity, lost revenue and more highly stressed employees who have to fill in for departed coworkers.

3. Time to Fill. This measurement monitors the average number of days it takes to fill a job once a vacancy occurs. Depending on the industry and the level of job, this number has been ranging from 52 to 119 days.

When it takes this long to fill a job, the vacancy means that work is not accomplished and/or significant additional costs like overtime, temporary help, or lost sales are being incurred.

4. Human Capital Value Added. This metric relates the revenue, operating expense, and compensation and benefit costs to the number of full time equivalents to derive the human capital value added.

Human Capital Value Added = Revenue - (Operating Expense
 - [Compensation Cost + Benefit Cost]) / Total FTE

This metric is the prime measure of people's contributions to an organization. It answers the question, what are workers worth?

5. Human Capital Return on Investment. This metric relates the revenue, operating expense, and compensation and benefit costs to compensation and benefit costs to derive the human capital ROI.

Human Capital ROI = Revenue - (Operating Expense -
[Compensation Cost +Benefit Cost]) / (Compensation
Cost = Benefit Cost)

This is the ratio of dollars spent on pay and benefits to an adjusted profit figure.

6. Return on Compensation. This metric relates the compensation and benefit costs to revenue to derive the total compensation revenue percent.

Total Compensation Revenue Percent = Compensation Cost
+ Benefit Cost / Revenue

If you monitor pay and benefits in comparison to revenue per employee, you can see the return on your investment.

7. **Labor Cost as a Percent of Revenue.** This metric relates the compensation, benefit, and other labor costs to revenue to derive the total labor cost revenue percent.

Total Labor Cost Revenue Percent = Compensation Cost + Benefit Cost + Other Labor Cost / Revenue

By looking at total labor cost versus total compensation revenue percent, you can see the complete cost of human capital. Total labor cost revenue percent shows not only pay and benefits, but also the cost of contingent labor.

8. **Training Investment.** This metric relates the total training cost to headcount to derive the training investment.

Training Investment = Total Training Cost / Headcount

This formula enables you to assess your organization's training investment on a per capita basis. By modifying the formula, you can compare the training investment to payroll, revenue, profit, or other measures.

9. **Acquisition Costs.** This metric relates the many of the assorted recruiting costs to operating expenses to derive the cost per hire.

Cost per Hire = Advertising + Agency Fees + Employee Referrals + Travel Cost of Applicants and Staff + Relocation Costs + Recruiter Pay and Benefits / Operating Expenses

Understanding the cost of hiring new employees is important, looking at the cost of bringing on new people for corporate growth or to factor into replacement cost for employee turnover management. The cost elements shown are all valid, but many more could be added for a truly complete and accurate evaluation.

10. **Healthcare Costs per Employee.** This metric relates the cost of healthcare benefits to the to the total number of employees to derive the healthcare costs per employee.

Health Care Costs per Employee = Total Cost of Health
Care Benefits / Total Employees

11. **Turnover Costs.** See the information on the Bliss-Gately Tool, Appendix B. From all we have seen, this tool is the most comprehensive measurement tool available. In fact, it is *so* comprehensive that many users will find it almost overwhelming. For those needing less information, the tool is designed, so it can be used without all the detail.

Special note: One of the major challenges today in human resource metrics is the lack of standardization in measuring turnover. It is our hope that the use of these formulas and the Bliss-Gately Tool will help bring a measure of consistency to this process.

Measuring turnover rates is a significant challenge. Do you measure voluntary and/or involuntary turnover? How about people who transfer from one department to another, but stay with the same company? How about employees who go from full-time to part-time or who are laid off? There are so many variables in the way employers look at this issue, that statistics can be—and are—manipulated to achieve whatever objective management wants.

Other Measures

Some other measures come into play in today's society, some with hard numbers attached and some that are "softer" in their evaluative factors. The price/earnings ratio is important to watch. Financial managers remind us that a company's earnings stream should be an overriding factor in monitoring corporate health. They warn, without sufficient cash flow, everything else may grind to a halt. Accountants will share with you a long list of measures that assess an organization's financial health. Many of these formulas are designed to monitor risk to protect against adverse circumstances.

We can't argue this point, however please be advised that other factors such as overly high turnover rates can be similarly life-threatening to an employer. If valued employees leave, you certainly can expect adverse circumstances. Productivity may suffer, output may suffer, and customer relationships may be at risk. Human resource measurements can help monitor potentially critical human resource risks.

Some employees and investors use social values as a measurement factor. Those social values include corporate citizenship, family support, and environmental sensitivity. This profiling is described as the Return on Social Investment (RSI). There is no generally accepted formula to measure this quantitatively.

In this appendix, we have looked at many different metrics and measurements for valuing a business. Choose the combination that works best for you.

APPENDIX B

The Business Cost and Impact of Employee Turnover

One of the most critical components of success for the business owner, regardless of size, is the ability to keep the cost of doing business at a minimum. Obviously, every owner wants to ensure the best possible profit margin for the sustained growth and success of the business. What many businesspeople fail to realize is that employee turnover can represent a very substantial cost and lead to serious erosion of the bottom line.

Would it surprise you to learn that it will cost at least 150 percent of a person's base salary to replace him or her? Actually, the more you pay a person, the higher that percentage will be, because the more you pay the person, obviously, the more you value the individual's contribution to the growth and success of your business. Most businesses will probably pay their top salesperson triple (or more) what they pay a bookkeeper. The business values the contributions of the salesperson at a higher level, at least in strict monetary terms, over those of the bookkeeper, although both perform valuable roles.

Let's say you have an employee with an annual salary of $50,000 who leaves a company. (The reasons for leaving are not important in this case; if the plan is to replace the employee, the costs will be the same.) It will cost the company a minimum of $75,000 to replace that person. This cost includes the savings realized because the person has left! And, the entire cost comes right off of the bottom line. We have developed a turnover cost projection model, now called The Bliss-Gately Tool, that identifies and calculates all the costs incurred.

The model groups into four major categories the business costs and impact of employee turnover: 1) Costs due to a person leaving; 2) Hiring costs; 3) Training costs; and 4) Lost productivity costs. For purposes of illustration, take the example of a financial analyst in a mid-sized company. This person is paid an annual base salary of $52,000, which works out to an hourly rate of $25, assuming a 40-hour workweek.

Costs Due to a Person Leaving

When this financial analyst announces that s/he is leaving (to avoid awkwardness, we'll use the pronoun "he" from now on), he has immediately begun to transition out of the company. Even though he has given you two or three weeks' notice, his mind and full attention are not on your business anymore; this mental departure is simply human nature.

At this point, costs include the following: Employees who must fill in for the person that leaves before a replacement is found; the lost productivity of the employee while he is still in his position, but not fully concentrating on his job; the cost of a manager or other executive having an exit interview with the employee to determine what work remains, how to do the work, why he is leaving, etc.; the cost of training the company has provided this departing employee; the cost of lost knowledge, skills, and contacts of the departing employee; the increased cost of unemployment insurance; and the possible cost of lost customers the departing employee is taking with him (or that leave because there is a negative impact on the service). The sum total of these costs can be as much as 85 percent of this position's base salary or $45,000.

Hiring Costs

Unless there is someone to promote or the perfect person just happens to come along at the right time, there will be some costs associated with identifying and hiring a replacement for the financial analyst position. These costs will include items like advertising, an employment agency fee, employee referral award, Internet posting, and other forms of announcing the availability of the position. More money may well have to be offered to attract the right candidate. At the next stage, interviews conducted by management and/or hiring department staff will cost money in terms of the time people spend arranging for interviews, conducting the interviews, calling references, having discussions about the candidates they met, and time spent notifying candidates who did not get the job.

The time spent on these activities will also cost money in lost productivity, because, with rare exceptions, these people who are hiring are not employed to be full-time interviewers. Also included here are any skills, personality, or assessment testing your company may utilize. Finally, there is the cost of conducting preemployment checks such as past employment histories, drug screening, educational verifications, and (possibly) criminal background checks. And don't forget, these assessments and reference checks may be conducted on more than one candidate for the opening. If an employment agency is used, the sum total of the additional cost will be at least 15 percent of this position's base salary or approximately $8,000. This fee will increase to about 38 percent of the position's base salary or $20,000.

Training Costs

Now that the person is hired for the financial analyst position, he can't be expected to know absolutely everything on the first day, can he? Costs to factor in for training include any new employee orientation that explains benefits, basic policies, company history, etc.; specific training for the person to do his job, such as computer training, product knowledge, industry knowledge, and the day-to-day duties to get the job done. Even though this training may be informal or on-the-job training, the time it takes for various people to impart this knowledge does cost money?especially since people who are knowledgeable enough to train others are probably also highly valuable to the company. Set the sum total of these costs at approximately 13 percent of the position's base salary or $7,000.

Lost Productivity Costs

Because the newly hired employee does not come fully trained, it will take some time before he is fully productive in his new position. This deficiency exists, even if someone has been promoted from within the company. The following formula can be used: The employee is only 25 percent productive for the first four weeks; 50 percent productive for weeks 5 to 8; 75 percent productive for weeks 9 to 12; and will finally reach full productivity after week 12. Since this person is being paid at the full rate of pay during this period, there are still more lost productivity costs. Naturally, for more senior-level positions, or those requiring longer periods of time to develop full productivity, the costs will be higher.

During this time of lost productivity, the person's supervisor is also spending more time instructing, reviewing work, and possibly correcting mistakes. (There will be some mistakes that are not caught right away and will cost money to correct down the line, such as with a customer who receives an incorrect price, invoice, or actual shipment, due to the new person's error.) Put the sum total of these costs at approximately 32 percent of the position's base salary or $17,000.

Adding the subtotals of each major category discussed above gives a total of $77,000 if an employment agency is not used and $89,000 if it is. The first figure is just about 150 percent of the original $52,000 base salary we used in this example. (And remember the additional costs of employee benefits and company-paid taxes on top of that, which can range from 20 to 30 percent of the base salary.)

If we were looking at a sales position, the costs would be significantly higher due to the value of lost sales or customers. To calculate this cost, take the costs listed above and add the average revenue per sales representative divided by the number of weeks the position is vacant. This total will be well above 200 percent of the salesperson's annual compensation.

The Employee as Resource, Rather Than Expenditure

For a company with $5 million in revenue and $250,000 in net income, we have just spent between $75,000 and $90,000 of that profit to replace someone! You may say that these are just "the costs of doing business" and to a certain extent, that's true. However, would you rather spend $75,000 on purchasing a new piece of equipment that can increase your manufacturing or service capacity, or use it just to maintain the status quo?

Many managers have focused only on the cash cost of employee turnover. They do not realize the entire cost and impact of turnover. The point is that the cost of time and lost productivity are no less important or real than the costs associated with paying cash to vendors for services such as advertising. This high value is something often overlooked or underestimated by employers; yet in today's tight job market, with companies competing for skilled workers, these costs are becoming more and more significant.

This attitude does not mean that *all* employee turnover can or should be eliminated. But given the high costs involved and the impacts on productivity and customer service, a well-thought-out program designed to retain employees can easily pay for itself in a very short period of time. Unless you are prepared to beat all of your competition on wages all of the time, it is a good idea to start taking a hard look at your benefits, your policies, and the "intangibles" that make your company a desirable place to work.

Bill Bliss of Bliss & Associates, Inc., Wayne, New Jersey, wrote the text in this appendix. Appreciating that he has captured our thoughts and committed them to paper so well, we felt it appropriate to share them directly with you. We are indebted to Bill for his insight, research, and collegiality. He and Robert Gately, an engineer with a keen eye for calculation and detail, constructed the Bliss-Gately Tool for measuring the cost of employee retention.

The Bliss-Gately tool is the finest we have seen for this purpose, so we commend it to you. It's a tool we have wanted to develop for years; we won't bother now—it's been done! The balance of this appendix is an explanation of the calculation lines of the analysis system. We refer you to figures 18, 19, and 20 as illustrations.

If you would like to use the Bliss-Gately Tool, you will find it available at *www.hermangroup.com/store/software.html*.

Business Costs & Impacts of Turnover

Summary

Instructions

To save all data about this job title click on the "Save Current Values to Records..." button, see above right. To print this page click on "Print this page" button, see above left.

Company: ABC Hospital

Contact: Katherine Madison   Title: HR

Job Title: Education Coordinator Hourly Rate $20.18

Part A - Costs Due to a Person Leaving

Line A1	$	4,855	Cost of employee(s) filling-in
Line A2	$	1,214	Lost productivity of fill-in employee
Line A3	$	65	Cost of exit interview
Line A4	$	202	Cost of manager's time
Line A5	$	4,048	Cost of training company has provided
Line A6	$	2,033	Lost departmental productivity
Line A7	$	-	Cost of severance and benefits continuation
Line A8	$	20,800	Cost of lost knowledge, skills and contacts...
Line A9	$	-	Increased cost of unemployment insurance
Line A10	$	-	Cost of losing customers
Line A11	$	(4,855)	Minus the savings in salary
Part A	$	28,362	Total Costs

Figure 50: Business Costs And Impacts Of Turnover Summary

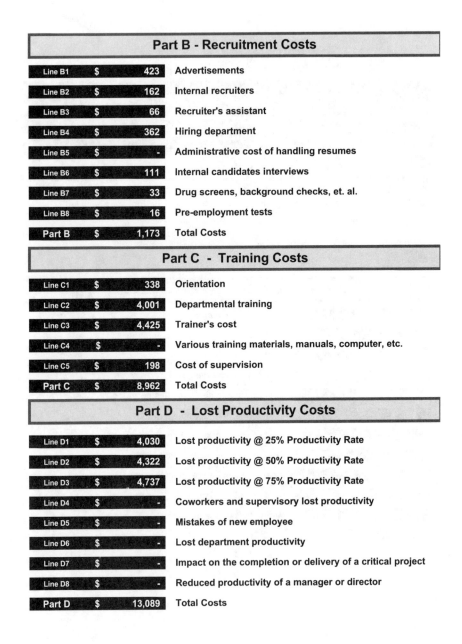

Part B - Recruitment Costs

Line B1	$	423	Advertisements
Line B2	$	162	Internal recruiters
Line B3	$	66	Recruiter's assistant
Line B4	$	362	Hiring department
Line B5	$	-	Administrative cost of handling resumes
Line B6	$	111	Internal candidates interviews
Line B7	$	33	Drug screens, background checks, et. al.
Line B8	$	16	Pre-employment tests
Part B	$	1,173	Total Costs

Part C - Training Costs

Line C1	$	338	Orientation
Line C2	$	4,001	Departmental training
Line C3	$	4,425	Trainer's cost
Line C4	$	-	Various training materials, manuals, computer, etc.
Line C5	$	198	Cost of supervision
Part C	$	8,962	Total Costs

Part D - Lost Productivity Costs

Line D1	$	4,030	Lost productivity @ 25% Productivity Rate
Line D2	$	4,322	Lost productivity @ 50% Productivity Rate
Line D3	$	4,737	Lost productivity @ 75% Productivity Rate
Line D4	$	-	Coworkers and supervisory lost productivity
Line D5	$	-	Mistakes of new employee
Line D6	$	-	Lost department productivity
Line D7	$	-	Impact on the completion or delivery of a critical project
Line D8	$	-	Reduced productivity of a manager or director
Part D	$	13,089	Total Costs

Figure 50: Business Costs And Impacts Of Turnover Summary

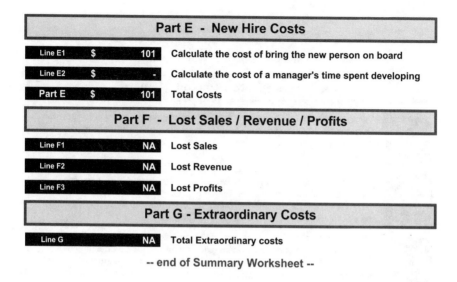

Part E - New Hire Costs		
Line E1	$	101	Calculate the cost of bring the new person on board
Line E2	$	-	Calculate the cost of a manager's time spent developing
Part E	$	101	Total Costs

Part F - Lost Sales / Revenue / Profits

Line F1	NA	Lost Sales
Line F2	NA	Lost Revenue
Line F3	NA	Lost Profits

Part G - Extraordinary Costs

| Line G | NA | Total Extraordinary costs |

-- end of Summary Worksheet --

Figure 50: Business Costs And Impacts Of Turnover Summary

Cost Inputs Worksheet

Enter the following data in the Cost Inputs Worksheet.

Part A - Costs Due to a Person Leaving

Line CIA1
Calculate the cost of the person(s) who fills in while the position is vacant. This can be either the cost of a temporary or the cost of existing employees performing the vacant job as well as their own. Include the cost at overtime rates.

Line CIA2
Calculate the cost of lost productivity at a minimum of 50% of the person's compensation and benefits cost for each week the position is vacant, even if there are people performing the work. Calculate the lost productivity at 100% if the position is completely vacant for any period of time.

Line CIA3
Calculate the cost of conducting an exit interview to include the time of the person conducting the interview, the time of the person leaving, the administrative costs of stopping payroll, benefit deductions, benefit enrollments, COBRA notification and administration, and the cost of the various forms needed to process a resigning employee.

Line CIA4
Calculate the cost of the manager who has to understand what work remains, and how to cover that work until a replacement is found. Calculate the cost of the manager who conducts their own version of the employee exit interview.

Line CIA5
Calculate the cost of training your company has invested in this employee who is leaving. Include internal training, external programs and external academic education. Include licenses or certifications the company has helped the employee obtain to do their job effectively.

Line CIA6
Calculate the impact on departmental productivity because the person is leaving. Who will pick up the work, whose work will suffer, what departmental deadlines will not be met or delivered late. Calculate the cost of department staff discussing their reactions to the vacancy.

Line CIA7
Calculate the cost of severance and benefits continuation provided to employees who are leaving that are eligible for coverage under these programs.

Line CIA8
Calculate the cost of lost knowledge, skills and contacts that the person who is leaving is taking with them out of your door (e.g., take 50% of the person's annual salary and then increase it by 10% for each year of service).

Figure 51: Business Costs And Impacts Of Turnover Descriptions

| Line CIA9 | Calculate the cost impact of unemployment insurance premiums as well as the time spent to prepare for an unemployment hearing, or the cost paid to a third party to handle the unemployment claim process on your behalf. |

| Line CIA10 | Calculate the cost of loosing customers that the employee is going to take with them, or the amount it will cost you to retain the customers of the sales person, or customer service representative who leaves. |

| Line CIA11 | Subtract the cost of the person who is leaving for the amount of time the position is vacant. |

Part B - Recruitment Costs

| Line CIB1 | The cost of advertisements (from a $200 classified to a $5,000 or more display advertisement); agency costs at 20 - 30% of annual compensation; employee referral costs of $500 - $2,000 or more; internet posting costs of $300 - $500 per listing. Include sign-on bonuses and relocation packages. |

| Line CIB2 | The cost of the internal recruiter's time to understand the position requirements, develop and implement a sourcing strategy, review candidates backgrounds, prepare for interviews, conduct interviews, prepare candidate assessments, conduct reference checks, make the employment offer and notify unsuccessful candidates. This can range from a minimum of 30 hours to over 100 hours per position. |

| Line CIB3 | Calculate the cost of a recruiter or a recruiter's assistant who will spend 20 or more hours in basic level review of resumes, developing candidate interview schedules and making any travel arrangements for out of town candidates. |

| Line CIB4 | Calculate the cost of the hiring department (immediate supervisor, manager, director, peers and others on the selection list) time to review and explain position requirements, review candidates background, conduct interviews, discuss their assessments and select a finalist. Also include their time to do their own sourcing of candidates from networks, contacts and other referrals. This can take upwards of 100 hours of total time. |

| Line CIB5 | Calculate the administrative cost of handling, processing and responding to the average number of resumes considered for each opening at $2 per resume or more. |

Figure 51: Business Costs And Impacts Of Turnover Descriptions

Line CIB6	Calculate the number of hours spend by the internal recruiter interviewing internal candidates along with the cost of those internal candidates to be away from their jobs while interviewing.
Line CIB7	Calculate the cost of drug screens, educational and criminal background checks and other reference checks, especially if these tasks are outsourced. Don't forget to calculate the number of times these are done per open position as some companies conduct this process for the final 2 or 3 candidates.
Line CIB8	Calculate the cost of the various candidate pre-employment tests to help assess a candidates' skills, abilities, aptitude, attitude, values and behaviors.

Part C - Training Costs

Line CIC1	Calculate the cost of orientation in terms of the new person's salary and the cost of the person who conducts the orientation. Also include the cost of orientation materials.
Line CIC2	Calculate the cost of departmental training as the actual development and delivery cost plus the cost of the salary of the new employee. Note that the cost will be significantly higher for some positions such as sales representatives and call center agents who require 4 - 6 weeks or more of classroom training.
Line CIC3	Calculate the cost of the person(s) who conduct the training.
Line CIC4	Calculate the cost of various training materials needed including company or product manuals, computer or other technology equipment used in the delivery of training.
Line CIC5	Calculate the cost of supervisory time spent in assigning, explaining and reviewing work assignments and output. This represents lost productivity of the supervisor. Consider the amount of time spent at 7 hours per week for at least 8 weeks.

Figure 51: Business Costs And Impacts Of Turnover Descriptions

Part D - Lost Productivity Costs

As the new employee is learning the new job, the company policies and practices, etc., they are not fully productive. Use the following guidelines to calculate the cost of this lost productivity:

Line CID1	Upon completion of whatever training is provided, the employee is contributing at a 25% productivity level for the first 2 - 4 weeks. The cost therefore is 75% of the new employees full salary during that time period.
Line CID2	During weeks 5 - 12, the employee is contributing at a 50% productivity level. The cost is therefore 50% of full salary during that time period.
Line CID3	During weeks 13 - 20, the employee is contributing at a 75% productivity level. The cost is therefore 25% of full salary during that time period.
Line CID4	Calculate the cost of coworkers and supervisory lost productivity due to their time spent on bringing the new employee "up to speed."
Line CID5	Calculate the cost of mistakes the new employee makes during this elongated indoctrination period.
Line CID6	Calculate the cost of lost department productivity caused by a departing member of management who is no longer available to guide and direct the remaining staff.
Line CID7	Calculate the impact cost on the completion or delivery of a critical project where the departing employee is a key participant.
Line CID8	Calculate the cost of reduced productivity of a manager or director who looses a key staff member, such as an assistant, who handled a great deal of routine, administrative tasks that the manager will now have to handle.

Figure 51: Business Costs And Impacts Of Turnover Descriptions

Part E - New Hire Costs

Line CIE1	Calculate the cost to bring the new person on board including the cost to put the person on the payroll, establish computer and security passwords and identification cards, business cards, internal and external publicity announcements, telephone hookups, cost of establishing email accounts, costs of establishing credit card accounts, or leasing other equipment such as cell phones, automobiles, pagers.
Line CIE2	Calculate the cost of a manager's time spent developing trust and building confidence in the new employee's work.

Part F - Lost Sales Costs

Line CIF1	For sales staff, divide the budgeted revenue per sales territory into weekly amounts and multiply that amount for each week the territory is vacant, including training time. Also use the lost productivity calculations above to calculate the lost sales until the sales representative is fully productive. Can also be used for telemarketing and inside sales representatives.
Line CIF2	For non-sales staff, calculate the revenue per employee by dividing total company revenue by the average number of employees in a given year. Whether an employee contributes directly or indirectly to the generation of revenue, their purpose is to provide some defined set of responsibilities that are necessary to the generation of revenue. Calculate the lost revenue by multiplying the number of weeks the position is vacant by the average weekly revenue per employee.
Line CIF3	Calculate lost profits based on Lost Revenue, Line F1.

Figure 51: Business Costs And Impacts Of Turnover Descriptions

	Part G - Extraordinary Costs
Line CIG1	Costs of key jobs such as ERP, head of a team, production development, etc., may have a high impact and could exceed $1 million. Enter your best estimate of this cost on this line.
Line CIG2	Turnover may excite competitors and they may seize the opportunity to get more employees to leave or go after our customers. Enter your best estimate of this cost on this line.
Line CIG3	A competitor may learn of your business secrets and ideas as well as learn who else to recruit. Enter your best estimate of this cost on this line.
Line CIG4	Turnover may send a message to customers that "we don't care" and thus give them an opportunity to look for new supplier. Enter your best estimate of this cost on this line.
Line CIG5	Turnover send a message to potential new recruits and current employees we are going down hill. High turnover rates impact your image and low help us recruit others. Enter your best estimate of this cost on this line.
Line CIG6	Turnover may send a message to potential new recruits and current employees that you are going down hill. High turnover rates may impact your image and prevent you from recruiting good employees. Enter your best estimate of this cost on this line.

-- end of Instructions Worksheet --

Figure 51: Business Costs And Impacts Of Turnover Descriptions

APPENDIX C

Research Methodology

This book was written by the leaders of two separate, yet complimentary, organizations. Roger and Joyce's firm, The Herman Group, has developed a considerable amount of anecdotal research as well as future-focused perspective. Tom's firm, Success Profiles, Inc., has engaged in more formal research involving a substantial amount of data gathering and analysis. *Impending Crisis* is a productive balance of the two approaches.

In this appendix, we share the research methodology underlying the work done by Success Profiles. This team's work, linked with the input from the Bureau of Labor Statistics and VHA, Inc., has generated clear evidence of the unprecedented challenge facing business leaders during the next decade. For our readers who desire a bit more background into the methodology, we offer this explanation.

Overview of Research

- Over a 10 year period, Success Profiles has performed extensive research into the business practices of over 600 organizations and has compiled data on the performance of over 5,000 individual business units.

- The standard statistical analysis includes tests for scale reliability, factor analysis, correlation analysis, and linear regression.

- The outcome metrics for business comparison include compound revenue growth, revenue per full time employee, profitability, and employee turnover.
- Once we perform the statistical analysis to determine which business practices have the greatest impact on business performance, we graphically illustrate the results in a way that is "management friendly" and easy to understand.
- Keep in mind that everyone knows that through statistical deception, one can virtually demonstrate correlations between *any* two factors. We have done everything possible to graphically illustrate the evidence in this book with integrity.
- This book is not solely dedicated to the measurement of business practices or the details of statistical analysis. The research data that we have shared is representative of the "Sweet Spot," the zone of effective practices that differentiates high performing organizations from average ones.
- Also, there is "no *one* practice" that will lead to exceptional performance. Companies that are usually good at one business practice almost always exhibit other great practices. It is a compounding effect that is most likely contributing to exceptional results.

Use of Statistical Analysis By Success Profiles

Norming the Data

Simply put, a norm is a benchmark or average for comparison. Some of the most valuable comparisons are those analyzing a company's performance compared to its *own* established norms. We accomplish this norming by conducting studies at reasonable intervals and as the studies continue, tracking the results throughout time. Success Profiles has established overall norms as well as the norms in a number of industries and is continuing to grow the best practices database for further comparison opportunities.

Centile Scoring

When benchmarking a company's scores, knowing how they compare to the norms is only one aspect of the overall analysis. To be an average company, after all, is not what companies should be striving for. Being the best is the ultimate goal, which brings us to the centile scoring method of comparison. A centile (often referred to as percentile) score tells you the percent of the normal population that is estimated to score at or below the level you did. For example, at the 60th percentile, there is approximately 60 percent of the norm group that would score at or below your level, while 40 percent would score higher than what you did. In analyzing the centile, it is important to realize that this score is a highly sensitive analysis and it is not uncommon for a centile score to be high or low, despite the raw score being quite close to the norm mean. This proximity is due to the bulk of the population falling within a relatively close range to one another.

A zero to five scale is used in scoring. Respondents are asked to rate performance with zero being "To no extent", one being "To a little extent", two being "To some extent", three being "To a considerable extent", four being "To a great extent", and five being "To a very great extent". Scores of five are worth noting, Success Profiles refers to these as the "delight factor" and show that the company was rated above and beyond in that specific area.

Scale Reliability

Reliability analysis allows market researchers the ability to develop the best questionnaire with the least amount of questions. The benefit of the reliability analysis is the identification of the questions that explain the greatest amount of variance within a specific group. Generally, the greater amount of variance explained by a given set of questions indicates a stronger relationship between the questions and a more accurate composite score for the grouping.

This relationship is demonstrated through the analysis of an alpha score for the group as a whole as well as the individual questions. Alpha scores are a measure of the amount of variance that is explained by a single question or group of questions with values ranging between zero (explains none of the variance) and positive one (explains all of the variance). Questions can be removed until the desired number of questions remains or the group's alpha score falls just above an acceptable level. The desirable level depends on specific criteria, but usually falls between 0.65 and 0.9. Alpha scores lower than 0.65 do not explain enough of the general module score and those scores higher than 0.9 are generally due to too much similarity in the questions within the module.

How Success Profiles uses Scale Reliability

Success Profiles uses the scale reliability analysis in two ways. The scale reliability is used to confirm the quality of questions used in their different modules in an effort to continually validate and improve the assessment designs. The analysis is also used to minimize the number of questions required for a customer or employee assessment while still ensuring the accuracy of the module scores.

Factor Analysis

A factor analysis can be performed to provide a detailed look at the underlying constructs of the assessment questions. A factor is defined as a variable or construct that is not directly observable through the use of one question, but instead is derived from the answers to a number of questions asked throughout the assessment. For example, a measure of teamwork might be identified through the rating or scoring of four or five specific questions dealing with the topic. Through this analysis, redundancy within the questions can be identified, as well as providing the company with the number of factors that are prevalent within the assessment. We derive this factor analysis by computing a score that measures the amount of variance. This variance is explained in the overall data by each specific factor. Factor analysis attempts to identify underlying variables, or factors, that explain the pattern of correlations within a set of observed variables. Factor analysis is often used in data reduction, by identifying a small number of factors that explain most of the variance observed in a much larger number of manifest variables. Factor analysis can also be used to generate hypotheses regarding causal mechanisms or to screen variables for subsequent analysis (for example, to identify co-linearity prior to a linear regression analysis).

How Success Profiles uses Factor Analysis

Success Profiles uses the Factor Analysis to identify the loading of their questions into specific modules. This analysis provides the company with a measure of the strength of the modules, as well as the proper placement of individual questions within an assessment.

Correlation Analysis

A correlation matrix is a statistical tool that helps to identify the type and strength of the relationship between two variables. We choose variables and use professional statistical software packages to produce a report of all of the relationships in question. During this process, a correlation coefficient is computed for each individual relationship of one variable to another.

The coefficient can range from –1 to +1, and the magnitude of the number is indicative of the strength of the relationship. That is to say, a coefficient near negative or positive one is considered a strong relationship between the two variables. If a negative coefficient is computed, there is an inverse relationship (as one variable increases or decreases, the other responds in opposite fashion). If the coefficient is positive, it indicates a direct relationship with both variables responding in the same way.

In most studies, a statistically significant relationship with a magnitude of .5 or higher or -.5 or lower is considered very strong and as the coefficient increases in magnitude, the relationship becomes more linear (as one variable increases, the other increases or decreases at a similar level). We must pay attention to any statistically valid relationship with a correlation coefficient score higher than .2 or lower than -.2.

How Success Profiles uses Correlation Analysis

Success Profiles uses the correlation matrices to determine strength of relationships in their Integrated Performance Measurement (IPM) tool. Running correlations on all of the financial, employee, and customer data shows us the specific relationships that exist. From the initial analysis, we can further examine certain relationships by lagging and leading particular variables. When variables are "lagged," the statistical package creates a new variable that moves the old values forward creating a time-series that scrutinizes the chicken-egg question of this type of data. "Leading" a variable is done for the same reason, but the new variable is moved backward, not forward, from its original position.

Linear Regression

Linear regression is a statistical procedure used to estimate the linear relationship between a dependent variable (variable being predicted) and one or more independent variables (variable used to help predict dependent variable). The stepwise regression technique can be used to select a small subset of variables that account for the vast majority of variation in a dependent variable. With this method, variables are entered into, or removed from the model one at a time, until we identify the best fitting model. Then, we produce a table displaying the strength of the model. In addition, at this time we generate the coefficients that may be used to determine a prediction equation with the questions included in the final model.

How Success Profiles Uses Linear Regression

We use the linear regression model to develop the cause and effect relationship (or lack thereof) between assessment questions and profit measures within an organization. Through continued feedback from employees and customers, we can begin to understand and forecast the effects that perceptions and business practices have on financial measures.

Five Principal Reasons People Change Jobs

(from *Keeping Good People*, Roger E. Herman, Oakhill Press)

1. It doesn't feel good around here. This "feeling" is a corporate culture issue in most cases. Workers are also concerned with the company's reputation; the physical conditions of comfort, convenience, and safety; and the clarity of mission.

2. They wouldn't miss me if I were gone. Even though leaders do value employees, they don't tell them often enough. If people don't feel important, they're not motivated to stay. No one wants to be a commodity, easily replaced by someone off the street. If workers are regarded as expendable, they'll leave for a position where they *are* appreciated.

3. I don't get the support I need to get my job done. Contrary to opinions heard all too often from management, people really *do* want to do a good job. When they're frustrated by too many rules, red tape, or incompetent supervisors or coworkers, people look for other opportunities.

4. There's no opportunity for advancement. No, we're not talking about promotions, although many deserving people would like to move up. The issue here is learning. People want to learn, to sharpen their skills and pick up new ones. They want to improve their capacity to perform a wide variety of jobs. Call it career security. The desire is for training and development. If workers can't find the growth opportunities with one company, they'll seek another employer where they can learn.

5. Compensation is the last reason people most leave. That's a brash statement, but it's true. Workers want "fair" compensation, but the first four aspects must be strong. When the other factors are addressed well, money has diminished importance. If they're not addressed appropriately, and money's high, you'll still hear people say, "You can't pay me enough to stay here." Even with these values in place, there are a lot of workers who feel they can better themselves just by chasing more income.

BIBLIOGRAPHY

There are a number of fine books that relate to the theme of this book. It is impossible for us to list them all. However, to help our readers learn more and take the action steps to make a difference for their organizations, we share this list.

Aldisert, Lisa. *Valuing People.* (Chicago: Dearborn Publishing, 2002).

Barrett, Richard. *Liberating the Corporate Soul: Building a Visionary Organization.* (Burlington, Massachusetts: Butterworth-Heinemann, 1998).

Bechet, Thomas P. *Strategic Staffing: A Practical Toolkit for Workforce Planning.* (New York: American Management Association, 2002).

Brian E. Becker, Mark A. Huselid, Dave Ulrich . *The HR Scorecard: Linking People, Strategy, and Performance.* (Boston: Harvard Business School Press, 2001).

Buckingham, Marcus and Curt Coffman. *First, Break All the Rules.* (New York, NY: Simon & Schuster, 1999).

Collins, James C. and Jerry I Porras. *Built to Last: Successful Habits of Visionary Companies.* (New York, NY: HarperCollins Publications, Inc., 1997).

Collins, James C. *Good to Great: Why Some Companies Make the Leap... and Others Don't.* (New York: HarperCollins Publications, Inc., 2001).

Dent, Harry S. *The Great Boom Ahead.* (New York: Hyperion, 1994).

Dychtwald, Kenneth, Ph.D. *Age Wave.* (New York: Bantam Doubleday Dell, 1990)

Gelinas, Lillee and Chuck Bohlen. *Tomorrow's Work Force: A Strategic Approach.* (Dallas: *VHA Research Series, 2002).*

Gordon, Edward E. *Skill Wars: Winning the Battle for Productivity and Profit.* (Boston:Butterworth-Heinemann, 2000).

Herman Roger. *Keeping Good People: Strategies for Solving the #1 Problem Facing Business Today.* Winchester, Virginia: Oakhill Press, 1999).

Herman, Roger E. and Joyce L. Gioia. *Lean & Meaningful: A New Culture for Corporate America.* (Winchester, Virginia: Oakhill Press, 1998).

Herman Roger E. and Joyce L. Gioia. *How to Become an Employer of Choice.* Winchester, Virginia: Oakhill Press, 2000.

Herman, Roger E. and Joyce L. Gioia. *Workforce Stability: Your Competitive Advantage.* (Winchester, Virginia: Oakhill Press, 2000).

LaFasto, Frank M. J. and Carl E. Larson. *When Teams Work Best : 6,000 Team Members and Leaders Tell What It Takes to Succeed.* (Thousand Oaks, California: Sage Publications, 2001).

Kaplan, Robert S. and David P. Norton. *The Balanced Score Card: Translation Strategy Into Action.* (Boston: Harvard Business School Press, 1996).

Ed Michaels, Helen Handfield-Jones, and Beth Axelrod. *The War for Talent.* Boston: Harvard Business School Press, 2001).

Mitchell, Don and Carol Coles. *The Ultimate Competitive Advantage: Secrets of Continually Developing a More Profitable Business Model.* (San Francisco: Berrett-Koehler Publishers, 2003).

Nelson, Bob. *1001 Ways to Reward Employees.* (New York: Workman Publishing, 1994).

Nelson, Bob. *Don't Just Do What I Tell You, Do What Needs to be*

Done: Every Employee's Guide to Making Work More Rewarding. (New York: Hyperion, 2001).

Niven, Paul R. *Balanced Scorecard Step-by-Step: Maximizing Performance and Maintaining Results.* (New York: Wiley, 2002).

Pfeffer, Jeffrey. *The Human Equation: Building Profits by Putting People First.* (Boston: Harvard Business School Press, 1998).

Pink, Daniel. *Free Agent Nation: How America's New Independent Workers Are Transforming the Way We Live.* (New York, Warner Books, 2001).

Reichheld, Frederick F. *The Loyalty Effect: The Hidden Force Behind Growth, Profits, and Lasting Value.* (Boston, Harvard Business School Press, 2001).

Ricchiuto, Jack. *Collaborative Creativity: Unleashing the Power of Shared Thinking.* (Winchester, Virginia: Oakhill Press, 1996).

Stack, Jack and Bo Burlingham. *The Great Game of Business.* (New York, NY: Doubleday, 1994).

Terez, Tom. *22 Keys to Creating a Meaningful Workplace.* (Boston, Adams Media, 2000).

Ulrich, David. *Results Based Leadership.* (Boston: Harvard Business School Press, 1999).

Whyte, William. *The Organization Man.* (Philadelphia: The University of Pennsylvania Press, July 2002).

Zemke, Ron, Claire Raines and Bob Filipczak. *Generations at Work: Managing the Clash of Veterans, Boomers, Xers, and Nexters in Your Workplace.* (New York: Amacom, 1999).

INDEX

ABOUT THE AUTHORS

Roger E. Herman is a strategic business futurist concentrating on workforce and workplace trends. He is a sought-after professional speaker and media resource on relevant trends, workforce stability, and becoming an Employer of Choice^SM. In 2000, *Successful Meetings* magazine selected him as one of the country's leading speakers—"worth his fee and then some."

Roger is author or coauthor of ten other books, including *How to Become an Employer of Choice*, which was runner-up for Best Business Book of 2000 in the Benjamin Franklin Awards Program. Roger serves as contributing editor for workforce and workplace issues for *The Futurist* magazine. He has written over 650 articles, and his column appears in a number of trade publications. With his partner, Joyce Gioia, Roger produces the Herman Trend Alert, a weekly e-advisory distributed as a public service.

An active consulting futurist, Roger was recognized as a Certified Management Consultant by the Institute of Management Consultants. He was also elected a Fellow of the Institute, the highest recognition of peers in the profession. The National Speakers Association designated Roger as a Certified Speaking

Professional. He is a Professional Member of the World Future Society and belongs to the Society for Human Resource Management. In addition, he is Senior Fellow of The Workforce Stability Institute.

Roger serves as chief executive officer of The Herman Group, a consultancy he founded in 1980. Based in Greensboro, North Carolina, the firm has offices in Melbourne, Australia, and Sao Paulo, Brazil.

Roger is a graduate of Hiram College and earned his master's degree from The Ohio State University. He is currently a member of the Hiram College Board of Visitors. During the Vietnam era, Roger served as a Counterintelligence Special Agent for the United States Army.

Thomas G. Olivo is president of Success Profiles, Inc., a consulting firm that specializes in marketplace research and business performance measurement. The firm designs and provides organizational performance measurement instruments and database management services to clients, management consulting firms, accounting firms, and affinity groups. The purpose of the service is to create, measure, and  manage "actionable knowledge." Tom and his team have worked with over 600 companies and developed a database of business practices that includes over 5,000 individual business units. Tom formed the firm in 1990.

For almost two decades, Tom has gained experience in identifying, measuring, and comparing the "commonalties" of highly successful athletes, business leaders, and organizations. Emphasizing the importance of high performance standards consistent with "best business practices," he has worked in a multitude of industries with hundreds of senior executives and managers.

Tom's work with Olympic athletes, coaches, and successful business leaders led to the development of several unique diagnostic instruments that measure business performance. His methodology, combined with a measurement framework and supporting research data, proves that consistent success in business today rarely occurs by accident. In fact, there are specific predictors, critical success factors, behaviors, and business practices that contribute to success among people and organizations. These characteristics can be identified, measured, and compared over time as performance indicators to improve business results.

Throughout his life, Tom has been very involved in competitive athletics. His collegiate career was highlighted by twice being honored as an NCAA All-American in the sport of springboard diving. As a coach, Tom has developed athletes at every level of competition. In 1985 he was recognized as an NCAA coach of the year.

Tom holds a bachelor of science degree in geology from the State University of New York, Cortland, with a minor in music history.

Joyce L. Gioia is President of The Herman Group, a management consulting firm based in Greensboro, North Carolina with offices in Melbourne, Australia, and Sao Paulo, Brazil. A consultant since 1984, she is recognized as a Certified Management Consultant by the Institute of Management Consultants.

A specialist in adding value, Joyce gained a national reputation for her

work in direct marketing, product launches, and arranging strategic alliances. At the age of 28, she became the youngest magazine publisher in the country. An award-winning marketing strategist, Joyce has arranged strategic alliances for MasterCard, AT&T, and other household names.

Recognized as an innovator, she is known for her ability to understand and explain consumerism trends in the United States and in other countries and regions. She intertwines this knowledge with her work in the field of human resources to bring a totally new dimension to workforce stability strategy.

Joyce is a graduate of the University of Denver and holds a Masters of Business Administration from Fordham University. She also holds a Masters in Theology and a Masters in Counseling from the New Seminar in New York City. She has taught marketing on the university level at numerous colleges and universities, including the City College of New York and New York University.

A frequent speaker for corporate and trade association audiences, Joyce is a Professional Member of the National Speakers Association. She is also a member of the Association of Professional Futurists, a Professional Member of the World Future Society, and a member of the American Society for Training and Development. A Fellow of the Workforce Stability Institute, Joyce is frequently cited in the national news media, including *The Wall Street Journal, The Christian Science Monitor,* and *Business Week,* for her expertise on workforce and workplace trends and internal marketing. She has written hundreds of articles for the trade media and is frequently quoted in those publications as well. Her concentration is communicating messages through organizational cultures to encourage people to remain productively with their employers for longer periods of time.